THE LAST YEAR OF THE
KRIEGSMARINE

THE LAST YEAR OF THE
KRIEGSMARINE

May 1944 – May 1945

V. E. TARRANT

ARMS AND
ARMOUR

Dedicated to the memory of my Grandmother
SARAH ANN COLES, 1900–1992
who clung to the Old Rugged Cross all her life,
finally exchanging it for a Crown.

Arms & Armour Press
An imprint of the Cassell Group
Wellington House, 125 Strand, London WC2R. 0BB

Distributed in the USA by Sterling Publishing Co. Inc.,
387 Park Avenue South, New York, NY 10016-8810

Distributed in Australia by Capricorn Link (Australia) Pty. Ltd.,
2/13 Carrington Road, Castle Hill, NSW 2154

First Published in 1994
This paperback edition 1996

British Library Cataloguing-in-Publication Data: A
catalogue record for this book is available from the
British Library

ISBN 1-85409-362-2

Designed and edited by DAG Publications Ltd.
Designed by David Gibbons;
edited by Michael Boxall; Printed and bound in
Great Britain by Hartnolls Limited, Bodmin, Cornwall.

Cover illustration by James Mitchell.
Prints of thie work are available
from Mirage Fina Art, 8 Huntersfield,
Sharington, Crewe, Cheshire CW2 5FB

Contents

CONTENTS

Preface

In 1991, Arms & Armour Press published Dr Alfred Price's *The Last Year of the Luftwaffe*. Following the success of this work the publishers, through the good offices of my literary agent Bob Tanner, at International Scripts, invited me to write a companion volume dealing with the last year of the *Kriegsmarine* (as the German Navy was called during the Nazi era). In his preface Dr Price explains his book's *raison d'être:* 'So much has been said and written about the Luftwaffe, but all previous accounts charting its path through the whole of the war seem to lose their thrust once they enter the final year. It is as if those writers, having delighted in describing the build-up of the force and its many triumphs, lose heart when the towering edifice began to come tumbling down.'

This is equally true of the final year of the Kriegsmarine. All the published works, both in English and German, that I consulted while researching my book deal with the demise of the Kriegsmarine in little more than a single chapter; an oversight of which, I have to confess, I myself was guilty in my *The U-Boat Offensive 1914–1945* (Arms & Armour Press, 1989). I therefore gratefully accepted the publishers' offer that has enabled me to correct my earlier oversight, especially with regard to the U-boats' inshore campaign which, I have discovered, has not been dealt with in any depth in any previous published work.

I decided to employ the artificial device of describing the progress of the inshore campaign in seven separate 'waves'; each dealing with the operations of U-boats deployed to British coastal waters during a particular month. I say artificial because in fact the boats sent out in any particular month were still in their operational zone when the next month's boats were arriving, so there was a constant overlap. But the device simplifies what would otherwise be a difficult and confusing narrative.

Because German surface ships played a decidedly secondary role during this period of the war, the main thrust of my narrative is concerned with the U-boats, S-boats and 'Small Battle Units' that carried out the main, and largely the only, offensive operations of the Kriegsmarine from May 1944 to May 1945.

A major problem facing any historian writing about German naval operations during the last year of the war is that many of the records are incomplete and in some cases, notably Mediterranean and Arctic operations, fragmentary or non-existent. Fortunately, a vast quantity of German naval Enigma signals, which were intercepted and 'read' by British cryptanalysts at Bletchley Park, have been preserved, and these reveal the German naval commands' strategic intentions and the course of the most important operations. In using this material I must express a debt of gratitude to Professor F. H. Hinsley and his associates for their priceless and monolithic work, *British Intelligence in the Second World War* (4 vols. in 5 parts, HMSO, 1979-88), which not only analyses the most important of the intercepted signals, but also provides a valuable guide into the huge and difficult to use corpus of Naval Intelligence Division records (which include the texts of decrypts of German naval radio traffic enciphered on the Enigma machine) preserved in the Public Record Office.

Fighting against impossible odds during the last year of its exis tence, the Kriegsmarine fought gallantly and honourably to the bitter end, in a desperate attempt to regain the initiative at sea which they could well have attained if enough of the new and revolutionary Electro-boats had entered service in time.

I wish to thank the following publishers for permission to quote copyright material as follows: Weidenfeld & Nicholson, from Dönitz's memoirs, *Ten Years and Twenty Days*; Victor Gollancz, from Peter Padfield's *Dönitz: The Last Führer*; Secker & Warburg, from Martienssen's *Hitler and his Admirals*; Hodder & Stoughton, from Correlli Barnett's *Engage the Enemy More Closely*. Crown Copyright material has been used by permission of the Controller of Her Majesty's Stationery Office. The photographs have been reproduced by kind permission of the Imperial War Museum; WZ-Bilddienst (Wilhelmshaven); and the U-boat veteran, Karl Wahnig, who kindly provided photographs from his private collection.

Introduction

By November 1942, the empire of Adolf Hitler had reached its zenith. It stretched from North Africa to the Arctic, from the English Channel to Stalingrad deep within Russia. Four hundred million people in Europe lay under the yoke of German rule. Between the Pyrenees and the Ukrainian steppes there were no other sovereign states but neutral Switzerland and Sweden. Even Hitler's allies, Italy, Roumania, Hungary, and to a lesser extent, Finland, had been reduced to little more than German puppets. In the ancient capitals of Europe – in Athens, Vienna, Brussels, the Hague, Paris, Belgrade, Prague, Oslo, Copenhagen and Warsaw – freedom and self-determination had been stifled by Nazi domination.

The German armed forces seemed invincible, but then in the space of a month the seemingly impossible happened. On 2 November 1942, Rommel's Afrika Korps was decisively defeated by Montgomery's Eighth Army at the Battle of El Alamein, and six days later Anglo-American forces invaded French North Africa, threatening Rommel's forces from the deep rear. This double blow was followed by an even greater catastrophe at Stalingrad. In a matter of only five days, from 19 to 23 November 1942, a massive Russian counter-offensive wiped two Roumanian armies off the Axis order of battle, shattered the German Fourth Panzer Army, and encircled 267,000 troops of the 'crack' Sixth Army at Stalingrad. By the time Sixth Army finally surrendered on 2 February 1943, further Russian offensives north and south of Stalingrad had expelled two German armies from the Caucasus and had destroyed the Hungarian Second and Italian Eighth Armies. By March the southern wing of the German front line had been pushed back 250 miles from the Volga to the Donets.[1] The twin reverses in North Africa (from where the Axis forces were finally expelled on 11 May 1943) and Russia, cost the Axis some 1,000,000 casualties and effectively broke the back of the German Army.

The last of the decisive defeats that turned the tide of war against Germany was the 'Black May' of the Kriegsmarine. In May 1943, 41 U-boats were destroyed, unsustainable losses that caused Grossadmiral Karl Dönitz, Commander-in-Chief of the Kriegsmarine, to withdraw his

U-boats from the North Atlantic and concede that Germany had lost the Battle of the Atlantic.

When war broke out on 3 September 1939, the Kriegsmarine had 57 U-boats in commission. Despite the loss of 154 of them from enemy action and accidental causes during the three years and four months up to the end of 1942, the number of U-boats in commission had risen to 403 by this date. The slaughter they had wrought on Allied shipping during these 40 months of war, 2,280 merchant ships grossing 11,422,350 tons, had brought Britain to the brink of defeat. During 1942 alone, when the Battle of the Atlantic reached its crescendo, the U-boats sent 1,155 vessels grossing 6,149,473 tons to the bottom together with their precious cargoes.[2] But, during the second half of 1942, the growing effectiveness of Allied anti-submarine measures began to turn the tide against the Germans. During the first half of 1942, only 21 U-boats had been destroyed; during the second half of the year losses trebled to 64 boats, and in the first five months of 1943, 97 boats were lost (41 of these in May alone). After 'Black May' the number of merchant vessels sunk by U-boats fell dramatically, while the number of U-boats destroyed by enemy action increased alarmingly. From the peak of 1,155 vessels grossing 6,149,473 tons accounted for in 1942 for the loss of 85 U-boats, the figure dropped to 457 vessels grossing 2,536,757 tons through the whole of 1943 for the loss of 242 U-boats; a ratio of 13.58 merchant ships sunk per U-boat lost in 1942, to 1.89 vessels sunk per U-boat lost in 1943.

The reason for this reversal of fortune was that the sum total of Allied A/S (anti-submarine) measures had reached a stage of development that proved to be a panacea against the U-boat menace. In addition to strongly protected convoys, more effective U-boat detection devices and anti-submarine weapon systems, well-trained escort groups and the breaking of the U-boat Enigma codes, new developments introduced in the spring of 1943 had finally proved decisive. The provision of an adequate number of Very Long Range aircraft and the innovation of merchant ships being converted to escort-carriers, meant that the 450-mile-wide mid-Atlantic gap, where the U-boats had been able to operate with impunity from air-attack, was suddenly closed.

'Air cover for even only a few hours in mid-Atlantic proved effective in breaking up attacking U-boat formations. Experience had shown that Allied surface escorts might become so disorganized by a concentrated attack by U-boat wolf-packs that the resultant breaks in the convoy protection formation rendered the escorts ineffective in defence and attack. But given air escort the surface escorts, however scattered, had time in which to rally while the U-boats were driven down by aircraft attacks and as a result became themselves disorganized.'[3]

Fregattenkapitän Günther Hessler summed-up the German appreciation of the situation:

'... failure in a whole series of convoy battles [during the first five months of 1943] had shown beyond doubt that the offensive power of the U-boat was incapable of dealing with the defence. This situation was due firstly to outstanding developments in enemy radar, and secondly to effective co-operation between surface escorts, support groups, and carrier-borne aircraft. Moreover, we had numerous indications that the Allies' huge construction programme for escort-carriers, escort vessels and aircraft had not yet reached its peak. On the other hand, there was no increase in the destructive power of the U-boat. Yet the crux of the U-boat campaign was the maintenance of the offensive against the Allied life-line [of seaborne supplies] in the North Atlantic. But now the staggering realization came upon us that we could no longer pursue this offensive in its existing form. Indeed, the latest experience [in the spring of 1943] had shown that the striking power of the U-boat threatened to collapse in every theatre of war.'[4]

The disastrous losses suffered by the U-boats during 'Black May' and the failure of Rudeltaktic (U-boats operating in wolf-packs) against the convoys during the spring of 1943, obliged BdU (Befehlshaber der U-boote = U-boat High Command) to concede defeat, and on 24 May Dönitz ordered the withdrawal of the U-boats from the North Atlantic convoy routes. Dönitz wrote in BdU War Diary:

'The situation in the North Atlantic now forces a temporary shifting of operations to areas less endangered by aircraft ... the Caribbean Sea, the area off Trinidad, the area off the Brazilian and West African coasts. With the boats at present in the North Atlantic, operations will be made against traffic between the USA and Gibraltar - as far as these boats are able to do this with their fuel. The North Atlantic cannot, however, be entirely denuded of boats. It is necessary, by means of single boats, to leave the enemy in ignorance as long as possible regarding these alterations in tactics. It is intended to attempt attacks on convoys only under particularly favourable conditions, i.e., in the time of the new moon... these decisions comprise a temporary deviation from the former principles for the conduct of U-boat warfare. This is necessary in order not to allow the U-boats to be beaten at a time when their weapons are inferior, by unnecessary losses while achieving very slight success. It is however, clearly understood that the main operational area of U-boats is, as it always was, in the North Atlantic. It is anticipated that after equipment with quadruples (the fitting of quadruple AA guns) from the autumn, the Battle of the North Atlantic will be completely resumed once more. In the meantime the excessive losses and the lack of success in operations against the latest convoys now force us to take these decisive measures until the boats are equipped with better defence and attack weapons.'[5]

To put it succinctly, although conceding defeat, Dönitz still planned to resume the campaign in the North Atlantic once his U-boats were better equipped with anti-aircraft guns. In his memoirs he explained why he felt that he had no choice but to call upon the U-boats 'to continue the unequal struggle'.[6]

On land the situation was going from bad to worse. During July 1943, the Allies invaded Sicily, Mussolini was arrested and a new government was formed, which immediately began looking for a way out of the war. In the same month an attempt to regain the initiative on the Eastern Front in the Battle of Kursk, resulted in a decisive defeat for the German Army. This proved to be Hitler's last great offensive of the war against the Russians, who promptly counter-attacked and from that moment on never lost the initiative. While from the skies over Germany Allied bombers were systematically reducing the great and ancient cities of Germany to piles of rubble. During a raid on Hamburg 40,000 of the inhabitants lost their lives in a 'firestorm' which devastated the city.

'Under these conditions', Dönitz lamented, 'what effect would the abandonment of the U-boat campaign have on our war situation as a whole? Could we afford to abandon it.'[7] The answer, he concluded, was a decided no, for if the U-boat campaign was abandoned the costs of the anti-submarine war to the Allies – the high merchant ship tonnage requirements, together with the large number of warships and aircraft required to protect the convoys, the strain on the naval bases, airfields, dockyards, labour and production – would become available for use against Germany elsewhere. Among other things it would allow the Allies the means to intensify the bomber offensive against German cities, causing even greater sufferings and higher casualties for the civilian population. Dönitz argued: 'Could the submariner stand aside as a spectator, saying there was nothing he could or would do, and telling the women and children they must put up with it? On the other hand there was really no doubt that, if we carried on, U-boat losses would rise to an appalling height, in spite of anything we could do to accelerate improvements on their defensive equipment and afford them effective protection. A continuation of the U-boat campaign would involve certain and deliberate self-sacrifice. I finally came to the bitter conclusion that we had no option but to fight on.'[8]

However, Dönitz's determination to fight on was fatally compromised by events on the cryptanalytical front. Throughout 1942 the Kriegsmarine's cryptanalysis service (B-Dienst) had achieved considerable success against the British Naval Cipher No 3, known to B-Dienst as the 'convoy cipher', and they had supplied BdU with accurate intelligence about convoy movements. In December 1942, increased security of this and other British ciphers, made the convoy cipher unreadable. However, by February 1943, after switching most of its cryptanalysis effort to breaking the changes to the convoy cipher, B-Dienst was again able to read, on most days, the Admiralty's daily U-boat disposition signal to the convoys at sea, and were able, as a result, to forecast the areas through which the convoys would probably be routed. Nearly all the U-boat dispositions ordered by BdU during the periods that Naval Cipher No 3 was being read were based either directly on B-Dienst's decrypts or, when these were delayed or incomplete, on the knowledge of convoy routes which BdU had built up from its study of earlier decrypts.

In June 1943 BdU was robbed of the considerable value of these decrypts when the Admiralty, responding to an anxiety expressed by the signals security authorities regarding the security of the heavily used convoy cipher, replaced Naval Cipher No 3 with Naval Cipher No 5, a more secure cipher, which proved to be unbreakable by B-Dienst.

To make matters worse, although BdU didn't know it, in December 1942 British cryptanalysts at Bletchley Park succeeded in breaking 'Triton' – the U-boat four-wheeled Enigma Key – which the British called the 'Shark' key. During the first half of 1943, the 'Triton' traffic sent by BdU to the U-boats was being read with a delay of between 24 to 72 hours, and sometimes much longer when the Enigma settings proved to be unusually intractable. However, by August 1943 and thereafter until December 1944, the British were able to read the BdU's Enigma traffic with little or no delay. The great bulk of the decrypts provided the Admiralty with vital intelligence regarding the departure times and dates of U-boats from and to their bases, the numbers and types of U-boats at sea, the movements and dispositions of their patrol groups and their operational orders.

In short, at a time when BdU was rendered blind as to convoy routing because of B-Dienst's inability to break the new British convoy cipher, BdU's intentions were fatally compromised by British cryptanalysts' ability to read concurrently the 'Triton' traffic, which provided the Admiralty with a crystal ball to divine corporate and individual U-boat movements and dispositions.

When Dönitz decided to resume the U-boat offensive against the North Atlantic convoys in September 1943, it was due in large measure to the British cryptanalytical success against 'Triton' that it was very quickly and roundly defeated.

'All the essentials for a successful campaign are to hand,' Dönitz had signalled to the U-boats as they set out to give battle. By essentials he was referring to the improved anti-aircraft guns (quick-firing twin 20mm) that had been fitted; the Wanze radar search receiver (a non-radiating search receiver designed to provide early warning of approaching radar-bearing aircraft, giving the boats time to dive to safety); and the new T5 Zaunkönig (known to the Allies as Gnat) acoustic torpedo, developed for use against fast escort ships.

Dönitz's optimism quickly foundered. 'Triton' decrypts allowed the Admiralty successfully to divert practically every threatened convoy away from the U-boat patrol lines. In addition to being deprived of contact with the convoys, the U-boats were overwhelmed by the Allied forces. Strong air escorts kept the boats almost continuously submerged; while the few (six boats) that tried to fight it out on the surface with the new AA armament were all sunk. On 12 November, Dönitz wrote despairingly in his diary: 'The enemy holds every trump card, covering all areas with long-range air patrols and using location methods against which we still have no warning ... The enemy knows all our secrets and we know none of his.'[9]

Once again BdU was forced to withdraw the U-boats from virtually the whole of the North Atlantic. This led to the abandonment of wolf-pack tactics, and from the middle of November 1943 until May

---

The Progress of the U-Boat Offensive Against Merchant Shipping from September 1939 to April 1944, Expressed in Four-Monthly Periods.

Column *1:*	Four-monthly period
Column *2/3:*	Number of ships (in brackets) and gross tonnage sunk by *U*-boats in all theatres
Column *4:*	Number of U-boats lost
Column *5:*	Ratio of number of ships sunk per U-boat lost

1	2	3	4	5
Sept-Dec 1939	(147)	509,321	9	16.33
Jan-April 1940	(135)	446,151	14	9.64
May-Aug 1940	(177)	926,859	6	29.50
Sept -Dec 1940	(208)	1,089,857	5	41.60
Jan-Apr 1941	(152)	860,097	7	21.11
May-Aug 1941	(182)	886,312	9	20.22
Sept-Dec 1941	(123)	552,305	20	6.15
Jan-April 1942	(302)	1,656,154	14	21.57
May-Aug 1942	(478)	2,308,057	27	17.70
Sept-Dec 1942	(375)	2,185,262	44	8.52
Jan-April 1943	(271)	1,590,145	56	4.83
May-Aug 1943	(128)	643,492	120	1.06
Sept-Dec 1943	(53)	276,667	65	0.81
Jan-April 1944	(50)	297,729	84	0.59
TOTALS	(2,781)	14,228,408	480	5.79

1944 the boats were dispatched singly to the north-eastern corner of the Atlantic with orders to act aggressively on their own initiative. During this period they managed to account for only 107 ships grossing 598,819 tons in all theatres (only eight of these in convoys, the remainder being unescorted stragglers from the convoys, or ships that had sailed independently), for the loss of 136 U-boats: a ratio of 0.78 ships sunk for every U-boat destroyed, which spelled the doom of U-boat warfare and definitely settled the Battle of the Atlantic in the Allies' favour.

It had now become blatantly obvious to the Germans that the existing types of U-boat, which had been designed largely to operate on the surface, were handicapped by blindness, slow speed and poor endurance now that Allied A/S measures were forcing them to spend much of their time submerged. It had, therefore, Dönitz concluded, become a matter of extreme urgency to arm the U-boat fleet with new types combining high submerged speed with the capacity to spend long periods under water, which would frustrate all the enemy's A/S tactics. Prototype boats incorporating the technology that provided these qualities were already under construction: and it was these new U-boats, together with developments in jet aircraft, flying-bombs and rockets, that convinced Hitler of the tide-turning powers of these 'miracle weapons' and caused him to prolong a war which he had already lost. As a result Germany was about to be dragged over the precipice to complete disaster, marking millions for doom in the terrible final year of Hitler's dictatorship – a year in which the Kriegsmarine would fight to the death.

Chapter 1

A BELIEF IN MIRACLES

By the beginning of May 1944, the bell was tolling loud and ominously for Nazi Germany. Apart from a large salient in the area of Minsk, the Red Army had liberated virtually all Soviet territory from the German invader, and the Russian juggernaut was now poised to sweep forward into Poland and Roumania. In Italy the Allies were advancing on Rome (which fell on 5 June), while the German forces in France were bracing themselves for an imminent cross-Channel invasion by the Anglo-American armies based in Britain.

The failure seriously to disrupt the North Atlantic convoys during 1943 had been a bigger disaster than was realized by the German High Command at the time. For it was during the twelve months of that crucial year that the vast stocks of weapons, munitions, supplies and troops were ferried almost unmolested across the Atlantic, to make possible the assault on Fortress Europe. Although Oberkommando des Herres (OKH = Army High Command) believed that the invading army could be defeated comprehensively by the ground forces once it had landed, the Oberkommando der Kriegsmarine (OKM = Navy High Command) regarded the coast itself as the principal line of defence and was resolved to oppose the invasion forces offshore and at the beachheads.

However, the naval forces available to repulse an invasion fleet were scant and ill-equipped. By this stage of the war the Kriegsmarine had no heavy surface units immediately available. War losses had reduced the surface fleet to one battleship (*Tirpitz*), two pocket-battleships (*Lützow* and *Admiral Scheer*), two heavy cruisers (*Prinz Eugen* and *Admiral Hipper*), and four light cruisers (*Nürnberg, Leipzig, Köln* and Emden). Of these, *Tirpitz* was in a non-operational state in Kaafiord in northern Norway, undergoing repairs to substantial damage sustained during an air raid by carrier-borne Barracudas on 3 April. *Hipper* was in dock at Gotenhafen (Gdynia) in the eastern Baltic, still undergoing repairs to damage sustained during the Battle of the Barents Sea in December 1943. All the remaining units were being employed as training ships in the Baltic, and their effectiveness as fighting units was extremely limited because the majority of their crews were trainees.

In addition, the Kriegsmarine had a large number of smaller surface units suitable for anti-invasion duties: 24 destroyers, 69 torpedo-boats (small destroyers) and 126 Schnellboote (fast motor torpedo-boats), but these were widely scattered throughout bases in northern and southern Norway, the Baltic, the Mediterranean and the French Channel and Biscay ports.

As for the U-boat fleet, although the total number in commission had reached the imposing figure of 449 by the beginning of May 1944, 63 per cent of these (287 boats) were still undergoing trials or were being used as training boats in Baltic waters. This left 162 Frontboote (operational boats), but a large percentage of these were undergoing refits and repairs or were in the process of being equipped with improved AA armament and other refinements, so that only 43 boats were fully operational on any one day in all theatres (Atlantic, Arctic, Mediterranean and Far Eastern waters). Moreover, the existing types of U-boats that were in service, mainly Type VIIs and Type IXs, had been rendered as good as obsolete in their existing state by Allied A/S measures, and would be at a serious disadvantage against an invasion fleet which was bound to be powerfully protected by masses of escort craft and aircraft.

As the U-boats provided the main striking force of the Kriegsmarine, new technology to improve the offensive and defensive capabilities of the existing U-boats and, more importantly, the early completion of new prototypes with high submerged speed and the ability to remain submerged for long periods, had become imperative if a successful attack on the Allied invasion fleet and its support convoys were to be realized. When the invasion came, Dönitz concluded, the U-boats would have to be there, because:

'The U-boat was the sole instrument which, with a few men aboard, could make a wholly disproportionate contribution to success by sinking, for instance, just one ship laden with munitions, tanks or other war material, even if it were itself lost in the process. How many soldiers would have to be sacrificed, how great an endeavour made, to destroy on land so great a mass of enemy material?'[1]

DEVELOPMENT OF THE WALTER BOATS
None of the various types of U-boat commissioned prior to the Walter boats were 'true' submarines. It would be more correct to call them submersibles. These 'conventional' types were designed to operate mostly on the surface, and the majority of U-boat attacks were carried out on the surface at night, in which they exploited not only their high surface speed but also their low, lean silhouette to avoid detection in the darkness. They only dived to evade a counter-attack by surface craft or aircraft, and it was only on rare occasions that conditions were conducive to a submerged attack. This was because of the very slow submerged

speed of the conventional types: a maximum of 8 knots could only be maintained for very short periods.

An experimental type of U-boat with the qualities of a 'true' submarine, one that could operate continuously submerged even during an attack, had been under development by its inventor, the brilliant engineer and scientist Professor Hellmuth Walter, since well before the war.

In 1933, when Walter was working on the design of a gas turbine for Germania Werft at Kiel, it occurred to him that it would be possible to provide U-boats with a high submerged speed by using a fuel containing its own oxygen, the combustion of which would not exhaust the limited amount of oxygen available in the boat.

The essence of the Walter system was a closed-circuit turbine activated by the thermal energy produced by the decomposition of a high concentration of hydrogen peroxide (H_2O_2) in a stabilized form called Perhydrol. This resulted in the formation of hot gas under considerable natural pressure sufficient in itself to drive a turbine. The system was a complex one by which the Perhydrol was forced up by water pressure from its containers stowed at the bottom of the hull to a porcelain-lined chamber where it encountered the catalyst necessary to bring about its decomposition. This resulted in steam and oxygen at a high temperature (1,765°F) which passed to a combustion chamber where they met to ignite the oil fuel, while water was sprayed on the gas to increase its volume and decrease its temperature to 986° F. This combination of gas and steam was then led to the turbine, and from there to the condenser, where the water was extracted and the residual carbon dioxide generated in the combustion chamber was drawn off.

The result was a power plant much more compact and lightweight than the conventional diesel/electric engines of similar power, which was completely independent of an external air supply, because the Perhydrol released oxygen when it disintegrated under combustion. A boat so powered would not have to spend long periods on the surface to replenish with air like conventional boats. The main disadvantage, however, was that the Walter system used tremendous amounts of Perhydrol (25 times more fuel per mile than diesel engines), and the Perhydrol, which reacted powerfully with any impurity present, was expensive (it cost eight times as much as fuel oil) and was difficult to manufacture and store. Impurities could serve as a catalytic agent, causing decomposition and a rise of temperature which could result in spontaneous combustion. Absolute clinical cleanliness, then, was essential in preparing and storing the concentrate. After a variety of tests, flexible synthetic rubber was found to be the most suitable container.

In October 1934, Walter submitted his plans to OKM. 'The following design', he explained, 'arises from the efforts to increase surface and submerged speeds of U-boats ... [allowing] them to attain speeds which will enable them to take favourable attacking positions against fast opponents...'[2] The specifications of the revolutionary U-boat envisaged by Walter, was for a boat of 300 tons displacement with a maximum surface speed of 26 knots and a hitherto undreamed of submerged speed of 30 knots, capable of a range of 2,500 nautical miles at 15 knots, of which 20 per cent could be carried out submerged (500 miles at 15 knots). In comparison with the conventional boats then under construction (Type IIA) which were capable of a maximum speed of 13 knots surfaced and 6.9 knots submerged, Walter's proposal seemed like a flight of fancy and OKM showed little interest in the project.

Three years later, having refined his design, Walter approached Kapitän zur See Karl Dönitz, commander of a U-boat training flotilla. Impressed by the potential of Walter's design, Dönitz made representations to OKM, and at the beginning of 1939 a contract to build a small Walter test vessel (V80), to determine speed-keeping and steering capabilities at high submerged speed, was given to Germania Werft. Of some 80 tons displacement, V80 was built at Kiel in the greatest secrecy, on a slipway surrounded by high wooden screens. The results of the trials, which were carried out in the spring of 1940, with Walter himself at the controls, were declared to be sensational: V80 attained submerged speeds in excess of 23 knots!

OKM's construction office was so impressed by the result that it suggested that an immediate start should be made with the construction of six coastal-size Walter U-boats. But there was scepticism in OKM's U-boat department that operationally reliable full-size boats using the Walter turbine could be produced quickly, together with a reluctance to sacrifice current production of conventional U-boats that were achieving adequate results and were urgently needed in greater numbers to prosecute the Battle of the Atlantic. As a compromise it was decided that a larger boat should be constructed by Germania Werft, further to test the potential of the Walter system.

The design for the new test boat, designated V300 (Type XVII) but later renamed *U791*, was drawn up by the Naval Constructor's Department. But the plans they submitted in September 1941, for a boat of 600 tons with a calculated submerged speed of only 19 knots, did not correspond to Walter's idea of a high-speed boat. Disappointed, he set about his own design for a smaller test boat of about 220 tons, capable of attaining a submerged speed of 26 knots. On 3 January 1942, Walter travelled to Paris to submit his rough plans to Dönitz, who was by now a Konteradmiral and Befehlshaber der U-boote (C-in-C, U-Boats). At this meeting Dönitz declared that 'the gift of a high-speed (U-boat) which had been bestowed on him overnight, as it were, by the Walter

Process' would justify his doing everything he could to make boats of this kind available. For Dönitz, the high submerged speed outweighed all other considerations, but he did impress upon Walter that the radius of action of the boat under design would have to be sufficient for operations to the north of the British Isles, and that it would have to carry at least four torpedoes. In a telex to OKM in Berlin, Dönitz requested that construction of new test boats be commenced as soon as Walter completed his design. The upshot was that in the summer of 1942 building contracts were awarded, on the submission by Walter of two slightly variant designs, to Blohm & Voss, Hamburg, and Germania Werft, Kiel, to build two test boats each. The two boats constructed by Germania Werft (Project WK202), *U794* and *U795*, displaced 236 tons and were capable of a submerged speed of 24 knots. The two boats constructed by Blohm & Voss (Project Wa2Ol), *U792* and *U793*, were slightly larger, displacing 277 tons with a submerged speed of 25 knots. Both types carried four torpedoes. The keels of all four boats were laid down in December 1942, but it was not until 28 September 1943 that the first true Walter boat, *U792* entered the water at Blohm & Voss. She was followed by *U794* , at Germania Werft on 7 October.

Numerous difficulties and breakdowns occurred in the Walter turbines in these two boats during their subsequent trials, but by March 1944 these had been ironed out sufficiently for Dönitz, together with Admirals von Friedeburg, Backenköhler, Thedsen and Godt, to put to sea in *U794* to experience at first-hand speed and diving trials at Hela in the Bay of Danzig. This must be the only occasion on which five admirals sailed together in one submarine! The results were impressive, *U794* reached a submerged speed of 22 knots, and at the end of the trials Dönitz declared: 'With more courage and confidence in the Supreme Naval Command, we could have had this [type of] boat one or two years earlier.' In later trials *U792* covered the measured mile, submerged, at 25 knots: a speed never quite achieved by any other boat. Unfortunately *U792* was shortly afterwards damaged in a collision and she was still under repair at the end of the war.

The conclusion was that the Walter turbine had shown its value despite the numerous initial difficulties. The other two boats, *U793* and *U795*, were commissioned in April. Work on the construction of these two boats had been skimped because of a shortage of shipyard labour, and they suffered from defects to such an extent that they were never used for anything other than experimental purposes. Of the four, only *U794* was fully commissioned into service, being used for sea training of future Walter boat crews at Hela.

The experience gained in the construction and model tests of these boats prompted Dönitz (by now Grossadmiral and C-in-C,

Kriegsmarine) successfully to press for the construction of 24 coastal-type Walter boats, based on the Wa2Ol and WK202 designs, but enlarged and developed for full operational deployment. Contracts for these 24 boats were given to Blohm & Voss and Germania Werft in equal quantities on 4 January 1943. Designated Type XVIIB (*U1405–U1416*, built by B & V) and Type XVIIG (*U1081–U1092*, built by GW), they displaced 312 tons (Type XVIIB) and 314 tons (Type XVIIG). These boats would be ideally suited for operations against the Allied invasion fleet, if they could be completed in time.

In September 1942, while the designs for Types XVIIB and XVIIG were being drawn up, Dönitz decided that an ocean-going Walter boat would be the ideal weapon with which to prosecute the Battle of the Atlantic. In a conference with Hitler at the Chancellery, Dönitz argued the case for the construction of such boats.

'Technical improvements in U-boats are required so that in tactical terms, in spite of the increase in Allied anti-submarine measures, we may retain at least the same success rate we have enjoyed hitherto [the conference took place eight months before the defeat suffered in 'Black May' of 1943]. Most important of all is the requirement that submerged

---

Characteristics of Type XVIIB and XVIIG Walter Boats

	Type XVIIB (*U1405 – U1416*)	*Type XVIIG* (*U1081 – U1092*)
Displacement (tons):		
Surfaced	312	314
Submerged	337	345
Dimensions (feet):		
Length	136¼	129¾
Beam	10¾	11¼
Draught	14¾	15½
Machinery:		
Walter single-shaft geared turbines,2,500shp; 8-cylinder		As Type XVIIB
Deutz diesel/electric motors, 210/77 bhp/shp		
Fuel Capacity:	75 tons H_2O_2	64 tons H_2O_2
Maximum speeds (knots):		
Surfaced	8.5	8.5
Submerged	21.5	21.5
Endurance (nm):		
Surfaced	3,000 @ 8 knots	3,000 @ 8 knots
Submerged	150 @ 20 knots	114 @ 20 knots
Armament:		
torpedo tubes	2 bow	2 bow
torpedoes	four 21in	four 21in
Crew:	19	19

speeds be increased and this is possible by the introduction of the Walter boats. A U-boat with high submerged speed has a greater chance of getting into a good firing position against a convoy despite enemy escort vessels. It would also mean that a U-boat would be more readily capable of evading its pursuers.'[3]

Impressed by the potential of the Walter boats, Hitler approved Dönitz's proposal, stating that, in his opinion, the introduction of the Walter boats, by virtue of their high submerged speed would mean incontrovertible success. This resulted in Professor Walter's submission of a design for a huge, 1,485-ton boat, designated Type XVIII, carrying 23 torpedoes and capable of a submerged speed of 24 knots, with a radius of action of 5,200 nautical miles at 12 knots surfaced and 250 miles at 20 knots submerged. A building contract for two prototypes, of this design (*U796* and *U797*) was given to Deutsche Werke, Kiel, in January 1943.

The Walter boats were the nearest the Germans came to realizing the dream of a 'true' submarine which, as opposed to the limited submersible qualities of conventional U-boats, would be capable of remaining submerged for the greater part of an operational patrol, being divorced from the need to spend lengthy periods surfaced to recharge the diesel/electric engines with air which made the conventional boats so vulnerable. But enthusiasm for the Walter boats began to wane because they were phenomenally complex and expensive to build and operate, and they relied on a questionable supply of fuel. For these reasons work on the two Type XVIII ocean-going boats was abandoned in the spring of 1944. However, it was the design work on the Type XVIII Walter boats that led to the concept of the 'Electro-boats', which proved to be a more successful venture.

THE DEVELOPMENT OF THE ELECTRO-BOATS

In March 1943, Heinrich Heep, an engineer involved in the development of the Walter boats, suggested to the Director of Naval Construction, Professor Oelfken, that a U-boat with high submerged speed could be produced by the simple expedient of trebling the battery capacity of the conventional diesel/electric engines, which could be achieved by utilizing the large, but streamlined hull of the Type XVIII ocean-going Walter boat.

Professor Oelfken submitted detailed plans for converting the basic Type XVIII design to Dönitz on 19 June 1943, arguing that: 'If we intend to build such a large boat [Walter Type XVIII] and consequently have so much [propulsion plant] space at our disposal, we can accomplish much more than hitherto by using conventional [diesel/electric] engine installations...'[4]

The calculations for the new 1,621-ton boat, known as an 'Electro-boat' because of its large battery capacity, showed that it would be capable of a submerged speed of 18 knots which, although 6 knots slower than the Walter Type XVIII, was 10 knots faster than that obtainable by conventional boats, and was sustainable for a much greater length of time. The new boats should be able to travel submerged at 18 knots for 1½ hours or 12–14 knots for 10 hours. In addition, the enhanced pressure hull of the Walter-type shell would give the Electro-boat a greater diving depth than existing types; and a new hydraulic loading system would double the rate at which torpedoes could be loaded and fired.

The assurance that Electro-boats could be constructed much more quickly and cheaply than boats powered by the complex and expensive Walter turbine, offered Dönitz the heady prospect of regaining the initiative at sea much sooner than he had hoped, and he pressed for the immediate introduction of the Electro-boats in large numbers. The final design for this large ocean-going boat, designated Type XXI, was for a U-boat displacing 1,621 tons, armed with 20 torpedoes, with a maximum speed of 15.6 knots surfaced and 17.18 knots submerged. By virtue of its deep-diving capacity, together with improved manoeuvrability and a long endurance at high silent-running speed (60 hours at 5 knots as compared to conventional boats' 20 to 30 hours at 1.5 knots), the offensive potential of this type, and the subsequent chances of eluding pursuit after launching an attack, or withstanding a protracted counter-attack by depth-charges, were greatly enhanced. The large fuel capacity of this type also extended the radius of action to the whole of the North and South Atlantic without reliance on rendezvous with U-tankers (Milchkühe) to refuel. These inherent qualities were further enhanced by the fitting of the newly developed Balkon Gerät (balcony device) hydrophone, a sophisticated passive echo chamber which could track, identify and range multiple targets at a range of 50 miles while the boat was totally submerged.

During the design work on Type XXI, Professor Oelfken began investigating the possibility of employing the hull shape of the Walter coastal boats to produce a coastal-size Electro-boat. The preliminary outline was placed before Dönitz at the same time as the presentation of the Type XXI design. Although the Grossadmiral was much more interested in the ocean-going type, he ordered the planning of the coastal Electro-boat, designated Type XXIII, to proceed, when it was pointed out to him that the large size of the Type XXI rendered it unsuitable for operations in the North Sea and other shallow-water areas, particularly the Mediterranean and Black Sea.

The design of the XXIII, in contrast to the ocean-going Electro-boat for which many innovations were planned, was kept very simple as regards installations and engines, and was to be assembled from well-tried components. The final design, which was ready by July 1943, was for a very small, 234-ton, boat armed with only two torpedoes, with a maximum speed of 9.7 knots surfaced and only 12.5 knots submerged. Radius of action was limited: 2,600 nautical miles at 8 knots on the surface, and 175 miles at 4 knots submerged.

Under the usual planning procedures, large U-boats of Type XXI required a development and building time of at least eighteen months, so it was reckoned that the first three prototypes of the ocean-going Electro-boat would not be completed until November 1944, and mass

Characteristics of Type XXI and Type XXIII Electro-Boats

	Type XXI	*Type XXIII*
Displacement (tons):		
Surfaced	1,621	232
Submerged	1,819	256
Dimensions (feet):		
Length	251¾	113¾
Beam	21¾	9¾
Draught	20¾	12¼
Machinery:		
	2-shaft 6-cylinder MAN single-shaft diesel/electric motors, 4,500/5,000 bhp/shp silent creep-speed electric motors, 226 shp	1-shaft 6-cylinder MWM diesel/electric motors, 575/600 bhp/shp; silent creep-speed electric motors, 35 shp
Fuel Capacity:	250 tons	18 tons
Maximum speeds (knots):		
Surfaced	15½	9¾
Submerged	17	12½
Endurance (nm):		
Surfaced	15,500 @ 10 knots	4,300 @ 6 knots
	11,150 @ 12 knots	2,800 @ 8 knots
Max. sustained	5,100 @ 15½	1,350 @ 9¾ knots
Submerged	365 @ 5 knots	175 @ 4 knots
	285 @ 6 knots	113 @ 6 knots
	170 @ 8 knots	70 @ 8 knots
	110 @ 10 knots	43 @ 10 knots
Diving depth (feet):	376	330
Armament:		
torpedo tubes	6 bow	2 bow
torpedoes	twenty 21in	two 21in
guns	two twin 2cm AA	none
Crew:	57	14

production would not commence until March 1945. This meant that the Type XXIs would not be ready for operational use before 1946 – 2½–3 years after Dönitz had ordered their production and far too late to influence the war at sea. In view of the critical situation, Dönitz demanded that the construction of Type XXI be pushed forward by all available means. During a conference with Hitler on 8 July 1943, he urged that three-shift, round the clock working be instituted at the shipbuilding yards, and that an extra 260,000 men, especially technical staff, be drafted in to speed up production.

Hitler put the matter in the hands of Albert Speer, Reich Minister for Armaments, who in turn called upon the expertise of Otto Merker, General Director of Magirus Werke in Ulm, who, being experienced in the automobile industry, was familiar with modern methods of mass production. Merker quickly came to the conclusion that unless the traditional method of constructing individual boats from start to finish on a single building slip were abandoned, nothing could be done to expedite building time.

As an alternative he suggested that the Type XXIs and Type XXIIIs be assembled from prefabricated sections, which could be put together like automobiles on an assembly line. If this process were adopted, he estimated that the first of the Type XXI Electro-boats would be ready by 1 April 1944. Mass production could then begin immediately, and by the autumn of 1944 a formidable rate of thirty Type XXIs would be delivered each month. Type XXIII construction time was estimated at seven months, and the first boats should, therefore, be ready by February 1944, with twenty boats a month following from March 1944. Despite scepticism as to the feasibility of the project by the conservative-minded Naval Construction Office, Speer approved Merker's proposal, and contracts for the prefabricated parts for 241 Type XXIs and 140 Type XXIIIs were sent out to industry in August 1943.

Because of the ever-increasing intensity and frequency of bombing raids on the shipyards, a policy of dispersal was decided upon for the construction of the individual sections of the prefabricated parts. The criteria for the firms selected (mostly in western Germany, with a smaller number in Silesia and Danzig) was that they be widely scattered throughout the interior of Germany, and have accessibility to navigable rivers and canals so that the Type XXI sections could be transported to the shipyards on barges. As the prefabricated sections of the Type XXIII were much smaller, it was planned to transport them by rail.

The pressure hull sections, complete with bulkheads, in crude form (without interior fittings) for Type XXI were to be completed by steel firms (50 per cent of Germany's steel-producing firms were involved). These crude sections were then to be transported to thirteen shipyards where the main and auxiliary engines and all electric wiring and pipe-work would be installed. The final assembly, when the completed sections would be welded together, was to be carried out at major shipyards experienced in U-boat construction. Three yards were chosen to complete the Type XXIs: Blohm & Voss, Hamburg; Deschimag, Bremen; and Schichau Werke, Danzig.

The programme for the Type XXIII coastal boats differed in that it was decided that the crude sections of the pressure hull would be built by the steel firms already chosen for the Type XXI programme, but both the installation of the interior fittings and the final assembly for the 50 boats intended for operations in the North Sea and British coastal waters would be carried out by Deutsche Werft at the firm's principal yard, Finkenwerder at Hamburg. Boats destined for operations in the Mediterranean and Black Sea would have their sections fitted out and assembled at Deutsche Werft's foreign outlets in Toulon (30 boats), Genoa (30), Monfalcone near Trieste (15) and Nikolayev near Odessa on the Russian Black Sea coast (15).

In Merker's plan the construction of the prefabricated parts of the ocean-going Type XXIs was divided into nine sections, with the following specifications:

SECTION 1. Stern with stern compartment: length 41½ feet; weight 65 tons.

SECTION 2. Electric motor compartments: length 33 feet; weight 130 tons.

SECTION 3. Diesel engine compartment: length 27½ feet; weight 140 tons.

SECTION 4. Crews' living quarters: length 17½ feet; weight 70 tons.

SECTION 5. Control room and galley: length 25 feet; weight 140 tons.

SECTION 6. Forward living quarters: length 39¼ feet; weight 165 tons.

SECTION 7. Torpedo stowage compartment: length 22¼ feet; weight 92 tons.

SECTION 8. Bows with torpedo tubes: length 46 feet; weight 110 tons.

SECTION 9. Conning-tower superstructure: length 46¼ feet; weight not known.

The smaller, Type XXIII coastal boats' had four prefabricated sections:

SECTION 1. Stern with steering installation, silent creep-speed engine and gearing: length 30 feet; weight 11½ tons.

SECTION 2. Main engines: length 19½ feet; weight 14 tons.

SECTION 3. Control room and part of the forward living
quarters: length 24½ feet; weight 18 tons.
SECTION 4. Bows with torpedo tube installation: length 32½
feet; weight 16¼ tons.

Merker's system promised to reduce the building time for the 1,621-ton
Type XXI to 260,000-300,000 man-hours per boat, compared to 460,000
man-hours for a boat of similar size by existing methods. To realize the
planned early completion of the prototypes and to ensure that sufficient
boats had been delivered by the autumn of 1944 to resume the Battle of
the Atlantic, no further conventional U-boats were to be laid down,
BdU reckoning that the completion of the 250 old-type boats already on
the stocks, in various stages of construction, would be sufficient to
maintain continuity in the supply of operational U-boats, and provide
enough reinforcements to cover losses, until the Electro-and Walter
boats became available.

Although the Electro-boats came closer than all the existing types
to being what Dönitz called a 'one-hundred-per-cent under-water boat',
they were not 'true' submarines because their propulsion units were not
divorced from reliance on the atmosphere (the Walter system was,
because it produced its own oxygen), so they still had to spend long
periods on the surface. However, during the early design stage of Type
XXI the suggestion had been mooted of fitting both the Walter and
Electro-boats with a flexible 'breathing-pipe'. This inspired the engineers Ulrich Gabler and Heinrich Heep, both leading ship designers, to
come up with the idea of a rigid air-pipe that could also be used in
rough weather when the waves would frequently wash over the top of
the pipe. The resulting snorkel, a rigid tube which enabled a U-boat to
take in air, expel diesel exhaust and charge her batteries while remaining submerged at periscope depth, consequently endowed the Electro-
boats with many of the qualities of a 'true' submarine. Here, then, was
the weapon, Electro-boats equipped with snorkel, that would, if they
could be completed in time, give the Germans the means to regain the
initiative at sea, and provide a strike-force capable of repelling an invasion fleet.

THE DEVELOPMENT OF SNORKEL

Hellmuth Walter's preliminary design for a high-speed U-boat, formulated in 1933, included the installation of an extensible air-shaft to
introduce atmospheric air into the boat while it was travelling just
below the surface. At about the same time Lieutenant-Commander J.
Wichers, of the Royal Netherlands Navy, also designed an extensible
air-tube to facilitate the use of diesel engines while a submarine was
submerged for long periods. In the lead up to the war Walter's concept

was laid aside as impracticable, but Wichers improved his design by adding a rudimentary head-valve with a spherical float to prevent water finding its way down the air-tube while the boat was under way.

By 1938 Wichers' invention had been fitted to two Dutch submarines, complete with automatic head-valves and a motor-drive for lifting and retracting the tube. The Germans became aware of Wichers' device when they overran Holland in May 1940, and captured submarines fitted with the air-tube (nine Dutch submarines had been so fitted by this time). But it was not until March 1943, when Walter and Dönitz were discussing the future development of the Walter boats, that Walter resurrected the idea. He submitted a design, based on his original 1933 idea, for an air-tube consisting of two pressure-resistant flexible hoses fastened together by metal bands, their lower ends secured rigidly to the boat and their upper ends terminating in a raft-like float housing a non-return valve. One hose was designed to supply air to the diesels, the other to conduct away the exhaust gases. Such a device was now of great value because enemy aircraft and surface radar were progressively forcing the U-boats to spend more and more time submerged, and Dönitz ordered experiments to be put in hand.

In the event Walter's design proved impracticable, but the concept was developed by the U-boat specialist engineers, Ulrich Gabler and Heinrich Heep, who designed a rigid tube fitted with a spherical float based on the Dutch design for an automatic head-valve (similar to a ballcock valve in a lavatory cistern) which would make the air-tube usable in rough Atlantic seas. The tube, which could be extended and retracted like a periscope, contained both a fresh-air shaft and an exhaust shaft, and was given the somewhat vulgar German term for a nose – Schnorchel.

The advantages of the snorkel were summarized in a report Walter made to Dönitz in May 1943, the 'Black May' of the Kriegsmarine. 'The outward and return journeys to base by U-boats could proceed almost without any danger. The detection of periscopes and snorkel by radar installations [in enemy aircraft and surface craft] would only be possible at close range and, on the high seas, would probably not occur at all ... Visual detection from aircraft would be difficult in normal sea conditions and, in any case, would be possible only at distances at which the U-boat would already have spotted the opponent. Snorkel could be of considerable worth to the high-speed underwater boats [Walter and Electro] ... they would hardly need to travel on the surface at all, and surface travel could be kept to an absolute minimum.'[5]

The first snorkels were constructed by Deutsche Werke, Kiel, in only three weeks, and were fitted to the 291-ton Type IIC training boats

U57 and *U58*. Initial tests carried out in August 1943 proved successful, and the installation of snorkels to conventional Frontboote began in the winter of 1943/4.

The first Frontboot to be fitted with snorkel was the 761-ton *U264* (Type VIIC), which was sunk by depth-charges by the RN sloops *Starling* and *Woodpecker*, west-southwest of Ireland on 19 February 1944, before she could make a report on her experience of snorkelling under operational conditions. The second boat to be fitted, the Type VIIC *U574*, was also lost (depth-charged by aircraft and destroyers north of the Azores on 13 March 1944), but not before her commander was able to radio a report on his experience with snorkel. He complained that it was impracticable to operate snorkel in an area where a U-boat hunt by surface craft was in progress, because the din of the diesels made it impossible to listen for the approach of enemy vessels' propellers. To alleviate this problem it became standard procedure to shut down the diesels every twenty minutes so that a hydrophone check could be made of the surrounding waters. There was also, he considered, a danger that the snorkel exhaust fumes might be located, or the sound of the boat's engines be picked up at long range while snorkelling was in progress. His reservations seemed to have been borne out by the

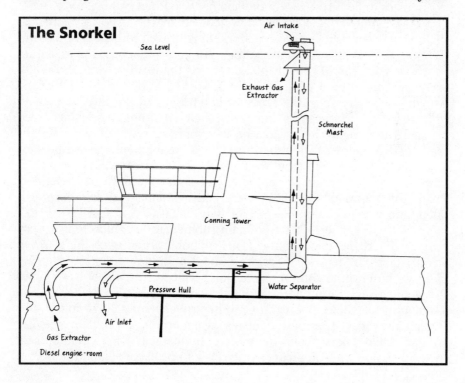

The Snorkel

loss of the boat, but the next commander to experience operational use of snorkel told a different tale. On 19 May 1944, when *U667* (Type VIIC) returned to a French Biscay base after a patrol in the North Atlantic, the commander reported that during the return passage he had proceeded submerged for nine days and, having thus avoided detection, was most enthusiastic about the new device. He also reported that the batteries could be sufficiently recharged in three hours of snorkelling to power the boat for the rest of the day, by running one diesel to charge the batteries while driving the boat with the other diesel at 3 to 4 knots.

A few months before the commander of *U667* waxed eloquent about snorkel, the potential tactical advantages that it would give the U-boats caused BdU to insist on the installation of the device to all Frontboote and boats under construction as quickly as possible. But this demand placed a further burden on the already over-stretched ship-building industry, and sub-contractors with little experience in marine construction had to be pressed into service to manufacture the individual parts. In some cases their work was far below standard, and production proceeded slowly, remaining a bottle-neck until the summer of 1944. As a result the decision was made that snorkel should be fitted as a priority to Frontboote, and only then to newly constructed boats. Even then, only thirty Frontboote had been so fitted by May 1944.

The innovation was never welcomed by the majority of the U-boat crews, because in practice snorkelling proved to be a very uncomfortable and dangerous undertaking. All too frequently waves would wash over the top of the air-intake causing the head-valve to close and the air in the interior of the boat to be sucked in by the diesel engines, which would create a low pressure condition causing intense pain to the crew and on occasions damage to their ear-drums. The danger also existed that if the air in the boat became foul as a result of heavy seas or bad depth-keeping causing the snorkel head to dip below the surface for any length of time, the crew would have to don escape apparatus until the boat could surface to ventilate. But if the presence of the enemy made this impossible the crew were in grave danger of being asphyxiated, and it is believed that one or two boats were in fact lost in this way. Moreover, being able to remain submerged for much longer periods confined the crew to the claustrophobic interior of the narrow, crowded boat, depriving them of the traditional practice of being allowed up into the conning tower for a welcome breath of fresh air or for a smoke. The long periods of submerged travel also prevented the jettisoning of cooking waste and other rubbish so that it rotted and fouled the boat. Use of the heads also became a problem because snorkel-fitted boats spent more time submerged, where the outside water pressure was too great for the waste to be expelled and until more powerful compressed air flushes were developed the crews were forced to use tins which made conditions even more unpleasant.

To overcome some of these problems, the design of the ocean-going Walter and Electro-boats was modified, the better to equip them for long periods of submerged travel. Air conditioning was installed, and a waste disposal system that could be used while the boat was submerged. There was even the luxury of a freezer so that meat and vegetables replaced the monotonous diet of tinned foodstuffs.

Although snorkelling remained problematic, by June 1944 BdU was of the opinion that the survival advantage of snorkel-fitted boats were so obvious that 'on account of the great number of air attacks, above all on U-boats without snorkel, and the extensive damage caused thereby, for the present further sailing of those boats not so fitted has been stopped'.[6] In the final analysis, it was the development of snorkel that endowed the conventional boats with a greater chance of survival, and gave the Electro-boats many of the qualities of a 'true' submarine, providing the Germans with the most useful of all Hitler's 'miracle weapons'.

RADAR DEVELOPMENT

At the outbreak of war all U-boats were fitted with the FuMO 29 Gema surface and air search radar set (so called after its manufacturer, Gesellschaft für Elektro-akustische und Mechanische Apparate) which operated on an 80cm wavelength, and had a range of approximately five miles for detecting surface vessels and ten miles for detecting aircraft flying at an altitude of 1,500 feet. Experience proved that the Gema set was not very effective: most U-boat crews discovered that an enemy vessel could be seen by the naked eye long before it appeared on the radarscope. For this reason, by March 1942 BdU had decided to replace the Gema set with a navalized version of the Luftwaffe's newly developed FUG 200 Hohentwiel (Owl) night-fighter radar set. The resulting FuMO 61 Hohentwiel-U, gave some 30 per cent better resolution than the Gema set and a 4-mile increase in range for the detection of low-flying aircraft. Development and production problems delayed the introduction of Hohentwiel-U, and it was not until two years after BdU opted for the set that the first two were fitted in *U311* and *U743* in March 1944. However Hohentwiel-U proved its worth. The first two boats equipped with the set found that they were able to pick up attacking aircraft at extreme ranges, and were able to man and range their guns in good time; on two occasions even managing to open fire before actually sighting the attacking aircraft. From April 1944 onwards, Hohentwiel-U brought great relief to the boats equipped with it. 'It showed the exact direction and range of an aircraft, thus making it possible to decide whether or not it was making a direct line for the boat and, if so, whether diving were practicable. The whole routine of the boat was therefore made much calmer and a safe yardstick provided for diving and AA defence.'[7]

RADAR DETECTOR DEVELOPMENTS

During 1941 the British began equipping their aircraft with 'Air to Surface Vessel' (ASV) radar. From the summer of 1942 U-boats increasingly reported surprise attacks by aircraft, even at night, when they would suddenly find themselves illuminated by powerful searchlights (Leigh Lights). Observations eventually showed the cause to be radar, and the Germans countered this development by fitting the U-boats, from July 1942 onwards, with a VHF-heterodyne radar detection receiver, designated FuMB 1 Metox (so named after the French manufacturer of the sets), which covered a broad range of wavelengths from 1.3 to 3.6 metres.

Initially the results were very successful; Metox effectively neutralized the threat of the ASV radar, and losses from aircraft dropped off considerably, especially from night sightings. It came as a severe shock, therefore, when during the early part of 1943, U-boats were once again subjected to surprise air attacks by night. By the end of July 1943, Dönitz had come to the conclusion that the enemy had found a way of homing-in on the emitted radiation of the Metox sets. He immediately forbade the use of Metox, and on 5 August suspended U-boat operations until the boats could be fitted with new non-radiating radar detection receivers. In fact enemy aircraft were not homing-in on radiation emissions from Metox; their success was due to the development of a new ASV radar (ASV Mk III/H_2S) which operated on the 9.7cm wavelength which Metox did not cover. But this was only part of the story, as Roskill, the official historian of the war at sea, points out:

'... radar development had undoubtedly restored the initiative to our ... air patrols, and it was making the passages to and from the operational U-boat bases increasingly hazardous. Moreover the German scientists believed at the time that we could not have overcome the technical difficulties involved in producing a centimetric radar set [which the ASV Mk III/H_2S was]. But the Allied successes in fact stemmed from wider causes than radar, and had Dönitz known about them his anxieties would certainly not have diminished. In the first place recent reinforcements had enabled us to organize ... far more regular air cover over and around the convoys ... and escort carriers had begun to accompany them throughout their passages, and were providing air cover in waters to which the shore-based aircraft could not yet reach. *Equally important was the fact that Allied intelligence was now working with great speed and accuracy* [author's italics]. This enabled convoys to be diverted clear of dangerous waters, and surface vessels or aircraft to be directed to the positions where they were most likely to find their quarry.'[8]

Roskill's comment that 'Allied intelligence was now working with great speed and accuracy' was a veiled reference to Allied cryptanalytical success in breaking 'Triton', the U-boat Enigma codes (a fact not admitted when Roskill's work was published in 1960). This was the major reason why the Allies were able to pin-point U-boat locations and attack them from the air, and Dönitz's belief that enemy aircraft had found a way of homing-in on the emitted radiation of the Metox sets was not only completely erroneous but led him down a blind alley, deflecting suspicion away from the insecurity of the U-boat Enigma which was to prove fatal.

Unaware that they had drawn the wrong conclusions, the Germans pressed ahead with the development of a non-emitting radar detector. A new receiver, FuMB 9 Zypern, more commonly known as Wanze GI (short for Wellenanzeiger = wave indicator) or Hagenuk, after its manufacturer, had been under development for some time and it was rushed into production in August 1943. It covered a narrower band than Metox, being sensitive between 1.3 and 1.9 metres.

Wanze G1 was rushed into service so quickly that it was not realized, until it had been fitted to a number of Frontboote, that it too radiated emissions, albeit much weaker than those emitted by Metox. This became apparent at the beginning of September when *U386*, equipped with Wanze Gl, was surprised and attacked by an aircraft at night. This forced BdU to order, on 5 November 1943, that its use be discontinued until its replacement, the nearly identical but non-radiating, Wanze G2 could be brought into service. As a temporary substitute a new and very simple, non-radiating radar detector, but with the handicap of a restricted range, the FuMB 10 Borkum, which covered the 3.3 to 0.8 metres wavelengths, was rushed out to the U-boat fleet.

A problem with Wanze G2 was that it didn't provide coverage of the 9.7cm wavelength (employed by the British ASV Mk III H_2S radar), but luckily for the Germans a NVK/Telefunken development had just reached the production stage. This was the FuMB 7 Naxos non-radiating radar detector which covered the high-frequency end of the spectrum between the 7cm and 12cm bands, but its effective range of 3 miles was too low to provide security from sudden air attack.

Individually, Wanze G2, Borkum and Naxos all had drawbacks, but used in combination, as they were at the end of 1943, they represented full coverage of the entire radar spectrum, or as the BdU War Diary expressed it: 'The installation of the detector-receivers Naxos,

Borkum and Wanze G2 guaranteed radar interception without the disadvantage of radiation emission over all hitherto essential wavelengths.'

Dönitz, still unaware of the true reason for the Allied successes, believed that this combination would put an end to the heavy losses suffered from air attack. He was quickly disillusioned. During the 10-month period August 1942 to May 1943, an average of 7.5 U-boats per month had been sunk by aircraft; during the subsequent 4-month period, June to September 1943, this rose to an average of 16 per month; and during the 8-month period, October 1943 to May 1944, when the combination of the three radar detectors was in operation, the losses from air attack averaged 9.5 boats per month; the decline from the previous quarter being attributable to the fact that far fewer boats sailed on operations.

The continuing high rate of loss from air attack goaded the Germans into pressing forward with further radar detector development. This led to the introduction of the FuMB 24 Fliege (Fly) and FuMB 25 Mücke (Gnat) during the spring of 1944. The former provided coverage of the 8cm to 20cm wavelengths, and was capable of detecting an aircraft's ASV radar at an altitude of more than 3,000 feet at a distance of 37 miles; while Mücke covered the very-high-frequency 2cm to 4cm band used by the 3cm American Meddo radar.

Although experience gained during the early months of 1944 had shown that 80 per cent of detected enemy radar transmissions were within the 10cm band (emanating from the ASV Mk III/H$_2$S and the Meddo sets), it was considered imprudent to dispense with Wanze G2 and Borkum, with the result that the conning towers' of the U-boats were cluttered with the aerials of Wanze, Borkum, Fliege and Mücke. To relieve this clutter the Fliege and Mücke sets were combined to form a system known as FuME 26 Tunis, which was first installed in May 1944.

Despite these advanced developments, U-boat losses from aircraft attack rose to an average of 14.36 per month after May 1944, but to the very end the Germans failed to realize that it was the insecurity of their Enigma ciphers that was their undoing. Moreover, although radar and radar detector developments gave the U-boats some security from aircraft attack, the increasing numbers of aircraft that the Allies were able to employ on A/S duties were such that no U-boat could stay on the surface for more than a few minutes; a debilitating handicap for conventional boats because of their slow submerged speeds.

THE INTRODUCTION OF 'SMALL BATTLE UNITS'

The attack on *Tirpitz* by British 'X-craft' midget submarines on 23 September 1943, which put the battleship out of commission for six months, came as a tremendous shock to the Germans. Up to this time the Kriegsmarine had shown no interest in midget submarines, the main tactical objective being the attacking of convoys by large ocean-going boats. But the damaging of *Tirpitz* and the realization that the Kriegsmarine had little with which to oppose an Allied invasion of northern Europe, caused OKM to begin investigating the possibilities of small surface, submersible and submarine attack-craft in the autumn of 1943.

This led to the formation in April 1944 of a special command under Konteradmiral Helmut Heye, the K-Verband (a contraction of Kleinkampfverbande) or 'Small Battle Unit Command', which was to develop the tactics and direct the operations of small attack-craft. In all, seven K-Verband craft entered service during the last year of the war.

HECHT (Pike) — This was a 3-man midget submarine, also know as U-boat Type XXVIIA, which was originally intended to carry limpet mines but was subsequently redesigned as a torpedo carrier for use against enemy shipping under way in coastal waters. Displacing 12 tons (submerged), 34 feet long on a beam of 5¼ feet, Hecht was capable of both surface and submerged travel. Powered by a 13shp single-shaft electric motor, it had a maximum speed of 5.6 knots surfaced and 6 knots submerged, with a range of 78 nautical miles at 3 knots surfaced and 40 miles at 6 knots submerged. Maximum diving depth was 164 feet and the boat was armed with one 21in torpedo (it was also capable of carrying one mine). Hitler approved the construction of fifty Hecht on 18 January 1944, and on 9 March Germania Werft was awarded a contract to build a prototype and an order for 52 production boats followed on 28 March. The first two Hecht (including the prototype) were delivered in May 1944, followed by one in June, seven in July and 43 in August. It had been intended to follow the initial contract of 53 boats by a further 189 (designated *U2111–U2300*), but Hecht did not prove a successful design, and the 53 boats completed were used only for training purposes.

SEEHUND (Seal) — This was a 2-man midget submarine, also know as U-boat Type XXVIIB, capable of both surface and submerged travel, and with a greater range of operation than Hecht. Propulsion, when surfaced, was provided by a 60hp single-shaft Bussing lorry engine, and for submerged travel a 25hp battery-powered electric motor, which gave the boat a radius of 300 nautical miles at 7 knots surfaced and 63 miles at 3 knots submerged. Displacing 14.7 tons (submerged), Seehund was 39 feet long on a beam of 5½ feet, and was armed with two 21in electric torpedoes slung beneath the boat. Three prototypes were ordered from

Howaldt in Kiel on 30 July 1943, and a large-scale programme was decided on for the production of 942 boats (designated U5501 to U6442), which were to be built by Schichau Werke, Elbing, Germania Werft, and Klöckner-Humboldt-Deutz at Ulm. In the event, raw material shortages, labour difficulties and conflicting priorities combined to reduce Seehund production, with the result that the three prototypes were not delivered until September 1944. These were followed by 35 deliveries in October, 61 in November, 70 in December and a further 116 during the first four months of 1945, for a grand total of 285 by the end of the war. Seehund, which had a maximum diving depth of 164 feet, proved relatively immune to depth-charge attack, its light weight causing it to be tossed aside by the explosion without serious damage.

BIBER (Beaver) — This was a tiny one-man midget submarine (the smallest U-boat in the Kriegsmarine) which displaced a mere 6.5 tons. It was 29¼ feet long on a beam of 5¼ feet, and was powered by a 32hp single-shaft Opel Blitz lorry engine for surface travel, and by an adapted 13hp battery-powered electric torpedo motor for submerged propulsion, which gave the boat a radius of 130 nautical miles at 6 knots surfaced and 8.6 miles at 5 knots submerged. It was armed with two 21in torpedoes slung beneath the boat. A major drawback with Biber was that despite having a diving depth of 65 feet, lack of compensation and trimming tanks meant that the boat could not be maintained at periscope depth, so attacks had to be carried out on the surface. Three prototypes, built by Lübeck Flenderwerke, were delivered in May 1944, and a further 321 followed from June to November of the same year.

MOLCH (Salamander) — This was a one-man, all-electric midget submarine, intended for coastal offensive operations. It was designed for submerged travel only, being powered by a 13.9hp single-shaft electric motor which gave the boat a radius of only 40 nautical miles at 5 knots. Displacing 11 tons, 35 feet on a beam of 6 feet, Molch resembled an enlarged torpedo. It was armed with two underslung 21in torpedoes. Lack of space prevented the installation of a gyro-compass, and all the pilot had to navigate by was a simple magnetic compass fitted to the mast outside the hull which could be observed from the interior through a Perspex window. The first prototype was delivered on 12 June 1944. By the end of the war a total of 393 had been delivered by Deschimag AG Weser, Bremen.

LINSEN (Lentil) — This was a radio-controlled motor boat developed from the Italian one-man assault boats. A Linsen unit comprised one control boat and two explosive motor boats, each of the latter carrying a

660-800lb explosive charge in the stern. Each explosive-boat carried a pilot who steered the boat to within striking distance, some 100 yards, of the target. The pilot then tripped switches that enabled the boat to be radio-guided by the control boat, and jumped overboard. The radio operator in the control boat, equipped with an ultra-shortwave transmitter, steered the unpiloted explosive boat the last hundred yards to the target. The control boat also had the task of picking up the ditched pilot. Linsen displaced 1.2 tons, was 18½ feet long, and was fitted with two 95hp V-8 automobile petrol engines, giving a maximum speed of 31 knots for 2 hours, or a cruising speed of 15 knots for 4.5 hours, and a radius of about 60 miles.

MANNED-TORPEDOES — These were cheap, easy to manufacture, simple weapons composed of a carrier body in the shape of a large torpedo, steered by a pilot who sat in a Perspex-covered cockpit in the bow section, protruding 18 inches above the water-line. Underneath was a standard 21in torpedo which was clamped to the carrier body. The cockpit was equipped with only very basic controls – start, stop, and a lever to turn the craft to port or starboard, and a trigger to fire the torpedo.

The first of these weapons to be developed, entering service in March 1944, was *Neger* (Nigger), so called after the name of its chief designer, the naval engineer Richard Mohr ('Mohr' is the 'polite' German word for 'Negro', although the pejorative 'Nigger' was used). Displacing 2¾ tons and 25 feet in length, Neger was powered by a 12hp single-shaft electric torpedo motor and was capable of travelling for 48 nautical miles at 4 knots in a surfaced awash condition (it had no submerged capability). In total about 200 Neger were constructed.

Further development in the concept of the manned-torpedo resulted in *Marder* (Pine Marten). This resembled *Neger* in every respect except that the carrier body was two feet longer to allow the incorporation of a diving-tank and a compressed-air pump. These installations gave Marder (which displaced 3 tons) a diving capacity of 100 feet. But because the craft could only remain submerged for a limited period, and since no navigational instruments other than a wrist-compass were provided, the diving capability was only practicable for evading attack, and *Marder* operated in travel and attack in a surfaced awash condition like *Neger*. The first *Marder* entered service in July 1944, and by the end of the war about 300 had been delivered.

The final development was *Hai* (Shark). Designed as a super *Marder*, the carrier-body of *Hai* was stretched by nine feet to a length of 36 feet to allow for extra battery capacity. This enabled the craft to achieve a speed of 20 knots for the final attack run, and increased the range to 63 nautical miles at a cruising speed of 3 knots. When the prototype underwent sea trials it proved to be so erratic in a seaway that no further *Hai* were constructed.

U-Boat Types

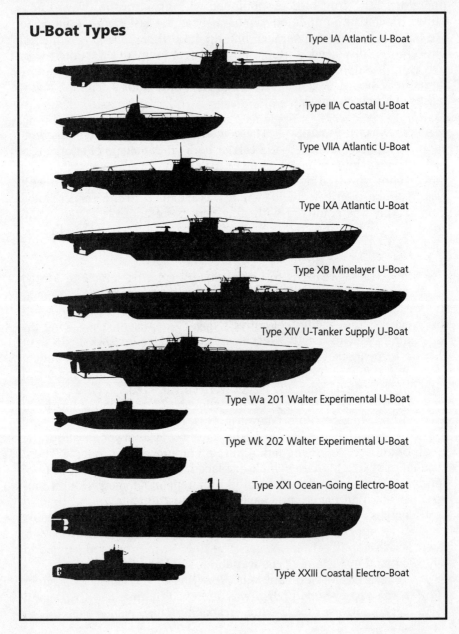

Type IA Atlantic U-Boat

Type IIA Coastal U-Boat

Type VIIA Atlantic U-Boat

Type IXA Atlantic U-Boat

Type XB Minelayer U-Boat

Type XIV U-Tanker Supply U-Boat

Type Wa 201 Walter Experimental U-Boat

Type Wk 202 Walter Experimental U-Boat

Type XXI Ocean-Going Electro-Boat

Type XXIII Coastal Electro-Boat

As the pilots of these manned-torpedoes had only an estimated 50/50 chance of surviving an attack on an enemy warship, they were manned entirely by volunteers for what were described as *Opfer-kampfer* (sacrifice missions) which was a euphemism for suicide missions.

In combination, the development of U-boats with high submerged speed, and developments in radar and radar detectors, snorkel, and the novelty of the midget-submarines and manned-torpedoes, convinced both Hitler and OKM that they had found the magical solution to turn the tide of war at sea back in Germany's favour. The introduction of the *K-Verband* units alone caused Hitler to fantasize about the enormous strategical consequences of the 'Small Battle Units' sinking from six to eight battleships of the Allied invasion fleet. At the very least, the Kriegsmarine now had the means to fight fanatically to the bitter end.

Conventional U-Boats in Operation During the Last Year of the War

Displacement, speed and endurance figures are expressed as: surfaced
submerged

Type		Displacement (tons)	Max speed (knots)	Endurance (n. miles/knots)	Torpedoes carried
VIIC		769	17.7	9,700/10	14
		871	7.6	80/4	
VIIC/41		This type was the same in all respects as Type VIIC with the exception of a stronger pressure hull for deeper diving (394 feet as opposed to 309 feet for Type VIIC).			
VIID		965	16.7	13,000/10	4 + 16 mines
	Minelayer	1,080	7.3	69/4	
VIIF		1,084	17.6	13,950/10	14
		1,181	7.9	75/4	
IXB		1,051	18.2	12,400/10	19
		1,178	7.3	64/4	
IXC		1,120	18.3	16,300/10	19
		1,232	7.3	63/4	
IXC/40		1,144	18.3	16,800/10	19
		1,257		63/4	
IXD/41		1,610	16.5	13,000/10	24
	U-Cruiser	1,799	6.9	115/4	
IXD/42		1,616	19.2	32,300/10	21
	U-Cruiser	1,804	6.9	57/4	
XB		1,763	17	21,000/10	15 + 66 mines
	Minelayer	2,177	16.4	93/4	
XIV		1,688	14.9	12,300/10	Nil
	U-Tanker	1,932	6.2	55/4	

Chapter 2

THE SOUNDING OF THE TOCSIN

NAVAL GROUP WEST

All the German naval forces (apart from the U-boats) based on French and Belgian ports were under the command of Vizeadmiral Theodor Krancke, C-in-C, Marinegruppe West (Naval Group West). From his HQ in Paris, Krancke exercised command over all surface vessels, naval coastal gun-batteries, naval radar stations and the 30,940 naval troops who garrisoned the German-occupied ports in the west. His command was divided into three areas: 'Channel Coast', under the command of Konteradmiral Rieve (HQ at Rouen), which stretched from the Belgian-Dutch frontier to St-Malo on the Brittany coast; 'Atlantic Coast', under the command of Konteradmiral Schirlitz (HQ at Angers), which covered the French Biscay coastline from Brittany to the Spanish frontier; and 'South Coast', under the command of Konteradmiral Scheurzen (HQ at Aix), which covered the French Mediterranean coastline. Although the majority of the U-boats that operated in Atlantic waters were based on the French Biscay ports, they remained under the command of BdU from its HQ (code-named *Koralle* = 'Coral') at Bernau, a small isolated village some nineteen miles north-east of Berlin.

In May 1944, Krancke had no major warships at his disposal with which to repel the Allied invasion fleet. All that he could call on were three destroyers, six torpedo-boats, 38 S-boats (*Schnellboote* = fast motor torpedo-boats which the Allies, for some illogical reason referred to as E-boats), 309 minesweepers, 116 assorted patrol craft and 42 artillery-barges (Marineartilleriefahrprahm = ferry barges armed with AA and light calibre naval guns designed to give support to German coastal convoys). These vessels were distributed along the Channel and Atlantic coasts from Ijmuiden in Holland to Bayonne near the Spanish frontier. Not all were immediately available as some were refitting. They were deployed as shown in the table. The large number of minesweepers in Marinegruppe West were necessary to keep channels swept for the U-boats and coastal convoys that plied between the French, Belgian, Dutch and German ports, particularly on the inshore route between Cherbourg and Dunkirk which required constant sweeping.

Up to the end of March 1944, the majority of the mines sown off the Channel and Atlantic coasts by the Allies had been laid by aircraft.

Deployment of Naval Group West, 6 June 1944

Channel Coast

Base	Torpedo-boats	S-Boats	Mine-sweepers	Patrol vessels	Artillery-barges
Ijmuiden		4			
Bruges			12	13	
Ostend		10	35		
Dunkirk			11		
Boulogne		8	11		16
Dieppe			12		
Fécamp					15
Le Havre	5		50	21	
Ouistreham to St-Vaast			12		11
Cherbourg		16			
St-Malo			20	23	
Totals	5	38	163	57	42

Atlantic Coast

Base	Destroyers	Mine-sweepers	Patrol vessels	Torpedo-boats
Brest		36	16	1
Bénodet		6		
Concarneau		19		
Lorient			16	
St-Nazaire & Nantes		16	15	
Les Sables-d'Olonne		20		
La Pallice	1			
Gironde estuary	4	49		
Bayonne			12	
Totals	5	146	59	1

From the beginning of April, when the Allies inaugurated an intensive minelaying campaign in preparation for the invasion, surface minelayers became more active, sowing 42 per cent of the 7,000 mines laid between the Baltic and the Bay of Biscay (mostly between Ijmuiden and Brest) during the seven weeks before D-Day. German records show that four merchant ships, fourteen auxiliary naval vessels (including minesweepers) and a tug were sunk after running on to these minefields, and five merchant ships, 22 auxiliary naval vessels, one torpedo-boat and a U-boat were damaged. At the end of May Vizeadmiral Krancke noted in the Marinegruppe West War Diary that: 'The enemy's air mining ... led to severe losses, and the ports of Cherbourg and Le Havre had to be closed for considerable periods because of the initial difficulty of clear-

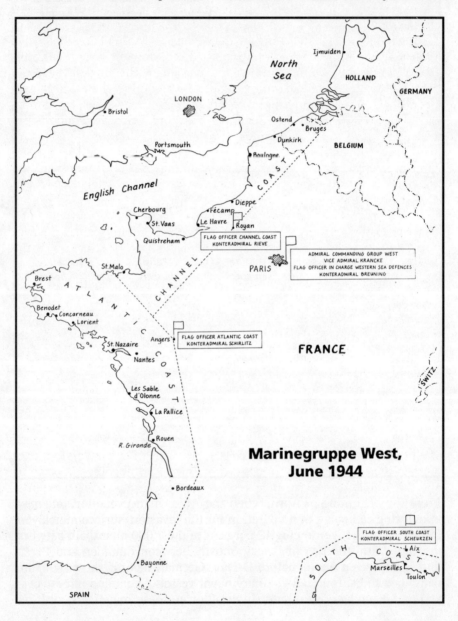

Marinegruppe West, June 1944

ing the mines which were fitted with new types of acoustic firing mechanism.'[1]

The intensified Allied mining caused a curtailment of seagoing activities by Krancke's forces, which not only prevented reconnaissance sorties and attacks upon the mass of Allied shipping and landing-craft on passage off the East and South coasts of England to the invasion fleet assembly ports, but also interfered with the intensive programme of German defensive minelaying in the Channel. Most of this defensive minelaying was in deep water, enlarging and strengthening a continuous 120-mile belt running down the middle of the English Channel from Boulogne to the Cherbourg peninsula. The mines were laid by torpedo-boats, S-boats and minesweepers fitted to carry mines, assisted by air-drops by the Luftwaffe. Secondary inshore fields and underwater obstacles were laid by R-boats (*Raumboote* = motor launches of between 60 and 140 tons used as coastal convoy escorts, and for coastal minesweeping and laying), converted landing-craft and minesweeping trawlers, along the Channel and Biscay coasts from Belgian waters to the Gironde.

For more than a year, Marinegruppe West had been concerned that the area of the Normandy coast between Cherbourg and Le Havre was exposed more particularly to invasion than other stretches of the European coastline for three main reasons:
1.   The two principal harbours of Le Havre and Cherbourg could be outflanked by a landing in the Seine Bay.
2.   The Cherbourg peninsula provided shelter against the prevailing westerly winds.
3.   The outlying rocks did not form any real obstruction to landings, as not only were there long stretches of beach clear of rocks, but many of the offshore rocky ledges were sufficiently submerged at high water to allow shallow draught vessels to pass over them.

However, the presence of these rocks led OKH to regard the area as far less threatened than either the Somme-Boulogne stretch of the coast or the north coast of Brittany. The known assembly of enemy landing-craft in the Plymouth area was thought (rightly) by Marinegruppe West to be for the ultimate purpose of a movement eastward to join the Portsmouth concentration of invasion shipping. The Army Command, however, regarded the Plymouth concentration as a clear intention of an Allied descent on Brittany, thereby lessening still further their attention to the Seine Bay defences, and their opinion prevailed. Consequently the construction of permanent coastal defence installations, particularly anti-tank obstructions, were notably backward in the Seine Bay area in comparison with other sectors of the Channel coast.

Marinegruppe West attempted to rectify this weakness of the Seine Bay defences by extensive mining. During the first three months of 1944, barrages of ground and moored mines were laid between Barfleur and the approaches to Le Havre. By April most of these ground mines had become inoperative (the ground mines were laid with period sterilizers), and many of the moored mines had been swept by the Allies. It was intended to renew both types of barrage during April, but delays in production in Germany and Allied bombing of the railway systems in Germany and France meant that no mines were available until May and then only in limited numbers. Extensive Allied air mining of Le Havre then caused a temporary but critical closing of the port.

To improve the situation it was decided to concentrate on a programme of laying offshore a mass of available KMA concrete ground mines. For this purpose 2nd and 6th Minesweeping Flotillas (fitted for minelaying) were ordered to Cherbourg from the Biscay ports of Concarneau and Bénodet to lay large numbers of these mines in the Seine Bay area, but because of the strong enemy surface and air patrols operating in the Bay of Biscay and in the Channel, few of these craft managed to break through to Cherbourg, which frustrated the planned scale of minelaying.

Although Krancke was unaware of it, the majority of the German minelaying sorties that did take place were known to the Allies from decrypts of Marinegruppe West's Enigma signals, which the Allies were reading almost concurrently. Specific information as to where the mines had been laid was also provided by Enigma decrypts of signals announcing that existing swept channels had either been closed or diverted. Moreover, the scale of this defensive minelaying was severely curtailed by the large number of layers that were lost or damaged on Allied minefields.

When, on the night of 19 May, Krancke ordered 5th Torpedo-Boat Flotilla and units of 6th Minesweeping Flotilla to leave Cherbourg for Le Havre on the evening of the 23rd to lay minefields on the eastern flank of Seine Bay, the signal was decrypted at Bletchley Park next morning, and the Admiralty dispatched a force of MTBs (motor torpedo-boats) and aircraft to intercept the German force, which they did during the early hours of 24 May.

During a confused action, the 924-ton torpedo-boat *Greif* was bombed and sunk by an Albacore of Coastal Command's No. 415 Squadron north-west of Ouistreham, the minesweeper *M39* was torpedoed by MTBs, and the torpedo-boat *Kondor*, the minesweeper *M84* and the R-boat *R217* were driven on to Allied minefields and badly damaged. The violence of the action is attested to by the fact that the German vessels fired 300 rounds of 4.1in ammunition and 17,000 rounds of 20mm AA. This disaster ended all further attempts at minelaying off the Normandy coast before D-Day.

One other weakness in the naval defence measures was the lack of suitable craft with which to maintain offshore patrols. The only vessels available were the artillery-barges of 6th Artillery Barge Flotilla, whose speed was insufficient to allow them to operate from either Cherbourg or Le Havre because the threat from Allied air patrols necessitated their return to port during daylight hours. Accordingly, they were based in the small local Seine Bay harbours of Courseulles, Port-en-Bessin, Grandcamp, Isigny and St-Vaast, but all these harbours were only usable at High Water. Consequently the threatened areas of coast remained unpatrolled for long periods. This was a disadvantage which Marinegruppe West was fully aware of, but unable to rectify.

SCHNELLBOOTE IN THE WEST

Krancke's main strike force for offensive action consisted of the the *Schnellboote* – fast motor torpedo-boats displacing between 80 and 100 tons, capable of speeds up to 42 knots, and armed with two 21in torpedoes and light AA guns. At the end of May 1944, Marinegruppe West had 38 S-boats disposed in five flotillas, under the command of *Führer der Schnellboote* (FdS) Kommodore Petersen, deployed between Ijmuiden and Cherbourg:

8th Flotilla (Ijmuiden)	4 boats operational
2nd Flotilla (Ostend)	5 boats operational
	5 refitting
4th Flotilla (Boulogne)	8 boats operational
5th Flotilla (Cherbourg)	5 boats operational
	4 refitting
9th Flotilla (Cherbourg)	7 boats operational

From 1 January to 24 May 1944, S-boats from these flotillas made a total of 315 sorties in 36 separate operations: involving fifteen torpedo attacks on Allied coastal convoys off the South and East coasts of England, which sank eleven merchant ships and damaged one; ten minelaying sorties that accounted for one Allied minesweeper; and nine anti-invasion reconnaissance patrols during which they sank one landing-craft and damaged two others that were taking part in an invasion rehearsal (700 American troops lost their lives). During these operations two S-boats were sunk and three damaged.

Although Allied decrypts of FdS Enigma signals revealed the majority of S-boat sorties, they were read with an average delay of fifteen hours after the S-boats had left port – too late to be of operational value. But the S-boat raids proved little more than a nuisance to the Allies, being too few to pose a serious threat to the huge armada gathering for the invasion. The Germans' only hope of inflicting serious damage rested with the U-boats.

U-BOATS IN THE WEST

Allied deception measures alerted the Germans to the possibility of an invasion of Norway and/or Denmark simultaneously with a landing in France, and to guard against this eventuality it was decided to hold a number of U-boats in southern Norwegian ports.

As early as February 1944, ten new Type VIIC U-boats that had sailed from Kiel bound for the Atlantic were diverted to the Norwegian bases of Bergen, Christiansand and Stavanger. These boats formed the nucleus of Group Mitte, under the command of Fregattenkapitän Schutze, and in March the strength of this group was increased to 22 boats.

Plans to use U-boats to prevent the enemy gaining a foothold in France, resulted in the formation of Group Landwirt on 22 March, consisting of fifteen Type VIIC boats based in the French Biscay port of Brest. This disposition, it was believed, would afford protection to the Brittany and Biscay coasts, and the boats were close enough to penetrate the English Channel, the most likely area of invasion. At the beginning of April six U-boats that had just reached the Atlantic from German ports were ordered to head for the Biscay ports to reinforce Group Landwirt, and from the middle of April all ocean-going U-boats refitting in the Biscay bases were held back as they became operational further to reinforce the anti-invasion group. As a result, an average of only four to six U-boats were operating in the Western Approaches to the British Isles during May.

BdU had intended to fit snorkels to most if not all the U-boats gathering in the Biscay ports, but, again, Allied bombing had severely curtailed production, and many snorkels were destroyed during the incessant bombing of the French railways, or lost in the chaos of stranded railway stock. As a result, only eight boats had been equipped with snorkel by D-Day.

Five of the snorkel-fitted boats in the Biscay bases (*U764*, *U441*, *U984*, *U953*, *U269*) were formed into a sub-group – Group Dragoner – and sent from 17 to 25 May to operate in the western sector of the English Channel to test the effectiveness of snorkel in coastal waters dominated by enemy aircraft, in advance of the planned incursion of U-boats into the Channel to operate against the invasion fleet. Although valuable experience was gained during the operation, in which the group patrolled as far east as St-Malo, both in the use of snorkel and the type of tactics suitable in a heavily patrolled area, BdU was disappointed that none of the boats scored a single success against the mass of naval and merchant shipping passing through their operational area. But none of the boats of Group Dragoner were lost or even attacked, which gave BdU conclusive evidence that snorkel-fitted boats could operate relatively safely in an area dominated by enemy aircraft. Indeed, BdU considered transferring all eight boats from the Biscay ports to the French Channel ports, but the idea was rejected because there were no bomb-proof U-boat pens at Cherbourg, Le Havre or Boulogne. Berthed in open docks so close to the English mainland, the U-boats would have presented sitting targets to Allied bombers.

By 5 June 1944, the eve of D-Day, the strength of Group Landwirt had risen to 36 U-boats. Of these, eight snorkel and nine non-snorkel boats were at Brest, and nineteen non-snorkel boats were distributed between the Biscay ports of St-Nazaire, Lorient and La Pallice. All were at six hours' notice for sea.

Other U-boats in home waters close enough to intervene against a cross-Channel invasion, were the 22 U-boats of Group Mitte, lying at six hours' notice in the Norwegian ports of Bergen, Stavanger and Christiansand (none fitted with snorkel); twelve snorkel-fitted boats outward bound from Norway to the Atlantic (seven of which were still

Group Landwirt (s = snorkel fitted)	
Brest:	U275(s), U269(s), U984(s), U621(s), U441(s), U764(s), U953(s), U212(s), U740, U821, U629, U413, U415, U256, U989, U963, U373
St-Nazaire, Lorient, La Pallice:	U981, U270, U260, U382, U714, U650, U437, U766, U255, U445, U262, U985, U758, U281, U228, U608, U993, U333, U970

to the east of the Faeroe Islands, the other five having reached positions south of Iceland); and three non-snorkel boats on weather reporting duty on the eastern side of the North Atlantic.

All these 73 U-boats were of conventional type, none of the Walter or Electro-boats having been completed in time to be thrown into the affray against the Allied invasion fleet.

TOO FEW TOO LATE

From mid-1943 onwards German industry had been strained to the limit, trying to cope with the huge demand for armaments of all kinds, a situation exacerbated by the ever-increasing intensity of the Allied bombing offensive on industrial centres, dockyards and lines of transportation. The extensive bomb damage to works and plant, and frequent rail and waterway transportation disruption, continually retarded the carefully timed delivery schedules of the prefabricated sections of Type XXI and XXIII Electro-boats, so that the building programme gradually dropped to five months behind schedule. The difficulties were compounded by the destruction of pontoons and cranes, and the heavy loss of life among dockyard workmen in the bombing raids and their flight from the frequently raided sea ports, particularly Hamburg.

In addition, the implementation of the revolutionary prefabrication methods of production caused great problems. Apart from bottlenecks in the construction of the main engines, electric motors and accessories, occasioned by damage through air attack, the unorthodox and untried methods used in the construction of the Electro-boats resulted in an inordinate number of defects in the boats delivered up to the autumn of 1944 (by which time the fundamental defects in the prefabrication system were finally eliminated), so that frequent interruptions for repair and modifications combined to lengthen crew training and working-up time in individual Electro-boats from the usual three months to nearly six months.

It soon became evident that, despite the very greatest efforts, the short delivery time of the Electro-boats predicted by Merker could not be met. Deutsche Werke in Kiel was especially affected by the bombing. This yard had been scheduled to complete the bow sections of the first two Type XXI boats by 20 February 1944, but preparatory work was interrupted when the yard's workshops were destroyed during three air raids between 13 December 1943 and 5 January 1944, so that construction of the two bow sections did not begin until March. Construction at this and other yards was further delayed by the late arrival of the crude pressure hull sections and faulty work in the prefabrication process. For instance, on 31 January 1944, Deutsche Werke, Hamburg-Finkenwerder, reported that the yard had received only one section each of the seven Type XXI crude sections III and seven sections VI, that should have been delivered by 29 January. Moreover, the two sections that had arrived were found to be defective: section III had various casings missing, and section VI was incomplete in respect of casings, drilled parts and various other components. A further crude section VI which arrived on 1 February had to have additional work carried out because it did not conform to the design dimensions. This additional work on these three sections took almost the whole of February to complete.

The assembly programme for Deutsche Werke, Hamburg-Finkenwerder, called for the completion of eight sections III and eight sections VI during the month of April, but by 1 April only five crude sections had been received instead of the stipulated sixteen. Similar problems were experienced at the other assembly yards. At Schichau, Danzig, crude sections for the first Type XXIs to be built at the yard were delivered on 20 February as planned, but many internal fittings were missing from each section. Late delivery of diesel engines compounded the yard's problems so that assembly work could not begin until the beginning of April.

However, it was at the Schichau yard that the first Type XXI Electro-boat, *U3501*, entered the water, on 19 April 1944, the day before Hitler's birthday, the launch being contrived to celebrate the event because *U3501* was nowhere near complete. She had no self-buoyancy, open parts of the hull being sealed with temporary wooden plugs, and it was necessary to tow the boat immediately into a floating dry dock. The consequence of this over-hasty launching was that *U3501* had to spend a long time in the badly needed dry dock, and she was not properly launched until 30 May. Fitting-out was not completed until 11 July, and she was not commissioned into service until 29 July 1944.

The directors of Blohm & Voss and AG Weser refused point-blank to take part in the prestige exercise, and would not allow their first Type XXIs to enter the water in the incomplete condition of *U3501* merely to impress Hitler with a bogus delivery date that simply could not be achieved.

The first true launch of a Type XXI was achieved by Blohm & Voss when *U2501* entered the water on 12 May. After fitting-out she was delivered to the Kriegsmarine on 15 June and was commissioned into service on 28 June 1944, one month before *U3501* was properly launched.

Only four Type XXIs had entered service by July (*U2501*, *U2502* assembled by Blohm & Voss; *U3501*, assembled by Schichau; and *U3001*, assembled by AG Weser). Numerous defects came to light during the trials of all four boats. For example, after commissioning *U2501* had to go back to the yard for ten days at the beginning of July because leaks in section II of the pressure hull had allowed sea water to enter the lubricating system of the gearing and electric motors. Furthermore, a series of breakdowns occurred in the propulsion plants in three of the boats. It had not been realized that an electric motor running in reverse would cause the diesel engine to go into reverse as well, and in so doing suck water in through the open exhaust-gas closures and through the submerged exhaust, resulting in an inrush of water into the cylinders that severely damaged the engines.

These teething troubles, and a plethora of other problems that subsequently came to light, in conjunction with the six months' training and working-up period needed by the crews before a Type XXI became fully operational and joined the *Frontboote*, meant that none was available to BdU until six months after D-Day.

Similar problems delayed the début of the Type XXIII coastal version of the Electro-boats, aggravated when weight checks revealed that the addition of various installations made the boats too heavy, robbing them of their buoyancy. On 23 February 1944 (by which time the first Type XXIIIs should have been delivered) it was decided that the only way to rectify this weight imbalance was to lengthen the pressure hull by an additional 7-foot section.

Assembly of the first Type XXIII, *U2321*, began at Deutsche Werke, Hamburg-Finkenwerder, on 10 March. She was launched just over five weeks later, on 17 April, and was commissioned on 12 June, a week after the Allies had invaded France. By July, only four Type XXI-IIs had entered service (*U2321*, *U2322*, *U2323*, *U2324*). Like the larger, Type XXI Electro-boats, these small coastal boats also suffered from numerous defects and teething troubles, although, being much smaller and of simpler design, their defects were easier to rectify.

The situation with regard to the twelve Type XVIIB and twelve Type XVIIG coastal Walter boats was even more depressing. On 14 August 1943, Dönitz decided to cancel seven of the Type XVIIBs under construction at Blohm & Voss and all twelve Type XVIIGs under construction at Germania Werft, so that all available labour at the two shipyards could be employed on the assembly of the Electro-boats. Work on the five remaining boats on the slips at Blohm & Voss proceeded slowly as labour was constantly diverted to other more pressing tasks, so the completion of the first Walter coastal boat, *U1405*, was delayed by six months: she was not launched until 1 December 1944. Of the remaining four boats, only two, *U1406* and *U1407*, were destined to be completed (February and March 1945 respectively).

ENEMY APPRECIATIONS

The Naval Intelligence Division (NID) of the British Admiralty were able to calculate fairly accurately the rate of U-boat construction from Enigma decrypts, which regularly disclosed the number of U-boats commissioned, and from regular photo reconnaissance (PR) flights by aircraft over the shipyards. The accuracy of the NID estimates is evinced by its calculation that from March 1941 until the end of January 1943 400 boats were completed, only seventeen short of the actual number.[2]

In January 1944, the NID suddenly became aware that the rate of U-boat construction had been declining steadily from the autumn of the previous year. This puzzling decline was the first indication that the Germans were up to something unusual. This was confirmed by Enigma decrypts that revealed that a U-boat had carried out submerged tests in the Strander Bucht off Kiel with an unknown and hitherto unheard of device called snorkel, and statements from prisoners of war rescued from *U841* (depth-charged by an RN frigate east of Cape Farewell on 17 October 1943) that a ventilation trunk was being developed together with a closed-circuit engine (the Walter turbine) to provide high-speed submerged propulsion. During February 1944, further PR flights indicated that only 183 U-boats were under construction as against 271 the previous September. On this evidence NID was able to deduce that so large a reduction could not be attributed to the effect of Allied bombing, and could only be explained by a switch in the German production priorities to new types of small submersibles and/or ocean-going U-boats with improved submerged performance provided by closed-circuit engines.

These ominous portents were given further credence in decrypts of reports sent to Tokyo from the Japanese Ambassador in Berlin, which quoted Hitler as saying that Germany was developing U-boats with increased submerged speeds; and POW statements that, in addition to developing a ventilation trunk called snorkel with which to equip the existing conventional U-boat types, Germany was also developing a coastal-size Walter boat and a larger type, both using closed-cycle propulsion, which not only gave the potential for high submerged speeds, but also the ability to remain submerged for lengthy periods of time. The partial evidence obtained obscured the difference between the Walter boats and the newly developed Electro-boats, with the result that the NID tended to associate all U-boat innovations with the name of Professor Walter.

Being preoccupied with the planning of the protection of the invasion fleet and the follow-up convoys, the Admiralty was alarmed by the NID reports, believing that the Walter boats had been developed specifically as an anti-invasion weapon and that a large number had probably already been built.

During the third week of April 1944, the examination of PR photographs provided evidence that yet another type of new U-boat, estimated as being some 245 feet in length, was being rapidly assembled from prefabricated sections. Two had been photographed at the Schichau yard in Danzig, of which one was already launched (*U3501*), four on the slips at AG Weser in Bremen and one in the Blohm & Voss yard at Hamburg. Further alarm was experienced at the Admiralty when NID reported that having examined previous photographs of the Schichau yard, the boat already launched at Danzig could not have been on the slips for more than six weeks, as against the minimum of five months for a conventional U-boat. It was also feared that this larger type might also be powered by closed-cycle engines.

Nothing was learned of the characteristics of this new type until the end of May, when decrypts of the machine cypher of the Japanese Naval Attaché in Berlin gave a detailed report of the technical specifications of Type XXI and Type XXIII. Later decrypts from this source also revealed full details of the Electro-boat building programme, the prefabrication process and the location of the final assembly yards.

These decrypts, which allowed NID to differentiate between the Walter and Electro-boats, were of 'inestimable value by showing that the propulsion of the Electro-boats was based on established methods, that is on diesels improved by the snorkel for proceeding at periscope depth and on more powerful electric motors for submerged passage. The decrypts also established that the Germans had failed to bring to a practical stage the innovation which the Admiralty had most feared – submerged propulsion using a form of [the Walter closed-cycle engines. On this evidence the Admiralty was able to dismiss the threat to the 'Overlord' convoys from Walter boats.'[3]

Most importantly, with regard to the 'Overlord' (code-name for the invasion) planning, the decrypts also disclosed that because of delays in the construction programme caused by the Allied bombing offensive, it was extremely unlikely that any of the Electro-boats would be completed by the time the invasion was scheduled to be launched.

As for intelligence regarding conventional U-boats, an analysis of U-boat movements revealed by Enigma decrypts established that the Germans were holding back the departure of ocean-going U-boats from the Biscay bases to the Atlantic in order to accumulate them as an anti-invasion force. By 9 April, NID had become aware that since 22 March no ocean-going U-boats had left the French Biscay ports where seventeen had been held for longer than their normal turn-round period, and that six U-boats that had recently entered the Atlantic from the Baltic on their first operational cruise were proceeding direct to the Biscay bases. NID had also become aware that an undetermined number of U-boats was being held back in southern Norwegian ports (Group Mitte).

By the end of May, NID estimated that there were 45 ocean-going U-boats in the Biscay ports, and that by D-Day they would be reinforced by a further 25 boats, making a formidable anti-invasion force of 70 U-boats, the majority of which, it was assumed, would be fitted with snorkel. This estimate was pessimistic in the extreme, as the strength of Group Landwirt on D-Day totalled only 36 boats of which only eight had snorkels. As it was uncertain to what extent these U-boats would be used to attack the initial Allied landings, or to harass the follow-up convoys in the Channel itself and in the western and south-western approaches to the Channel, intensive A/S surface and air patrols were spread all over the Channel and the vast area of the approaches.

PR had provided NID with fairly accurate assessments of the surface forces in Marinegruppe West. These did not present a serious threat to the huge armada set to ferry the Allied troops to the Normandy beaches, but concern was felt that the Kriegsmarine might risk all their available heavy units, pocket-battleships and cruisers, in a foray into the Channel if the Germans were determined to stake everything on an all-out attack on the follow-up troop and supply convoys. NID tended to exaggerate the threat by assuming that all the Kriegsmarine's heavy units – except *Tirpitz*, which was known to be non-operational in Kaafiord – were fully effective.

On 10 May, the Admiralty's Operational Intelligence Centre (OIC) warned, in a worst-case hypothesis, that the pocket-battleships *Admiral Scheer* and *Lützow*, and the heavy cruisers *Hipper* and *Prinz Eugen*, supported by destroyers, might, as a desperate measure, leave the Baltic to carry out an attack on the assault forces; or move to northern Norway for a concerted breakout into the Atlantic, in an attempt to divert some of the Allied naval forces covering and supporting the invasion. The OIC also warned that the four light cruisers *Leipzig*, *Köln*, *Nürnberg* and *Emden*, might make sorties into the North Sea to attack the follow-up convoys off the East Coast of England. These fears diminished somewhat when, on 30 May, as a result of regular PR flights over the Baltic bases, it was realized that *Hipper* was in dry dock at Gotenhafen undergoing an extensive refit, and that *Köln* also appeared to be laid up.[4]

The threat posed by all these units would, no doubt, have been discounted altogether if the Admiralty had known that the pocket-battleships and cruisers had very limited effectiveness as fighting units because the greater part of their crews were undergoing basic training.

By the eve of D-Day, the net result of all the intelligence assessments convinced the Admiralty that the only serious threat to the maritime forces involved in 'Overlord', was that posed by the U-boats that had been accumulated by BdU in the Biscay bases. But the massive sea and air A/S forces that had been deployed to counter any interference by U-boats, which included escort-carriers, 286 destroyers, frigates and smaller A/S vessels, and 21 squadrons of aircraft which flew day and night patrols over the Bay of Biscay and the western Channel approaches with such intensity that every square mile of sea was covered at least once every half-hour, made even this threat pale into insignificance.

The scene was set for the most decisive operation the Kriegsmarine would be called upon to perform in the last year of its existence. If it failed to sink enough of the Allied landing-craft carrying troops and armoured vehicles to the beachheads, or destroy the follow-up troop

---

Warship Dispositions in Marinegruppe West on the Eve Of D-Day

The minesweeping flotillas were made up of purpose-built Minesweepers (*Minensuch-boote*); Mine Clearance Vessels (*Sperrbrecher*) which were ex- merchant vessels specially strengthened, and varying in size from 1,000 to 6,000 tons; Motor Launches (*Raumboote*); and fishing vessels, varying in size from 150 to 500 tons, such as trawlers (*Fischdampfer*), whalers (*Walboote*) and drifters (*Fischkutter*)

Channel Coast (from Ijmuiden to St-Malo)

Ijmuiden	8th S-Boat Flotilla 4 boats
Bruges	8th R-Boat Flotilla 12 boats
	18th Vp Flotilla 13 boats (*Vorpostenboot* = patrol vessel)
Ostend	36th Minesweeping Flotilla 35 boats
	2nd S-Boat Flotilla 5 boats + 5 refitting
Dunkirk	2nd R-Boat Flotilla 11 boats
Boulogne	4th S-Boat Flotilla 8 boats
	4th R Boat Flotilla 11 boats
	2nd Artillery Barge Flotilla 16 boats
Dieppe	14th R-Boat Flotilla 12 boats
Fécamp	8th Artillery Barge Flotilla 15 boats
Le Havre	5th Torpedo-Boat Flotilla 5 boats
	15th Vp Flotilla 21 boats
	38th Minesweeping Flotilla 50 boats
Ouistreham	10th R-Boat Flotilla 12 boats
Isigny	
St-Vaast	6th Artillery Barge Flotilla 11 boats
Port-en-Bressin	
Cherbourg	5th S-Boat Flotilla 5 boats + 4 refitting
	9th S-Boat Flotilla 7 boats
St-Malo	46th Minesweeping Flotilla 20 boats
	2nd Vp Flotilla 23 boats

---

and supply convoys vital to the Allied build-up, any remaining hope of Germany's winning the war would founder.

While the Germans on the French coast watched and waited, 3,000,000 troops, 6,500 vessels and some 10,000 aircraft readied themselves on the other side of the Channel to launch the greatest invasion in history.

Atlantic Coast (from Brest to Bayonne)

Brest	One torpedo-boat (*T24*)
	40th Minesweeping Flotilla 28 boats
	24th Minesweeping Flotilla 8 boats
	7th Vp Flotilla 16 boats
Concarneau	6th Minesweeping Flotilla 7 boats
	6th Sperrbrecher Flotilla 12 ships
Bénodet	2nd Minesweeping Flotilla 6 boats
Lorient	14th Uj Flotilla 16 boats (*U-bootsjagelboote* = A/S vessels)
St-Nazaire	6th Vp Flotilla 15 boats
Paimboeuf	10th Minesweeping Flotilla 8 boats
Nantes	26th Minesweeping Flotilla 8 boats
Les Sables-d'Olonne	42nd Minesweeping Flotilla 20 boats
La Pallice	One destroyer (*Z23*, refitting)

Gironde estuary:

Royan	Three destroyers (*Z24, Z32, ZH1*)
	8th Minesweeping Flotilla 8 boats
	2nd Sperrbrecher Flotilla 10 ships
Paullac	28th Minesweeping Flotilla 8 boats
Blaye	44th Minesweeping Flotilla 23 boats
Bordeaux	One destroyer (*Z37*, refitting)

Southern Biscay:

Bayonne	4th Vp Flotilla 12 boats

Chapter 3

THE STRATEGY OF DESPAIR

FOUR AGAINST A THOUSAND

On 4 June 1944, Major Lettau, the chief meteorologist at Luftflotte III's Paris HQ, issued a forecast that the Allies would not launch the invasion of France within the next fortnight, because of the prevailing gales and rough seas in the Channel, which showed no signs of abating until the middle of the month.

On the strength of this report, Generalfeldmarschall Erwin Rommel, C-in-C, Army Group 'B' (which included the troops manning the 'Atlantic Wall'), left his HQ in Paris on the following morning to travel to his home near Ulm, intending to spend some time with his family. Before he left he issued instructions that both the Luftwaffe and Kriegsmarine should survey the harbours along the entire southern coast of England, to report on the state of Allied preparations. But on that critical day, 5 June, the weather was so bad that the Luftwaffe in France was grounded and all the Kriegsmarine patrols were driven back into harbour by the storms. So rough was the sea that all the naval patrols and minelaying operations scheduled for that night were cancelled. Not that any of this unduly bothered Vizeadmiral Krancke who noted in Marinegruppe West's War Diary that it was 'doubtful whether the enemy has yet assembled his invasion fleet in the required strength'.[1] On the same day, Feldmarschall von Rundstedt, C-in-C, West, expressed the opinion in his weekly situation report that: 'As yet there is no immediate prospect of the invasion.'

At 2115 that night, the French Service of the BBC began broadcasting the usual coded messages to the French Resistance. Normally the transmission of these messages lasted only five to ten minutes, but that night it ran for twenty minutes, at the end of which the spokesman declared: 'To-day the Supreme Commander directs me to say this: In due course instructions of great importance will be given to you through this channel, but it will not be possible always to give these instructions at a previously announced time. Therefore you must get into the habit of listening at all hours.'

This broadcast was monitored at Marinegruppe West's HQ, but Krancke wrote in the War Diary that he did not attach any special significance to it, believing that the BBC messages referred to acts of sabotage to be carried out by the Resistance as former messages had done. However, his suspicions were aroused when, from 2200 onwards, the few naval radar stations along the coast that had not been destroyed by enemy bombing (only eighteen out of 92 were still operating) reported that they were being jammed. When Krancke reported this ominous occurrence, von Rundstedt scouted the suggestion that this portended the start of the invasion, because he did not believe that the Allied armada would risk putting to sea in such appalling weather.

Even when reports began to reach Paris from Normandy, in the early hours of Tuesday 6 June, that Allied airborne troops had begun landing north-east of Caen and on the Cherbourg peninsula, Krancke was not convinced that this was part of a major operation. To quote his concurrent entry in the War Diary: 'It is not considered that this is a large-scale invasion: C-in-C West [von Rundstedt] and Luftflotte Ill are of the same opinion. *Increased defensive patrols in the Seine Bay have not been ordered on account of the unfavourable tide conditions and the weather* [author's italics]. No further signs of an enemy landing.' When Krancke made this entry in his diary, some 6,500 Allied vessels, including 4,250 landing-craft packed with assault troops, tanks and armoured vehicles, in some 75 convoys each five miles long, were approaching the Normandy coast undetected and undisturbed.

It was not until 0320 on that fateful morning, when the throb of thousands of ships' engines were heard entering Seine Bay, that Krancke woke up to the fact that a major operation was in progress. In response, at 0348, he ordered 8th Destroyer Flotilla to move north from the Gironde to Brest; the twelve operational boats of 5th and 9th Schnellboote Flotillas at Cherbourg to patrol off Cap de la Hague and Pointe de Barfleur; and 5th Torpedo-Boat Flotilla to leave Le Havre and attack the landing-craft which had been reported off Grandcamp and Port-en-Bessin on the western side of Seine Bay (the US assault area off Utah and Omaha Beaches).

The S-boats from Cherbourg began leaving their bomb-proof concrete bunkers at 0500. First to leave was 9th Flotilla, but as the boats approached Pointe de Barfleur, on the eastern tip of the Cherbourg peninsula, the crews were confronted with the awesome spectacle of the mighty Allied invasion fleet, 6,500 vessels filling the entire horizon. In an act of impotent defiance they fired their torpedoes from maximum range and fled back to base.

9th Flotilla was already well out to sea before the S-boats of 5th Flotilla began passing the outer breakwater of the harbour, but they were immediately subjected to a heavy attack from Allied fighter-bombers and were forced to return to the safety of their bunkers to avoid destruction.

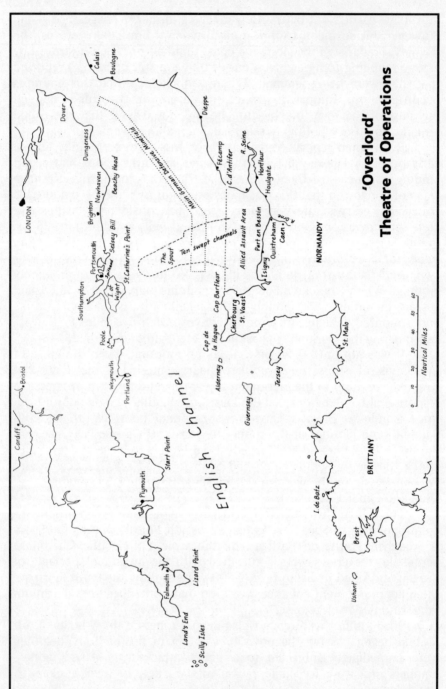

'Overlord'
Theatre of Operations

Fifteen minutes after the S-boats began leaving their bunkers, 5th Torpedo-Boat Flotilla sallied forth from Le Havre. Having lost *Greif* to enemy action on 24 May, and with *Kondor* still in dock undergoing repairs to the mine damage she had suffered on the same day, 5th Flotilla could muster only four boats – *Jaguar*, *Möwe*, *Falke* and *T28* – to attack the huge mass of enemy shipping pouring into Seine Bay. At 0530, just as the Allied warships began bombarding the German defences along a 50-mile stretch of the Normandy coastline, the four German torpedo-boats began their attack on the 1,213 enemy warships of the assault phase, which included seven battleships, two monitors, 23 cruisers and 168 destroyers and frigates.

Their egress from Le Havre had caused them to run directly into the eastern-flank bombarding force, consisting of the battleships *Warspite* and *Ramillies*, the 15in gun monitor *Roberts* and the cruisers *Arethusa*, *Scylla*, *Mauritius*, *Danae*, *Frobisher* and *Dragon*, which were screened by half-a-dozen destroyers. Luckily for the Germans their approach was obscured by a smoke-screen laid by Allied aircraft which, streaking low across the port side of the British warships, dropped smoke-bombs to screen the bombarding force from the German heavy gun batteries grouped around Le Havre. The four torpedo-boats took full advantage of this fortuitous veil and, working up to full speed, they were able to fire a total of fifteen torpedoes from the edge of the smoke-screen before they were spotted by the Allied ships.

Two torpedoes passed between *Warspite* and *Ramillies*, and the destroyer *Largs* only managed to avoid a torpedo by putting her engines into emergency full astern. The torpedo missed *Largs'* bows by a few feet and came to rest, before sinking, just short of the destroyer *Virage*. The Norwegian destroyer *Svenner* was not so lucky, being hit amidships by one of the torpedoes, which broke her back and sent her to the bottom. Although she sank very rapidly the majority of her crew were saved.

As soon as they had launched their torpedoes, the German torpedo-boats turned back into the smoke-screen, pursued by a forest of shell splashes as the bombarding warships turned their secondary armaments upon them. Zig-zagging at high speed through the dense fog of the smoke-screen, the four boats managed to get back to Le Havre unscathed.

This brief sortie represented the Kriegsmarine's second and last attempt to prevent the Allies gaining a foothold on the Normandy beaches on 6 June. In Marinegruppe West's War Diary, Krancke noted ruefully that: 'It was only to be expected that no effective blow could be struck at such superior enemy forces with the limited forces at my disposal.'

By the time the sun set on D-Day, the Allies had succeeded in breaking through the Atlantic Wall of Hitler's 'Fortress Europe' on a front of 30 miles. More than 132,000 Allied troops had poured ashore and penetrated inland to a depth of between two and six miles. The Germans had been taken completely by surprise, their coastal defences had been overwhelmed, and the Kriegsmarine and Luftwaffe had been rendered powerless to intervene by the crushing Allied sea and air superiority.

AN IMPOSSIBLE MISSION

The 8th Destroyer Flotilla, under the command of Kapitän zur See von Bechtolsheim, was at anchor at Royan in the mouth of the Gironde when it received Krancke's order, dispatched at 0348 on the morning of the 6th, to move north to Brest. The 8th Flotilla comprised five large destroyers, but two of these were undergoing refits (*Z37* at Bordeaux and *Z23* at La Pallice) so that only three, *Z32* (flagship), *Z24* and the ex-Dutch destroyer *ZH1*, were immediately available for operations.

While von Bechtolsheim's destroyers prepared for sea, British cryptanalysts were busy decrypting Krancke's Enigma signals. At 0620 the Admiralty was informed that 8th Flotilla had been ordered to Brest, and Coastal Command aircraft stationed at Davidstow Moor in Cornwall were dispatched to reconnoitre the mouth of the Gironde, with the result that von Bechtolsheim's three destroyers were observed steering out into the Bay of Biscay at 1230. During the afternoon a fur-

Characteristics of 5th Flotilla Torpedo-Boats, 6 June 1944			
	Jaguar	*Möwe &Falke*	*T28*
Displacement (tons):			
Standard	933	924	1,294
Dimensions (feet):			
Length	304	278¾	315
Beam	28	27½	31
Draught	9	9	9
SHP:	23,000	23,000	32,000
Radius (nm):	3,100	3,100	5,000
	@ 17 knots	@ 17 knots	@ 19 knots
Max. speed (knots):	33	32	33½
Armament:			
Guns	three 4.1in	three 4.1in	four 4.1in
	four 20mm	four 20mm	four 37mm,
	AA	AA	nine 20mm AA
Torpedo Tubes	six 21in	six 21in	six 21in
Complement:	129	129	198

ther decrypt revealed their course, speed and estimated time of arrival at Brest, and the Admiralty ordered an air strike.

At 2030 on the 6th, 8th Flotilla, steaming in line ahead at 25 knots with *ZH1* leading *Z32* and *Z24*, had reached a position 40 miles south-west of St-Nazaire when look-outs sighted a large group of low-flying aircraft in the process of splitting up into sub-groups and deploying so as to attack out of the setting sun. In all, 31 Beaufighters and eight Mosquitos (from Nos. 404, 248 and 144 Squadrons) launched attacks on the three destroyers with their cannon and 25lb rocket projectiles. Blazing away with their AA guns and taking violent evasive action, the three destroyers survived the attack, suffering only superficial damage to their superstructures, which were riddled with holes from cannon fire (three men were killed and 21 wounded). A second strike by eleven Beaufighters (from Nos. 404 and 144 Squadrons) at 0130, when the German ships had reached a position off Penmarch Point, south of Brest, also failed to inflict serious damage, and the three destroyers made the safety of Brest during the course of the night.

Next morning, Wednesday 7 June, while the flotilla was patching up the damage, von Bechtolsheim received a signal from Vizeadmiral Krancke ordering him to sail from Brest at 1830 on the following evening (8 June), with the object of making an offensive sweep during the early hours of the 9th, to the north-east of the Cherbourg peninsula against the invasion fleet's south-bound follow-up convoys.

Enigma decrypts not only alerted the Admiralty to the Germans' intentions, but also revealed the route and intended speed of the German flotilla. On the strength of this prompt intelligence the Admiralty ordered 10th Destroyer Flotilla, which was patrolling in the area of the Hurd Deep, to steer south-west to intercept the German warships as they rounded the Brest peninsula into the Channel.

Von Bechtolsheim's destroyers, reinforced by the torpedo-boat *T28*, sailed from Brest on schedule and rounded Ushant at 0100, steering a north-easterly course into the Channel. At 0120 the force was in the process of turning on to a more easterly course (they were then some 30 miles west-north-west of Ile de Batz) when look-outs in *Z32*, the leading destroyer, sighted shadowy shapes in the darkness, 5,000 yards off the port bow. As von Bechtolsheim turned to port to close, the shadows altered course to starboard and their true nature was suddenly revealed as their silhouettes were thrown into sharp relief by the moon appearing fitfully through a gap in the clouds. They were the four destroyers of the 19th Division of 10th Flotilla: the RN destroyers *Tartar* and *Ashanti*, and the Canadian destroyers *Huron* and *Haida*.

Horrified, von Bechtolsheim swung his squadron 90 degrees to port to escape to the westward. As they turned, *Z32*, *ZH1* and *Z24* fired four torpedoes each, but *T24*, the last ship in the line, held her fire because she could not see the targets. Simultaneously with the German turn away, the British destroyers fired starshell to illuminate their targets in a garish glow, which they then subjected to a withering hail of gun-fire. *Z32* was set on fire forward and one of her boilers was wrecked, and *ZH1* was riven by shellfire. One shell exploded in her starboard engine room, severing the main steam pipe which filled the engine room with clouds of scalding steam. Another shell penetrated a boiler room which quickly flooded. All power was lost and *ZH1* came to a standstill, wreathed in clouds of steam and smoke from her numerous fires.

The British destroyers conformed to the German movements by turning to port, and the range fell rapidly until it was so close that both sides added to the pyrotechnics of the gun flashes and explosions by bringing their AA armaments into play. *Z24* was hit by five shells, and sprayed with pom-pom rounds which killed nine men on the exposed bridge. Her forward gun-loading room, wheelhouse and charthouse were wrecked, and all the charts and signal books were destroyed. In addition, four men were killed when a shell exploded in the radio room, wrecking both the long-wave and short-wave radio sets. To escape further punishment *Z24* made smoke and turned sharply away out of the line on to a south-westerly course. As she turned she suffered further hits, one of which set the after funnel on fire, giving a point of aim to the British gunners until it was extinguished. In the confusion of gun-flashes, exploding shells and thick oily smoke pouring from the funnels of *Z24*, the last ship in the German line, the torpedo-boat *T24*, conformed to *Z24*'s sharp turn to port and followed in the destroyer's wake to the south-west.

Suddenly finding himself alone, von Bechtolsheim attempted to break away to the north-west, losing all touch with the rest of his flotilla because *Z32*'s radio room and aerials had been destroyed. This turn to the north led *Z32* on to the guns of the four destroyers of 20th Division, 10th Flotilla: *Piorun, Eskimo, Javelin* and the Polish destroyer *Blyskawica*. In the darkness von Bechtolsheim mistook the leading British destroyers for Glasgow-class cruisers. Swinging his flagship through a 180° turn to starboard at 0142, in an attempt to escape southwards, he launched four torpedoes at the oncoming enemy squadron, made smoke and began zig-zagging. But, illuminated by starshell, *Z32* was hit by twenty shells before she ran out of range of the enemy squadron, which turned away east-north-east to avoid the four torpedoes that *Z32* had fired while turning away.

Having run clear of 20th Division, *Z32* turned eastward at 0200 in an attempt to gain contact with the rest of 8th Flotilla, but ran into

Tartar and *Ashanti* of 19th Division (*Haida* and *Huron* were pursuing *Z24* and *T24* to the south-west). In a short, sharp, violent action from 0205 to 0215, *Z32* raked *Tartar* with gunfire. Four shells burst in rapid succession about *Tartar*'s bridge, bringing down her foremast and radar gear and causing heavy casualties; *Tartar* turned away, burning and shrouded in clouds of smoke. During this exchange *Z32* was hit by three shells. A magazine was set on fire and had to be flooded; her sick-bay and a pump-room were wrecked; and her after torpedo-tubes and a 5.7in gun were damaged. At 0215 she broke away to the north-west to escape further damage from *Ashanti*'s gunfire.

When *Ashanti* turned to starboard to chase *Z32*, she came upon the disabled and drifting *ZH1*, still wreathed in smoke from the fires which her crew were unable to bring under control. When she began firing her one remaining 4.7in gun, *Ashanti* promptly fired two torpedoes from point-blank range which blew off *ZH1*'s bows as far back as the breakwater. Realizing that his ship was doomed, *ZH1*'s commanding officer, Korvettenkapitän Barkow, gave orders for the ship's company to take to the boats and for scuttling charges to be activated. The charges exploded at 0240, tearing *ZH1* apart in a spectacular ball of fire, and the burning wreck quickly disappeared beneath the waves in a hiss of steam. Barkow, two other officers and 36 men were lost; 140 were rescued by British destroyers, and one officer and 27 men managed to row to the French coast in one of the ship's boats.

Schnellboote: Characteristics of Representative Classes			
	Class S101-S135	Class S138-S150, S159-S169, S171-S185, S187-S194	Class S151-S158
Displacement (tons):			
Standard	100	105	57
Dimensions (feet):			
Length	115	115	91¾
Beam	16¾	16½	14
Draught	6½	6	5
BHP:	6,000	7,500	2,850
Radius (nm):	700 @ 30 knots	700 @ 30 knots	350 @ 30 knots
Max. speed (knots):	39	42	34
Armament:			
Guns	two 20mm AA	one 40mm AA one 20mm AA	one 20mm AA one 15mm AA
Torpedo Tubes	two 21in	two 21in	two 21in
Complement:	23	23	21

In the meantime, *Z32*, which had turned to the north-east at 0215, swung round to the south-west at 0219, shaping course for Brest. Thirty minutes later she ran into the Canadian destroyers *Haida* and *Huron* which, having given up the chase of *Z24* and *T24*, were steering northwards to rejoin 10th Flotilla. Suddenly illuminated by starshell and surrounded by shell splashes from the two Canadian destroyers and *Ashanti*, the latter having worked around to the west effectively blocking the route to Brest, *Z32* swung round on to an easterly course and increased speed to 31 knots. Von Bechtolsheim's only hope now rested in passing between Jersey and Guernsey to reach the refuge of Cherbourg. A high-speed chase to the east ensued, which ended an hour and forty minutes later (0430), when von Bechtolsheim, realizing that the two Canadian destroyers would overhaul him long before he reached the Channel Islands, turned 90 degrees to starboard on to a south-westerly course and made smoke, hoping to shake off his pursuers in the darkness, and reach Brest by hugging the Brittany coast.

Fifteen minutes later *Haida* and *Huron*, conforming with *Z32*'s change of course, came into range. Illuminating *Z32* with starshell, they opened fire with their forward guns. Returning fire with her stern guns and launching torpedoes, *Z32* ran for her life, but at 0500 a shell penetrated her starboard engine room which quickly flooded, slowing the destroyer to 15 knots and putting paid to any remaining chance of escape. At 0515, by which time she had expended all her ammunition

Characteristics of 8th Flotilla Destroyers, June 1944

	Z24 and *Z32*	*ZH1**
Displacement (tons):		
Standard	2,600	1,628
Dimensions (feet):		
Length	390	384
Beam	40	34
Draught	10	11½
SHP:	70,000	49,500
Radius (nm):	5,000	5,400
	@ 19 knots	@ 19 knots
Max. speed (knots):	38½	37½
Armament:		
Guns	three 5.9in	five 4.7in
	one 4.1in	four 37mm AA
	fourteen 20mm AA	four 20mm AA
Torpedo Tubes	eight 21in	eight 21in
Complement:	321	236

*ZH1 - ex-Dutch *Gerard Callenburgh* (completed 1940).

and torpedoes and was receiving fearful punishment, von Bechtolsheim swung his flagship to port and drove her on to the rocks of Ile de Batz, a small island situated a few miles north of Roscoff. When *Z32* came to rest at 0520, with her forward section impaled on the rocks and with a heavy list to starboard, her crew scrambled off the destroyer to escape the gunfire of *Haida* and *Huron* which bombarded the wreck for ten minutes before withdrawing to the north. The survivors, who included von Bechtolsheim, were rescued later in the morning by German motor-launches. Considering the degree of punishment she had received, *Z32*'s casualties (30 men killed out of a complement of 321) were sur-prisingly light.

Later in the day 24 Beaufighters from Nos. 144 and 404 Squad-rons (which had attacked the 8th Flotilla on its passage from the Gironde to Brest three days earlier) launched a bombing attack on the wreck of the *Z32*. Sixty-five hits scored with 250lb and 500lb bombs and 60lb rockets battered her beyond all hope of being patched-up and refloated.

The two surviving warships of 8th Flotilla, the damaged *Z24* and the unscathed *T24*, made good their high-speed escape to the south-west, reaching Brest during the evening of 9 June.

In Marinegruppe West's War Diary, Krancke remarked somewhat philosophically that: 'The transfer of the 8th Destroyer Flotilla from the south, made enemy counter-measures inevitable. The employment of four enemy cruisers [*sic*] demonstrated the enemy's tactics of only attacking in overwhelming strength. The 8th Flotilla fought coura-geously and the loss of two destroyers, whilst very painful, has been alleviated by the relatively high number of survivors rescued. The high risk was clear to me beforehand.'

Krancke's 'high risk' strategy, which had led to the destruction of 8th Flotilla, left him with only one card to play – the *Schnellboote*.

ANTS AGAINST LEVIATHAN

After returning to Cherbourg from their abortive dawn sorties on D-Day, the S-boats of 5th Flotilla (under command of Kapitänleutnant Johannsen) and 9th Flotilla (under command of Kapitänleutnant Mirbach) were forced to remain inactive in their bomb-proof bunkers during the hours of daylight, while their frustrated crews, unable to intervene, anxiously followed the news of the battles taking place on the Normandy beaches.

During the afternoon of D-Day, *Führer der Schnellboote* (FdS), Kommodore Rudolph Petersen, following events from his HQ at Scheveningen in Holland, received Enigma coded orders from Vize-admiral Krancke to attack the invasion fleet that night with all available

S-boats at Cherbourg. Krancke also ordered 4th S-Boat Flotilla (eight boats under command of Kapitänleutnant Fimmen), based at Boulogne, to patrol off the Pas de Calais to give advance warning should the Allies attempt a further landing north of the Seine. For Krancke, like Hitler, von Rundstedt and Rommel, was inflexibly wedded to the long-standing theory that the Allies would effect two landings in France, and that the first would be a feint. By the close of D-Day, despite the huge naval assault fleet crammed into Seine Bay, Krancke and the German High Command still believed that the landing in Normandy was merely a diversion to entice their reserves west of the Seine as a prelude to the main attack in the Pas de Calais, which provided the shortest route to the German frontier.

Prior to D-Day, orders from Krancke's HQ in Paris to Petersen's HQ in Scheveningen, and from Scheveningen to the *Schnellboote* bases on the Channel coast, had only partially employed the Enigma cipher, most of the operational instructions being passed via land-lines, so the interception and 'reading' of the FdS Enigma had not provided NID with much intelligence of practical operational value. But the crippling disruption of land communications by Allied bombers meant that now FdS Enigma traffic was increasing to such a level that the Admiralty was getting advanced warning of S-boat operations for each successive night, stating which flotillas would be operating, from which base, the number of boats involved and the nature of the operation.

Consequently the Allies were able to strengthen their patrols in threatened areas and lay minefields along the S-boats' intended approach routes. From the point where the follow-up convoys converged in mid-Channel (the 'Spout') and then southwards along the swept channels leading to the anchorages in Seine Bay, the Allies had instituted defensive 'walls' of standing patrols, consisting of destroyers, frigates and MTBs, on both the western and eastern flanks. On receipt of FdS Enigma decrypts, announcing the intended attack by twelve S-boats from Cherbourg against the US assault area on the western side of Seine Bay during the night of D-Day, the patrols along the western 'wall' off Pointe de Barfleur were alerted and strengthened, and MTBs laid a minefield off Barfleur on the S-boats' probable line of approach.

Despite their foreknowledge of the operation, the Allied patrols did not sight the twelve S-boats that put out from Cherbourg just after midnight, 6/7 June. Divided into four groups of three boats, they rounded Pointe de Barfleur, and, despite losing *S139* on a mine laid only a few hours earlier, they managed to reach a point just south of St-Vaast by 0130 and fire three spreads of torpedoes which hit and sank the tank landing ship *LST 715* and one LCT (tank landing craft) on the northern edge of the US assault area. During their high-speed withdrawal, they ran into two MTBs supported by the frigate HMS *Stayner* off Pointe de Barfleur at 0230, and in the brief skirmish that followed, in which the S-boats fired all their remaining torpedoes while blazing away with their 20mm and 13mm machine-guns, *S140* was driven on to the same mine-field that had accounted for *S139* and she blew up and sank.

Meanwhile the eight S-boats of 4th Flotilla, which had sailed from Boulogne to patrol the waters off the Pas de Calais, attempted to approach the 'Spout' in search of targets but were driven off by gunfire from the destroyer *Hambledon*, which they attempted to torpedo with-out success.

Sorties of a similar nature and of varying degrees of success were subsequently carried out every night up to and including the night of 12/13 June. Although the Allies were forewarned of these nocturnal for-ays, the small groups of incredibly fast, highly manoeuvrable craft proved extremely difficult to detect and engage.

During the four nights of successive operations from 7/8 to 12/13 June, the S-boats sank three tank landing ships, one tank landing craft, one infantry landing craft, one motor torpedo-boat, one motor gunboat, the US tug *Partridge*, three small merchant ships grossing 1,812 tons, a component of the artificial Mulberry harbour, and the frigate *Halstead* which was so badly damaged by a torpedo that she was written off as a constructional loss. In addition they badly damaged the US destroyer *Nelson*, one tank landing craft and one tank landing ship. The price paid for these pin-pricks was the loss of four S-boats (*S136*, *S178*, *S179*, *S189*) and damage to ten others.

Extracts from the FdS War Diary illustrate the nature of S-boat operations carried out from 7/8 to 12/13 June:

'10th/11th June – The 5th S-Boat Flotilla left Cherbourg at 2300 with 6 boats, to carry out torpedo attacks on the east coast of the Cherbourg Peninsula. *S112* stopped owing to a rudder defect. At the same time the S-boats were attacked by a destroyer [HMS *Duff*] and MGBs. In order to relieve the situation, torpedoes were fired at the destroyer. One MGB probably sunk by a torpedo. During the engage-ment *S136* disappeared to the eastward. Breakthrough no longer possi-ble owing to strong enemy counter-measures. Flotilla operated against destroyer 'belt' to the north of Barfleur, in an attempt to relieve 9th Flotilla and also *S136*. At 0206 a torpedo salvo was fired at two destroy-ers. One claimed sunk [*sic*]. Several engagements ensued with destroy-ers and MGBs. Flotilla attacked with bombs. Proceeded West. At 0223 proceeded to Cherbourg to land one severely wounded man. Fate of *S136* unknown. Presumed sunk. [*S136* was sunk by gunfire from the destroyers *Sioux*, *Duff* and *Krakowiak*.] It was believed that *S136* had torpedoed a steamship before being sunk by destroyers.'[2]

'12th/13th June – The 9th S-boat Flotilla left Cherbourg at 2300 with 4 boats to carry out a torpedo attack west of the Seine Bay. Successfully broke through the enemy patrol lines by hugging the coast. Chased by destroyers east of Barfleur. Northbound convoy sighted shortly afterwards: attack impossible. Chased off to the east. Intended to attack southbound convoy from the eastward. Beaten off to the south-east by several destroyers and two MGB groups. Engaged by destroyers west of Barfleur. *S138* hit and set on fire, but she was able to maintain speed. Remaining boats attacked destroyers with gunnery armament. Thereupon more destroyers were sighted approaching from the north, and S-boats made off to the south-east. Owing to bad visibility further operations impossible, and boats entered Le Havre at 0230.'³

The majority of the S-boat sorties involved torpedo attacks, but they also engaged in minelaying sorties, sowing small fields on the Allied convoy routes in the Channel. Apart from laying conventional moored contact, magnetic and acoustic mines, they also laid three new types of pressure-operated mine (*Druck*) which the Allies collectively referred to as 'Oyster' mines. A large stock of these mines – pressure, acoustic-pressure and magnetic-pressure – had been stockpiled since they entered production in the later part of 1943, including 2,000 that had been stored in underground hangers at an airfield at Le Mans. The Germans purposely held back the operational use of these mines until D-Day, fearing that if they were used beforehand the Allies would devise a counter-measure as they had for the magnetic and acoustic mines only a short time after they had been used operationally. By holding back the Oyster mines until the Allied invasion actually materialized, they hoped to derive maximum effect from what proved to be a deadly innovation – the Oyster mines proved to be virtually unsweepable.

Their detonation mechanism consisted of a rubber bag that acted as an air reservoir, designed to communicate the water pressure created by a vessel passing over the mine to a thin aluminium diaphragm. When water pressure pulled the air bag away from the diaphragm, a switch was closed and actuated the mine. This basic pressure mechanism could be combined with either a magnetic or acoustic unit.

From 11 to 14 June more than 200 Oyster mines were laid in Seine Bay by S-boats, R-boats and two squadrons of minelaying aircraft based at Le Mans. By 21 June, 44 Allied ships had been sunk or damaged by mines (conventional and Oyster) which proved to be the most effective threat to the invasion fleet than anything else in the Kriegsmarine's arsenal.

On the night of 8/9 June, 4th Flotilla changed bases, moving from Boulogne to Le Havre, their vacated berths in the bomb-proof bunkers at Boulogne being taken over by the S-boats of 2nd Flotilla which moved down the coast from Ostend. Four nights later, when the Germans began blocking Cherbourg harbour and destroying the port installations to prevent them being used by the Allies who were advancing northward up the peninsula from the invasion beaches, 5th and 9th Flotillas joined the 4th at Le Havre (three boats refitting were forced to remain at Cherbourg).

This concentration of three S-boat Flotillas at Le Havre was to prove fatal. Their sorties had become such a source of anxiety to Admiral Ramsay, the Allied naval commander of the assault forces, that he called for an exceptionally heavy bomber raid to be made on their forward bases. Through decrypts of FdS Enigma the Allies knew that there were three flotillas at one base, and during the evening of 14 June they mounted the largest daylight operation hitherto undertaken by RAF Bomber Command.

The raid was entirely unopposed because the Germans had banned the use of AA fire in the Le Havre area, to safeguard Luftwaffe minelaying operations scheduled to take place over Seine Bay. The bombers attacked in three waves. In the first wave three Mosquitos laid marker flares over the concrete bunkers, which were then attacked by 22 Lancasters dropping 12,000lb Tallboy bombs. They scored several hits on the bunkers, but only one bomb penetrated the roof. The second wave, 209 Lancasters preceded by ten Mosquitos which dropped marker flares, followed close on the heels of the first, and the third wave, 116 Lancasters, followed three hours later as dusk was falling. The total absence of Flak and Luftwaffe enabled the Lancasters to bomb the port with great accuracy, although the Notre-Dame district near the docks was devastated by 'overs' (700 houses and a tobacco factory were destroyed, the local prison was damaged, and 76 civilians were killed and 150 injured). However, the greater part of the 1,230 tons of bombs fell on the harbour area, sinking twenty minesweepers and patrol-boats, nineteen tugs, three torpedo-boats (*Falke*, *Jaguar* and *Möwe*) and fourteen S-boats (*S169*, *S171*, *S172*, *S173*, *S187*, *S188* of 4th Flotilla; *S84*, *S100*, *S138*, *S142* and *S143* of the 5th Flotilla; and *S66*, *S146*, and *S150* of the 9th Flotilla). In addition *S144* and seven other craft were badly damaged, and heavy casualties were suffered by German naval personnel, including Kapitänleutnant Johannsen, commander of 5th S-Boat Flotilla. Only one S-boat (*S167*) was left operational in Le Havre. For some reason the S-boats were not berthed in the bunkers when the raid began, their places being occupied exclusively by R-boats.

Vizeadmiral Krancke described the effects of the raid as a 'catastrophe' and next morning he recorded in the War Diary that: 'it will hardly be possible to carry out the operations planned with the remaining forces... the naval situation in the Seine Bay has completely altered since yesterday's attack on Le Havre'. The 'remaining forces' were further depleted that very evening when 155 Lancasters, 130 Halifaxes and 12 Mosquitos struck at 2nd S-Boat Flotilla at Boulogne. The 2nd Flotilla escaped the holocaust inflicted at Le Havre, because the boats were safely ensconced in the concrete bunkers, but a depot ship and 26 light craft (including seven R-boats) were sunk and eight others were badly damaged together with the floating dock and harbour installations. This was the heaviest raid that Boulogne suffered during the entire war: great destruction being caused to the port and surrounding areas where some 200 civilians were killed. By 16 June the number of S-boats in the invasion area available to the FdS had been reduced to ten operational boats (one at Le Havre, four at Boulogne and five at Ostend) and four damaged boats undergoing repair (one at Le Havre and three at Cherbourg). To replace the losses Kommodore Petersen ordered 6th S-Boat Flotilla, operating in the Gulf of Finland, to leave the Baltic for Boulogne, but it did not arrive until the end of June. In the meantime, the surviving S-boats continued their nightly attempts to interdict the beachhead area (suffering damage to S190, S175, S181 in the process), but their reduced strength and the ever-increasing strength of the Allied air and sea patrols prevented them from causing any further damage to Allied shipping during the remainder of June.

The damage they had inflicted was insignificant given the volume of Allied shipping that was crossing the Channel daily, and was certainly not enough to have any effect on the build-up in France, for by 18 June 629,000 troops, 95,000 vehicles and 218,000 tons of ammunition and supplies had been landed.[4] By this date, not counting the shipping that had arrived in Seine Bay on D-Day, 93 troop ships, 636 merchant ships and 1,300 landing ships and craft had crossed the Channel safely. The only remaining hope of interrupting the build-up in Normandy and denying the Anglo-American armies already ashore of supplies, ammunition and reinforcements, now rested with the U-boats and the small battle units of the *K-Verband*.

Chapter 4

GREAT EXPECTATIONS

GROUP HOLZBEIN'S ODYSSEY

The advent of D-Day found Dönitz on vacation with his family in Badenweiler, a hillside resort in the Black Forest. He was woken in the early hours by a telephone call from his staff at the *Koralle* HQ near Berlin, telling him that the invasion had begun. He arrived back at his HQ at 1113 to chair a conference on the situation, declaring that 'the war has entered its decisive phase for Germany'.[1]

BdU staff had already ordered the 36 U-boats of Group Landwirt in the Biscay bases, and the 22 U-boats of Group Mitte in southern Norway, to come to immediate notice for sea, and the five snorkel-fitted boats south of Iceland on their way into the Atlantic were ordered to turn about and make for western French waters at high speed. A further seven Atlantic-bound boats in various positions to the west of Norway were instructed to mark time and await further orders.

During the conference Dönitz asserted that 'In this hour of crisis the role of the U-boats is decisive to the outcome of the war, and every available boat must be flung into the battle regardless of cost.'[2] The primary task was to attack the invasion fleet off the Normandy coast, but as the enemy was certain to employ a large number of air and surface A/S forces to protect the western flank of the assault forces, BdU was of the opinion that only the eight snorkel boats of Group Landwirt, based at Brest, would have any chance of forcing their way into the central waters of the English Channel to attack the great mass of shipping plying across the Channel between an area to the south of the Isle of Wight and Seine Bay. However, realizing that these eight snorkel boats would have a better chance of breaking through if more U-boats were crossing the western approaches into the Channel at the same time, Dönitz decided to take a risk and send the nine non-snorkel boats based at Brest into the danger area.

The remaining nineteen U-boats of Group Landwirt (none fitted with snorkel), based at St-Nazaire, Lorient and La Pallice, were ordered to form an anti-invasion patrol line in the Bay of Biscay, in case the Allies attempted a landing on the French Atlantic coastline.

While the Brest-based boats were preparing for sea, their commanding officers received a grim order from BdU:

U-Boat Dispositions, 10 June 1944

'Every enemy vessel supporting the landing, even though it may be carrying only 50 men or a tank, is a target. Press home your attack, even at the cost of your boat. Should it be necessary to close the enemy landing fleet, pay no regard to the danger of shallow water, mines or other hazards. Each soldier and weapon destroyed before reaching the beachhead diminishes the enemy's chance of victory. A U-boat which inflicts losses on the invasion forces fulfils her highest mission and justifies her existence, even though she herself may be destroyed.'[3]

All seventeen of the Brest-based boats sailed between noon and midnight on 6 June, with orders to proceed at high speed on the surface to their operational areas -the snorkel boats to a position north-east of Cherbourg (the 'Spout'), the remainder to an area on the western side of the Channel between Start Point and the Scilly Isles. Although a high-speed surface dash invited attack from enemy air patrols, BdU considered the risk justifiable as a slow submerged passage at six knots would delay the force from being brought to bear in time to influence events.

All BdU's operational decisions during the course of D-Day were known to the Admiralty, and the resulting 'Ultra' messages,[4] issued by the OIC to the naval commands, graphically illustrate the depth of insight into BdU's intentions that possession of the U-boat 'Triton' Enigma had given the Allies.

TIME OF DISPATCH TO ALLIED COMMANDS:

'0533   Six U-boats which have recently left the Baltic via south Norway ordered to halt and stay in positions.

0807   At 0513 all U-boats informed that the Allies were landing in Seine Bay.

0919   Five U-boats which have recently entered the Atlantic from Norway ordered to Biscay at highest speed, but submerged by day.

1402   Seven U-boats on hand in the Arctic ordered to return to Narvik and remain at immediate readiness, leaving nine on patrol off Jan Mayen.

1945   A total of 18 U-boats have sailed from the three bases south of Brest.

2057   *a.* One U-boat, probably non-snorkel, ordered to operate between the Scillies and the Lizard. *b.* Unknown number of snorkel U-boats ordered at noon to leave (probably) Brest via a given position between Ushant and Land's End to the area between Cherbourg and Portland.'

Although the decrypts did not furnish the Admiralty with the departure times of the Group Landwirt U-boats, this omission was not serious because extremely strong A/S patrols were already in position to counter the expected exodus of U-boats from the Biscay ports. By 1850 on the evening of D-Day, Beaufighters of Coastal Command had sighted five of the outward-bound U-boats from Brest, and they sighted another fourteen, all but two rounding Ushant, during the night of 6/7 June. As a result the seventeen boats making for the Channel, designated Group Holzbein by BdU to differentiate them from the nineteen boats of Group Landwirt forming a patrol line in the Bay of Biscay, were subjected to the most intensive air attacks hitherto encountered by a single group of U-boats in the entire war. During the night of 6/7 June more than fifty air attacks were made on the surfaced U-boats of Group Holzbein.

The log of the commander of *U415*, Kapitänleutnant Kurt Neide, gives a graphic account of the ferocity of the attacks:

'7th June 1944.

0140	Sea 1 to 2, swell, moonlight, good visibility. Dropped escort off Brest. Course 270 degrees, full speed (15 knots).
0145	Next astern attacked by aircraft. I open fire with her. Aircraft shot down by *U256*. Radar audible on all bearings, strength 3 to 4.
0220	Radar no longer audible to starboard, so assume aircraft on run in. Sunderland approaches from green 40. I open fire. Four bombs fall just ahead and detonate under the boat. Liberator attacks simultaneously from the starboard beam, firing her guns which hit my bridge. She drops no bombs. The Sunderland's bombs have brought my diesels to a standstill. The boat rises high in the water and settles by the stern, so that water enters the conning-tower hatch. Order "Clear lower deck; clear away rubber dinghy". Radio out of action so cannot report. Manned emergency radio transmitter on bridge, Rubber dinghy and life-buoys are being cleared away. Boat remains afloat, so order all ammunition on to the bridge. Rudder jammed to starboard.
0228	Sunderland renews attack from starboard, firing her guns and dropping bombs from low altitude. Bombs straddle us amidships. Directly afterwards the Liberator flies in from the port bow. I open fire. My twin machine-guns shoot well and the aircraft crashes in flames. My *Wanze* and *Fliege* [radar sets] have been shot out of action. Some time later the Senior Engineer reports all clear for diving on one electric motor, so I order all hands below and commence return passage...'[5]

U415 's experience was typical of the five other boats that were damaged by air attack during that first night out from Brest, and were forced to return to base (*U413*, *U256*, *U989*, *U963*, *U212* – only the latter being snorkel-fitted). All the attacks were made by aircraft from No. 19 Group, Coastal Command, which lost four aircraft shot down by Flak while making low-level attacks.

The depletion of six boats from Group Holzbein caused BdU to order the remaining eleven boats to proceed submerged for the rest of the passage into the Channel, although their daily run was thereby reduced to fifty miles a day. Despite this change in tactics, the group suffered further losses two nights later (8/9 June), when the non-snorkel boats were forced to surface to recharge their batteries, and those so fitted had to come up to periscope depth to take in air through their snorkels. Two boats, *U373* and *U629*, were sunk within half-an-hour of each other by a single RAF Liberator of No. 224 Squadron commanded by Flying Officer K. Moore (both boats had surfaced to recharge their batteries). Some of the group were attacked by surface vessels that night. *U984* was detected 30 miles north-west of Ushant by the ASDIC of a group of Canadian destroyers which subjected her to a 24-hour depth-charge attack and pursuit until she finally managed to shake them off. During the attack *U984* fired three Gnat torpedoes at the destroyer HMCS *Saskatchewan*, one of which exploded in the destroyer's 'foxer' gear towed astern; the other two missed their target. *U953* was also attacked by destroyers from this group on the morning of 8 June. Her commander, Kapitänleutnant Karl-Heinz Marbach, fired four Gnat torpedoes in three attacks – at 0945 against HMCS *Qu'Appelle*, at 0947 against HMCS *Restigouche*, and at 0950 against HMCS *Skeena* – all of which exploded in the wakes of the destroyers which were towing 'foxers'. The log of the commander of *U984*, Oberleutnant zur See Heinz Sieder, recounts the effect that this ordeal had on the crew:

'Although enemy radar is still audible, I decide to snorkel a little to ventilate the boat. We have now been submerged continuously for nearly 42 hours without a change of air, and for the last 12 hours breathing conditions have been extraordinarily bad. The men have literally been gasping for breath. A certain amount of relief has been obtained by breathing through potash cartridges, with the aid of escape apparatus mouth-pieces. I am now close to the French coast, my batteries completely exhausted, so decided to return to Brest to recharge and top up with torpedoes...'[6]

U984 reached Brest on 9 June, and sailed again on the 12th to rejoin Group Holzbein. *U953* was also forced to return to Brest because her snorkel had been damaged: she arrived on the 18th and sailed again on the 24th. The original group of seventeen boats had, by the morning of 9 June, been reduced to five snorkel and two non-snorkel boats. The latter two, *U740* and *U821*, were ordered to return to base by BdU, which had now decided that it was too risky for non-snorkel boats to operate in the Channel. In BdU's War Diary Dönitz commented that 'on account of the large number of air attacks and the extensive damage suffered above all on U-boats without snorkel, all further operations by these boats [in the Channel] has been stopped for the present'. Neither *U740* nor *U821* made it back to Brest, both being caught on the surface by aircraft and sunk: *U740* at 0840 on the 9th, by a Liberator of No. 120 Squadron south-west of the Scilly Isles; *U821* at noon on the 10th, off Ushant by four Mosquitos of No. 248 Squadron which riddled her with cannon fire, leaving her to be finished off by depth-charges from a Liberator.

The heavy losses made Dönitz fear that he was demanding the impossible from the crews of the five remaining snorkel boats of Group Holzbein. Operational experience with snorkel was too scanty to lay down instructions for its use, or to state what procedures should be adopted in the narrow waters of the Channel where opportunities for re-charging batteries by snorkeling might be few and far between because of the numerous A/S patrols. Günther Hessler, an officer on Dönitz's staff, explains how problematic the situation appeared to BdU at the time:

'No operational experience had been gained in the shallow waters of the Channel since 1940 ... for all we knew, the enemy might now possess depth-charges or other weapons of such devastating effect in shallow water that a U-boat's detection would ensure her destruction. Thus the boats, fitted with snorkel installation with which they were still unfamiliar, were being sent to face an unknown threat in an area considered, even in 1940, as too dangerous for such operations.

'Operational control was rendered difficult and onerous by the problem of communicating with U-boats, even in normal operations, and during Group Dragoner's brief sortie into the Channel in May there had been many instances of boats missing important messages through having to snorkel, despite careful timing of long-wave routines. It was most likely, therefore, that in the present circumstances the boats would have few opportunities to transmit, and that BdU would have to rely entirely upon radio intercepts and the reports of returning commanders for a picture of the situation. Such intelligence could be long out of date, and it is not surprising that we were unable to make up our minds on the viability of U-boats operating in the Channel, either before or after the invasion.'[7]

However, the gravity of the situation was such that Dönitz felt he had no choice but to attack the Allied supply traffic with every available snorkel-fitted U-boat regardless of the cost in German lives. To this end, four of the five snorkel boats, that had reached a position south of Iceland on their passage into the Atlantic (*U767*, *U1191*, *U988*, *U671*), and had been ordered to make for western French waters on the morning of D-Day, were ordered (on the morning of 9 June) to proceed surfaced at high speed to the latitude south of Ireland and continue into the Channel, there to reinforce the five remaining boats of Group Holzbein. In addition the remaining snorkel boat, *U719*, which had reached a position south of Iceland, was ordered into the North Channel, while *U247*, one of the seven boats ordered to mark time to the west of Norway, was sent to the Minch in an endeavour to tie down enemy A/S forces in that area.

As Dönitz had feared, enemy A/S patrols were so prolific that the U-boats were attacked on almost every occasion that they attempted to snorkel, and were afforded very few opportunities to attack the Allied follow-up convoys. Three boats, *U269*, *U275* and *U984*, were forced to put into St. Peter Port, Guernsey, on 13, 15 and 18 June respectively, their batteries and crews completely exhausted by being denied the chance to snorkel for any length of time. For instance, *U275* was almost continuously hunted and depth-charged from 0915 on 8 June until she reached St. Peter Port on the 15th. During those seven days she had only managed to snorkel for short periods during the hours of darkness.

'A study of the logs of the surviving U-boats during their June sorties into the Channel highlights their difficulties and complete lack of mobility. Never more than a 50-mile daily run was achieved and in most cases considerably less. The constant air cover made them chary of snorkelling by day and the drain on battery power forced them to lie bottomed when the tidal stream was adverse. Roving groups of surface craft kept then in a constant state of harassment and hindered snorkel charging at night. In desperation some U-boat captains surfaced at night to charge while manoeuvring at speed on various courses to avoid detection but more often than not they had to dive soon after, either because of sighting searchlights or on warning of approaching aircraft in their radar detectors, with the battery still far from charged. Inexperience of snorkelling led to frequent violent changes in the air pressure inside the boat or to blowbacks of stifling and noxious exhaust gases. Except for boats taking refuge and a slight rest in Guernsey, none dared to radio their base either to give their positions or experiences, and as a result the U-boat Command was unable to plan concerted operations, less dangerous routes or more favourable attack areas and was quite unaware of losses or of very slow progress when on passage.

'This handicap was indeed to remain a feature of all U-boat operations until the end of the war. The whole organization had been based on the principle of free inter-communication between the boats at sea and the headquarters ashore. From now onwards it was impossible to exercise control and operations degenerated into blind independent unco-ordinated sorties.'[8]

The three boats that sought refuge in St. Peter Port were all attacked by fighter-bombers, their arrival having been revealed by Enigma decrypts, but all three escaped damage by submerging and lying on the bottom of the harbour until the attack was over, and were able to leave within 24 hours. *U269* and *U984* resumed the attempt to reach the assigned operational area to the north-east of Cherbourg, but *U275* was attacked by a USN Liberator when she was only five miles clear of the harbour and, her oil tanks damaged, was forced to make for Brest which she reached on 24 June.

The return of *U275* to base reduced Group Holzbein to five boats, and the hope of reinforcements in the shape of the four boats diverted from the Atlantic crawling into the western approaches at a submerged speed of 6 knots. Of these nine boats only two, *U621* and *U764*, reached the intended operational area north-east of Cherbourg, where they succeeded in mounting four attacks. At 0803 on 15 June, *U621* sank a straggler from a convoy – the 1,490-ton tank landing ship *LST 380* (fully laden with tanks) – off Pointe de Barfleur. Two hours later she fired a spread of torpedoes at two US battleships, all of which detonated prematurely. Having expanded all her torpedoes, she began the return passage to Brest where she arrived on 23 June.

On the same day (15 June) *U764* managed to penetrate the screen of a convoy of six LSTs to the north of Seine Bay and fired a spread of three torpedoes, all of which detonated prematurely. Driven off to the west by the resulting counter-attack of the convoy escort, she managed to account for one of her pursuers – the 1,085-ton RN frigate *Blackwood* – which she torpedoed at 1910 off Cap de la Hague with a T5 *Zaunkönig* torpedo. *Blackwood*'s bows were blown off, and although she was taken in tow she sank at 0410 next morning, 23 miles south-east of Portland Bill. *U764* was damaged during a depth-charge attack, shortly after she had torpedoed *Blackwood* and she was forced to return to Brest which she reached on 23 June.

U767, one of the four boats diverted into the Channel from the Atlantic, also scored a success on 15 June, torpedoing and sinking the 1,370-ton RN frigate *Mourne* at 1145, 45 miles south-south-west of the Lizard.

No further successes were scored until ten days later (25 June) when *U984*, which had left St. Peter Port on the 19th after a 24-four respite, ran into a patrol group forty miles north of Jersey and torpedoed and damaged the RN frigate *Goodson* (which was towed into Portland). Four days later, on the afternoon of 29 June, she struck again, this time at a convoy of American Liberty ships, employed as transports, which she encountered 30 miles north of Pointe de Barfleur. *U984*'s commander, Heinz Sieder, managed to torpedo four of the liberty ships – *Edward M. House* (7,240 tons), *Henry G. Blasdel* (7,176 tons), *John A. Treutlen* (7,198 tons) and *James A. Farrell* (7,176 tons). All four were towed into English ports, but all bar *Edward M. House* were declared total constructional losses. Having expended all her torpedoes, *U984* began the return passage to Brest, arriving there on 4 July.

By the end of June only two (*U953* and *U671*) of the 21 U-boats that BdU had sent into the Channel, were still attempting to attack the Allied follow-up convoys. Of the eight snorkel-fitted boats that had sailed from Brest on D-Day, five (*U212*, *U275*, *U764*, *U621*, *U984*) had returned or were *en route* to Brest, and two had been sunk (*U441* had been depth-charged by aircraft of No. 304 Polish Squadron (RAF) 34 miles north-east of Ushant on 18 June; and *U269* had been depth-charged by the RN frigate *Bickerton* south-east of Start Point on 25 June). Of the nine non-snorkel boats that had sailed from Brest, five (*U256*, *U413*, *U415*, *U989*, *U963*) had returned, and four had been sunk (*U740*, *U821*, *U629*, *U373*). The four boats that had been diverted into the Channel from the Atlantic fared no better (all four had left German ports during the middle of May on their first operational cruises). Three had been sunk: *U767* (which had sunk the frigate *Mourne* on the 15th) had been depth-charged by the RN destroyers *Fame*, *Inconstant* and *Havelock*, south-west of Guernsey on 18 June; *U1191* had been depth-charged by the RN frigates *Affleck* and *Balfour*, 25 miles south-east of Start Point on the 25th; and *U988* had been depth-charged by aircraft and the RN frigates *Essington*, *Duckworth*, *Domett* and *Cook*, forty miles south of Start Point on the 29th. The sole survivor of this group, *U671*, in accordance with her instructions, had kept close to the English coast on her final eastward run towards the 'Spout' and had reached a position some twenty miles south-west of Beachy Head by 4 July without much difficulty. But on that day, while lying on the bottom, she was detected by ASDIC and subjected to a depth-charge attack by a group of patrol vessels. Damaged, *U671* was compelled to make for the nearest port, and managed to reach Boulogne on the 5th. As there were no U-boat technicians at Boulogne, a party of thirty men had to be sent from St-Nazaire. Working under great difficulties, they managed to ready *U671* for sea by the end of the month, but her return to the operational area was short-lived for on 4 August she was sunk by the RN frigate *Stayner* and the RN destroyer *Wensleydale* south of Brighton.

The only remaining boat of Group Holzbein still operating in the Channel, *U953*, ended this phase of U-boat operations by sinking the 1,927-ton British freighter *Glendinning* at 0805 on 5 July. She arrived back in Brest on the 21 July.

The two boats that BdU had sent into the North Channel (*U719*) and Minch (*U247*) in an endeavour to tie down A/S forces in those areas, fared no better than Group Holzbein. *U719* was sunk on 26 June by the RN destroyer *Bulldog* off the north-west coast of Ireland, and *U247*, constantly harried by surface patrols, only managed to sink the 207-ton trawler *Noreen Mary*, before making for Brest, where she arrived on 27 July.

So ended BdU's first attempt to prevent the Allied build-up in Normandy, which Dönitz had confidently expected would 'make a wholly disproportionate contribution to success [in defeating the invasion forces] by sinking ships laden with munitions, tanks and other war material'. For the loss of ten U-boats, and damage to practically every other boat that had ventured into the Channel, all that had been achieved was the sinking of two frigates, four freighters and one tank landing ship, and the damaging of one frigate and one freighter. The dense air and surface A/S patrols had effectively and systematically stifled any chance the U-boats might have had of causing any significant damage to the huge Allied invasion force, and on 5 July the millionth Allied soldier stepped ashore in Normandy, and Dönitz was left with the inescapable conclusion that his great expectations of what the U-boats could achieve had been nothing more than an even greater delusion.

BAY OF BISCAY OPERATIONS

The nineteen non-snorkel U-boats of Group Landwirt based at Lorient, St-Nazaire and La Pallice, put to sea on D-Day to form a reconnaissance line between the latitudes of Brest and Bayonne, in case the Allies attempted a second landing on the French Biscay coast. Initially they took up positions off the coast on the 200-metre line (where the depth of water reached some 650 feet). From north to south they were disposed as follows: between Brest and Lorient *U993*, *U981*, *U608*, *U333*, *U270*; between Lorient and St-Nazaire *U281*, *U228*, *U260*, *U985*; between St-Nazaire and La Pallice *U255*, *U262*; between La Pallice and Bayonne *U758*, *U437*, *U445*, *U650*, *U766*, *U970*, *U714*, *U382*.

From the outset these boats were subjected to constant air attacks. On 7 June *U970* was depth-charged and sunk west of Bordeaux by a Sunderland of No. 228 Squadron and *U333* was damaged by aircraft from the same squadron. On the same day *U955*, inward-bound from the Atlantic, was sunk by a Sunderland of No. 201 Squadron. *U437*, *U445* and *U228* were also attacked by aircraft, but in each case they not only survived but also shot down their assailants.

On 8 June, a Luftwaffe meteorological aircraft sighted a south-bound convoy 120 miles west of Brest. Acting on the possibility that this could be an Allied invasion force, BdU ordered the U-boats to move closer inshore to the 100-metre line (where the depth of water did not exceed 325 feet), from where they would be better positioned to attack landing-craft as they approached the shore. Some hours later the convoy was identified as a group of fishing vessels; nevertheless, it was decided that the U-boats should remain on the 100-metre line, where they could lie on the bottom for long periods and thereby shorten the time needed for surfacing to recharge their batteries, even though their reconnaissance value was consequently much reduced. Normally U-boats were forbidden to bottom in water of 100 metres or less because of the danger from ground mines, but this ban was now lifted since the danger of ground mines was regarded as less of a menace than that from air attacks on boats surfacing for lengthy periods to recharge their batteries. Although this procedure reduced to a minimum the time spent on the surface, the boats were still located and attacked almost every night. But BdU dared not recall them to harbour, fearing that an enemy landing on the Biscay coast, or the mining of the approach channels, could trap the boats, effectively sealing them up in the ports. So BdU chose the lesser evil, leaving them exposed to the danger of air attack at sea.

By 12 June it had become evident, from the scale of the landing in Normandy, that the danger of an imminent landing on the Biscay coast was unlikely, and rather than risk further loss or damage Dönitz recalled all the boats on the reconnaissance line to their bases, observing in his War Diary: 'otherwise the strong enemy air activity will lead to high losses which would only be acceptable if an immediate landing on the Biscay coast were expected. As this is no longer considered an acute danger the boats will remain at readiness in the concrete shelters in harbour.'[9]

Some of Dönitz's staff at BdU suggested that rather than keep the eighteen surviving Landwirt boats lying idle in the pens, they should be sent into the North Atlantic, even though their prospects of attacking convoys would be extremely poor, as their appearance in those waters might induce the enemy to withdraw substantial A/S forces from the Channel to deal with them. Dönitz rejected the proposal, believing that the enemy possessed such a wealth of A/S vessels as to render such a withdrawal from the Channel unnecessary. In his opinion, the sending of non-snorkel boats into the Atlantic would only result in further heavy losses, whereas if they remained in western France they would have some prospect of inflicting damage on the enemy in the event, which was still regarded as a possibility, of a landing on the Biscay coast. All eighteen boats remained in the bomb-proof pens at Lorient, St-Nazaire and La Pallice, while work pressed ahead with the utmost vigour to equip them all with snorkel.

GROUP MITTE

Allied deception measures caused the Germans to believe that strong forces had been assembled in Scotland and at English ports on the East Coast, with the intention of invading Norway (no such forces existed). For this reason the 22 U-boats of Group Mitte, based at Bergen, Stavanger and Christiansand, were held in readiness to repel an invasion fleet. Between 8 and 10 June, eleven boats of Group Mitte put to sea and, with the six boats marking time to the west of Norway, formed a reconnaissance line between the latitudes of Trondheim and Lindesnes. During the second week of June additional snorkel-fitted boats, on their first operational cruise, were dispatched from Kiel to bring the strength of Group Mitte up to thirty boats, of which sixteen were kept at sea on the reconnaissance line.

Like the boats of Group Landwirt in the Bay of Biscay, the boats patrolling off the Norwegian coast were subjected to frequent air attacks. On 11 June, *U980* was caught on the surface north-west of Bergen and sunk by Canadian Canso aircraft of No. 162 Squadron (RCAF). Two days later (13 June) *U715* was depth-charged and sunk by aircraft of the same squadron east of the Faeroes. She earned the dubious honour of being the first U-boat to be attacked and sunk while snorkelling at periscope depth: after being mortally damaged by depth-charges, she surfaced and some of her crew managed to shoot down the attacker before the boat foundered. Later in the day *U480*, positioned a little to the north of *U715*, was attacked by an aircraft from the same squadron, but she managed to shoot down her assailant and escape unscathed. *U290* was not so lucky: she was shot up by a Mosquito on 14 June and had to return to port with nine of her crew seriously wounded. Two days later (16 June) *U998* was badly damaged east of the Shetlands by a Mosquito from No. 333 Norwegian Squadron (RAF) and had to return to Bergen where she was paid off and later broken up. *U804* was also damaged by a Mosquito from the same squadron when she went to the assistance of *U998*: with eight of her crew badly wounded she was also forced to put back to Bergen. On 17 June, No. 333 Squadron notched up another kill when a Catalina sank *U423* north-west of Christiansand.

The loss of four boats (*U998* being a constructional loss) and two having to return to port damaged in the course of seven days, was the result of the U-boats on the reconnaissance line choosing to fight it out on the surface with their Flak against the attacking aircraft. No specific instructions on the employment of this tactic can he found in German records, and it may have been that over-confidence among U-boat captains on their first war cruise (most of the boats being of recent commission) resulted in their defiance of air attack. On the other hand, there is plenty of evidence that the newly fitted snorkels were giving trouble so some of the surfaced encounters may well have been involuntary.

The heavy losses incurred caused BdU to order the surviving non-snorkel boats to remain submerged except when recharging their batteries. The depth of the water off the Norwegian coast was too great to permit lying on the bottom, thereby conserving battery power, but some of the boats took advantage of density layers to drift, stopped and trimmed. Nevertheless, despite all precautions, another three boats (two of them snorkel-fitted) fell victim to attacks by aircraft. On 24 June, *U1225* was caught on the surface 120 miles north-east of the Shetlands by a Canso of No. 162 Squadron (RCAF). The aircraft was badly shot up by *U1225*'s Flak on the run-in, but staggered on to straddle and sink the U-boat with depth-charges. Immediately afterwards the Liberator became unmanageable, the starboard engine fell off and, burning furiously, the aircraft ditched in the sea. The crew got clear but were in the water for 21 hours, two of them dying of exposure, before the arrival of an Air Sea Rescue launch. The captain, Flight Lieutenant D. E. Hornell, died soon after being pulled on board the launch. He was awarded a posthumous VC. On 26 June, *U317* was depth-charged and sunk by a Liberator of No. 86 Squadron north-east of the Shetlands. Four days later, at 1750 on the 30th, *U478*'s periscope was sighted by a Canso of No. 162 Squadron, north-east of the Faeroes. The periscope dipped before an attack could be mounted, but a second Canso returned to the area three hours later and caught *U478* on the surface. As the aircraft ran into attack, *U478* opened a hot fire with her Flak which hit the aircraft and severed all the depth-charge release circuits. Denied the means of attacking, the Liberator circled the U-boat while homing a Canso from No. 86 Squadron which attacked at 2115 and sank *U478* with depth-charges. During this period two other boats (*U743* and *U396*) were damaged by aircraft attacks and forced to return to port.

By the end of June, when it became apparent that the threat of an Allied invasion of Norway was unlikely, BdU, not wishing to expose the boats on the reconnaissance line to further loss, decided to reduce the number of boats patrolling between Trondheim and Lindesnes to five. The remainder were recalled to Bergen and Stavanger, eight of the older, non-snorkel boats being paid off and laid up so that their crews could return to Germany to man the first of the Type XXI Electro-boats which were entering service. Group Mitte was further reduced in strength when *U971*, *U678* and *U480* were ordered into the English Channel, and five boats were transferred to the Baltic to operate against Russian coastal traffic.

ORDEAL IN THE CHANNEL

At the beginning of July, the Germans captured an enemy track chart which furnished them with a fairly accurate picture of the Allied supply organization to Normandy. It revealed that nine convoys sailed from the English and French sides of the Channel daily and, of those bound for Seine Bay four sailed from Portsmouth, three from the West of England and two from the Thames. These convoys followed buoyed routes and were timed to arrive in the unloading area between 1400 and 1800, while it was still light. There were no night sailings. The flanks of the convoy routes were protected by destroyer patrols, and the convoys were escorted by a variety of smaller patrol vessels. This information, taken in conjunction with an optimistic report from the commander of the recently returned *U984*, which had sunk three transports and damaged another together with the frigate *Goodson*, caused Dönitz to send a second wave of snorkel boats into the Channel with orders to refrain from attacking A/S vessels but concentrate on the invasion supply ships in the area of the 'Spout'.

From 2 July to 16 August, a total of twenty snorkel boats were sent into the Channel: seven of them were boats from Brest that had survived the first attempt – two of them, *U413* and *U989*, having been hurriedly fitted with snorkel during the interim; ten were from Biscay ports, being sent straight to sea after re-commissioning from lengthy dockyard refits; and three were from Group Mitte whose passage had taken them north of the Faroes and to the west of Ireland.

The crews of these boats suffered terrible hardships during their sorties into the Channel. They couldn't risk raising their snorkels to ventilate the boats in daylight, and consequently the atmosphere, which was normally pretty foul in a snorkel boat, was further polluted by the stench of decaying waste food and other refuse. A few boats had been equipped with a new type of air-pressure heads which included a sump and large-bore discharge pipe through which waste matter could be evacuated after being chopped up; others tried to solve their problems by packing refuse into tins and laboriously disposing of them at night through the ASDIC decoy discharge tube. One inventive commander hit upon the idea of stowing all the boat's refuse, including packing cases, in an empty torpedo tube and firing it every three or four days. This had the disadvantage that the tube could no longer be used for its proper purpose, and had to be isolated so as to avoid fouling the remainder; but this procedure, known as a *Mallschoss* (rubbish shot), was subsequently adopted by most of the boats, and thereafter, when a boat returned to base, the first dockyard workman to arrive on board no longer recoiled from the open hatch.

Since all crew's movements consumed oxygen, a boat's routine was usually adjusted to the snorkelling pattern – clean ship, torpedo maintenance and meals being put off until the night snorkelling period when there was sufficient fresh air for all. For most of the time and unless on watch, crew members generally lay on their bunks, and a few commanders even extinguished the lighting to discourage conversation and other oxygen-consuming activities. This measure proved to be psychologically unsound, since it allowed the minds of the crew to dwell too much on outside noises. During operations in the Channel, the din endured by the U-boat crews surpassed anything experienced hitherto; the buzzing and screaming of various types of noise-boxes (foxers), the pinging of ASDIC and the whirring of propellers were continuous, while the detonations of innumerable bombs and depth-charges shook the boats constantly. It was almost impossible to estimate the range of a noise-source; the faintest humming could spell danger, and a sustained noise often drowned the whirr of approaching propellers. On occasions a destroyer would suddenly be heard directly overhead, or depth-charges would explode nearby without warning. Even the bravest – and one must grant that these pale-faced U-boat men were brave – could not fail, eventually, to become adversely affected.

The crews found themselves in very serious straits if A/S vessels remained in the close vicinity, giving them no opportunity to snorkel. For instance, during the evening of 5 July 1944, *U763* attacked a convoy of cargo ships south of the Isle of Wight, and sank the 1,499-ton Norwegian freighter *Ringen*. This provoked a violent counter-attack on the part of the convoy escort, as Kapitänleutnant Ernst Cordes recorded in his log:

'6th July 1944. 1645. South of Isle of Wight. Bottomed again in 55 metres. Enemy still has contact. I shall wait here till night. Depth-charges are now fewer and farther between. Thirty-four detonated in our near vicinity between 1600 and 2000. Despite the addition of oxygen [from escape apparatus] and the use of potash cartridges, the air has become perceptibly fouler. A very great quantity of air was consumed by members of the crew who had to be moved in order to keep the boat trim during my attempt to shift position. The crew are becoming more exhausted. It is nearly 30 hours since the boat was last ventilated. The first cases of vomiting occur, and I issue each man with a potash cartridge. Breathing becomes distressed. The enemy search group is still active overhead ... The intervals between depth-charges are getting longer, but detonations are nearly all very close ... During the 30 hours of the pursuit, 252 depth-charges were counted in the near vicinity, 61 at medium range and 51 at long range ...'[10]

A snorkel failure or defect could also cause serious difficulties, as the log of Kapitänleutnant Klaus Becker, commander of *U218*, which was engaged in laying mines off Land's End, illustrates:

'0400	Bomb or depth-charge concussion has apparently fractured a tappet lever on the port diesel. Starboard diesel started; but owing to insufficient exhaust pressure the safety valve [on the snorkel] lifts and the exhaust gases escape into the boat, filling all compartments and necessitating the wearing of escape apparatus.
0500	Surfaced to ventilate the boat.
0503	*Naxos* [radar] gives three separate warnings, amplitude 4 to 5. Dived to 80 metres [260 feet].
1200	Several men suddenly taken ill during the forenoon. By noon two-thirds of the crew are suffering from severe headache and stomach-ache, nausea and retching, and are no longer fit for duty. The remainder, also complaining of bad headaches, keep things going. There are several cases of fainting through over-exertion and carbon-monoxide poisoning.
1230	Rise to periscope depth in an attempt to ventilate with port diesel.
1240	Port diesel starts, but exhaust pressure is too low to empty the snorkel mast. The safety valve lifts again, filling the boat with exhaust fumes which causes further cases of carbon-monoxide poisoning.
1250	Electric compressor started in an attempt to draw out the fumes and replace them through the snorkel valve. The state of the crew continues to deteriorate.
1400	Surfaced to change the air in the boat. I cannot wait until dusk.
1406	Dived. The boat is thoroughly ventilated. By evening there is only a slight improvement in the state of the crew. Milk is issued to counteract the effects of the poisoning. Six men, in a state of collapse, given injections of lobelyn sympatol to stimulate heart action...'[11]

U218 reached Brest on 9 July, her mines having damaged one ship, the 7,177-ton British freighter *Empire Halberd*.

By the middle of 1944, the majority of the most experienced U-boat commanders had either been killed or were employed in U-boat training establishments, with the result that the average age of the commanders of the *Frontboote* was only 24. These young officers had received their commands after only four years' service at the most, and few of them had any experience of navigation in the difficult tidal waters of the Channel. The same was true of the navigating officers, nearly all of whom had joined their boats direct from the training school. Moreover, in the Channel operations, the U-boat commanders and navigators had to cope with the added difficulty of operating almost continually submerged.

　　Although the periscope could be used for terrestrial navigation, it was necessary to approach very close to the shore to take sightings because the lens was so close to the surface, and as this invited destruction by mine or A/S forces few commanders would take the risk. Alternatively, to obtain a fix from radio beacons on shore, the boats would have to surface sufficiently to bring their aerials above water, which would expose the conning tower to location and attack. Speed was therefore vital when obtaining a fix from the beacons, but, as many of the beacons on the French coast had been destroyed by Allied bombing, it took a long time to obtain a fix and the commanders seldom ventured to expose their boats for so long a period. In these circumstances they had no choice but to navigate by dead reckoning, which proved a difficult task, since, apart from the Hurd Deep, there were no well-defined depth lines in the Channel. Furthermore, the tidal rates and directions marked on the charts were primarily for surface navigation and not for the water strata between 100 and 150 feet below the surface in which the boats were operating. Commanders sometimes found themselves in tidal races so strong that they had difficulty in holding a selected position, let alone intercepting a convoy. A submerged U-boat could not anchor to prevent herself from drifting, and only at about the time of slack water could she rest on the bottom, trimmed by the bow, allowing her stern to swing with the tide. On occasions when the batteries became exhausted, commanders were compelled to bottom regardless of the state of the tide and thereby risk damage to rudder and screws, by dragging.

　　The situation was compounded by the boats' gyro-compasses and echo-sounders having to be switched off to reduce noise every time A/S vessels approached. After some hours of manoeuvring, to dodge or shake off enemy patrols, commanders and navigators were frequently left with no idea of their position. Such a situation led to *U763*'s experience – probably unique in the history of U-boat warfare. After sinking the freighter *Ringen* on the evening of 5 July, *U763* was subjected to a 30-hour hunt. Having to remain submerged throughout, often bumping along the bottom, and having to resort to frequent evasive manoeuvres while being subject to unknown tidal drifts, she finally managed to shake of her pursuers at dawn on the 7th. Believing that the boat had been carried by strong currents to the vicinity of Alderney, Ernst Cordes, *U763*'s commander, decided to steer northwards, believing that this course would get the boat clear of the notoriously dangerous waters surrounding Alderney. That evening *U763* struck the bottom in shoaling water, and when Cordes took a cautious look through the periscope to ascertain his position he received the shock of his life, discovering that he had unwittingly entered Spithead – the most closely guarded waters in the world. This incredible episode is fully documented in *U763*'s log:

'7th July 1944.

1200	After having been pursued with asdics and depth-charges for nearly 30 hours, our greatest worry is the fixing of our position. No echo-sounding could be taken during that time and our alterations of course and the set of the tide have taken us a considerable distance. Dead reckoning puts us 20 to 30 miles north of Cherbourg ...
1654	Touched bottom in 40 metres [130 feet].
1902	Bottomed in 40 metres. This shallow depth makes me wonder if we are actually further to the southward. There is a 9-knot current there. Though we are trimmed by the head, the boat is lying very badly. Rise to periscope depth. Course 330 degrees. Land in sight to port, bearing 300 degrees true ...
2258	It is beginning to grow dark. As visibility is bad to starboard, I can make no further check. There are no stars. From a study of the chart it appears certain that the current has carried us between the Channel Islands. Sounding continuously and utilizing the northerly set, I try to snorkel clear to the northward. Visibility ahead is good enough ...

8th July 1944.

0041	The soundings do not agree with the chart. An attempt to fix by radio beacon produces one position only (Brest), which passes through the area in question and, together with the soundings, appears to confirm our estimated position. So long as I have sufficient water and visibility there is no point in surfacing. Carry on snorkelling in order to have batteries sufficiently charged, by daylight, to enable me to obtain a fix at periscope depth.
0337	Touched bottom in 16 metres [52 feet]. Stopped snorkelling. I determine to surface, since our estimated position cannot possibly be correct. The farther we proceed to the north-

west the shallower the water becomes, whereas according to the chart it should become deeper. I wonder if the echo-sounder is reading correctly.

0356 It is almost a flat calm, moonlight and misty. Surfaced ... About two and a half miles on the port quarter, four destroyers are lying in the moonlight. Land lies on both beams. The shapes of several steamships are visible to port. I turn off to the north-west, assuming that I have the enemy-occupied Cherbourg Peninsula to starboard and the Channel islands to port. The echo-sounder must be out of order and the current must have carried us into shallow water.

0433 Submerge again when the echo-sounder shows 30 metres · [100 feet]. Bottomed at 35 metres. After pondering over what I have seen, it suddenly occurs to me that we have fetched up close to the English coast. The direction of the Brest position line on the chart shows that in all probability we are at Spithead, however unlikely this may sound...'

That night and the following forenoon *U763* remained bottomed, and entirely unmolested, off St. Helen's while making good her minor defects.

'9th July 1944.

1525 Left bottom. 1548. Periscope depth at silent running speed. Using the periscope sparingly and just awash, I discern three small vessels anchored in the stream.

1605 An anchored landing craft – *US 264* – lies on the starboard beam, and ahead of her the hospital ship, No.62. I pass between them to the other side where, on the port bow, I sight two old 2,000 to 3,000-ton steamers, in ballast, lying at anchor. On south-easterly courses the water becomes shallower. A fix by cross-bearings shows that I am in danger of being left high and dry by the tide. I therefore turn about and make for a 20 metre patch.

1802 Bottomed again in 17 metres [55 feet]. Low water is at 2204, so that I am no longer in danger of being stranded ... '

Despite the opportunities that presented themselves – though there were no really worth while targets – Cordes could not attack in case one of his newly developed *Lut* torpedoes failed to explode and fell into enemy hands.

'We have inexplicably got the boat in here unnoticed and will get her out intact, for she must not fall into enemy hands.

2220   Action stations.

2250   Leave bottom. Rise to periscope depth. I keep to the starboard side of the fairway. Returning landing craft and what I presume to be two destroyers, pass us on the opposite course ...

2338   Course 140 degrees. We have not been observed. The water gets gradually deeper ... '[12]

Having extricated herself without being detected, *U763* set course for base. After a lively passage during which she was attacked by surface vessels and aircraft, she reached Brest on 14 July. 'One must give her captain and crew full credit for the endurance and resource displayed throughout what must have been a very harrowing experience. Her unintended and undetected entry into perhaps the most closely guarded waters in the world remained quite unknown to [the British] until the German records were examined after the war.'[13]

The experiences of most of the other U-boats operating in the Channel were no less harrowing. *U212* arrived in the area of the 'Spout' on 14 July, remained there for a week without effecting anything, and was sunk on the 21st by the RN frigates *Curzon* and *Ekins*, 47 miles south-east of Brighton.

U741 was subject to a chapter of accidents. On 12 July she ran into sweep wires in mid-Channel, which snapped her jumping wire and fouled her port propeller. Next night, while snorkelling to the north of Seine Bay, an unidentified vessel passed over her, wrecking the snorkel and both periscopes. Blinded, *U741* managed to grope her way submerged across Seine Bay to enter Le Havre on 16 July.

U672 sailed from St-Nazaire on 6 July, and took twelve days to reach a position 32 miles south of Start Point where she was promptly depth-charged by the RN frigate *Balfour*. She was so badly damaged that her commander was forced to surface during the night of 18/19 July and abandon the boat. The crew took to the dinghies before she foundered and were picked up by British Air Sea Rescue launches next day. On 20 July, *U413* also fell victim to A/S patrols, being depth-charged by the RN destroyers *Forester*, *Vidette* and *Wensleydale* south of Brighton.

U309 reached the 'Spout' on 19 July with most of her crew sick and exhausted from snorkelling difficulties during her passage up the Channel. Nevertheless, she attacked a convoy to the north of Pointe de Cap Barfleur on the 20th, firing a spread of three *Lut* torpedoes. Hearing one detonation after 9 minutes and 30 seconds, her commander, Oberleutnant Hans-Gert Mahrholz, claimed to have sunk a 6,800-ton freighter, but in fact all three torpedoes missed their targets. Four days later, at 2100 on the 24th, Mahrholz attacked another convoy, firing three *Lut* torpedoes. Detonations were heard in the submerged U-boat after 5 minutes 35 seconds and 8 minutes 40 seconds, followed by sinking noises, but in fact Mahrholz had only succeeded in damaging the 7,217-ton British freighter *Samneva*. On 25 July, her crew completely exhausted, *U309* turned back for Brest which she reached on 3 August.

U621 reached the 'Spout' on 23rd July, having averaged daily distances of between 40 to 50 miles during her passage to the operational area. On the 26th she had trouble while snorkelling, which resulted in drastic drops in the air pressure inside the boat causing a large number of her crew to faint. Three days later (29 July) she attacked a convoy to the north-east of Pointe de Barfleur and sank the 2,938-ton infantry landing ship *Prince Leopold*. Next morning she succeeded in damaging the 10,048-ton freighter *Ascanius*. Remaining in this area, enduring numerous depth-charge attacks, she sighted nothing until 2 August when she attacked but missed ships in a south-bound convoy. Next day another unsuccessful attack on a south-bound convoy exhausted her supply of torpedoes, and she returned to Brest, arriving on 11 August.

U275, which sailed from Brest on 16 July, had an uneventful passage until 1600 on the 25th when she was suddenly attacked by a surface vessel sixteen miles north-west of Alderney. Well-placed depth-charge explosions continued until midnight when she managed to evade her assailant. But she had been reduced to a parlous state, with snorkel, periscopes, main motors, batteries and rudder mechanism all damaged. Unable to snorkel, batteries nearly empty and not daring to surface because of continual hydrophone contacts of surface vessels in the vicinity, *U275* bottomed when the tides were adverse and drifted eastwards when they were favourable. She continued in this mode until the early morning of 1 August, when she surfaced just before daylight off the mouth of the Somme to recharge her completely flat batteries and ventilate the boat. Fortunate enough to lie undisturbed on the surface for two hours, she managed to charge her batteries sufficiently to crawl, aided by the easterly current, to Boulogne, which she reached at 0045 on 2 August.

Of the three boats that sailed from Biscay ports on 22 and 23 July (*U214*, *U333*, *U667*) to operate in the western part of the Channel, only one survived. *U214* was located by the RN frigate *Cooke*'s ASDIC as she approached Start Point, where she had been instructed to lay mines, and was sunk by depth-charges from the frigate south of the

91

Eddystone light on the 26th. *U333*, which had been ordered to patrol between the Lizard and the Scilly Isles, met her doom on 31 July, south-west of the Scillies, when she was depth-charged by the RN sloop *Starling* and the frigate *Loch Killin*. *U667*, which was to patrol from Land's End up to Trevose Head off the north Cornish coast, was the only one of this group of three to reach her operational area and complete her mission. She arrived on 7 August and next day attacked a convoy off Trevose Head, sinking the 7,176-ton US Liberty ship *Ezra Weston* and the Canadian corvette *Regina*. She escaped the subsequent counter-attack, and the air patrols dispatched to hunt her down spent nine days searching for her but only sighted her once, momentarily; they were unable to prevent her from attacking a convoy off the north Cornish coast on 14 August, when she torpedoed and sank the 1,653-ton tank landing ship *LST 921*. *U667* left her patrol area on the 17th, but when she arrived off La Pallice on 25 August her luck ran out and she foundered after hitting a mine in the approaches to the harbour.

By 14 August, eight U-boats were operating in the Channel. Six of them had reached the 'Spout' – *U984*, *U741* (which sailed from Le Havre after repairs), *U413*, *U480*, *U764* and *U275* (which sailed from Boulogne after repairs) – while *U989* was advancing up the Channel and *U218* was making for Start Point to lay mines. One of these boats, *U480*, was the sole survivor of the three Group Mitte boats that had been ordered into the Channel, the other two having been sunk (*U971* depth-charged north of Ushant by the RN destroyer *Eskimo* and the Canadian destroyer *Haida* and aircraft from No. 311 (Czech) Squadron; while *U678* was depth-charged by the Canadian destroyers *Kootenay* and *Ottawa* and the RN corvette *Statice*, 23 miles south-south-west of Brighton on 6 July).

On 15 August *U741* attacked a convoy some 40 miles south-east of St. Catherine's Point, and sank the 246-ton infantry landing craft *LCI 99*. Having fired her torpedoes, she bottomed but was soon located by the RN corvette *Orchis*'s ASDIC and destroyed by depth-charges.

U480, also operating to the south-east of St. Catherine's Point, attacked a convoy on 19 August and sank the 2,360-ton freighter *Saint Enogat*, and next day *U764* attacked a convoy in the same area and sank the 638-ton freighter *Coral*. *U480* followed-up her previous success by sinking the Canadian corvette *Alberni* on the 21st; the RN minesweeper *Loyalty* on the 22nd; the 7,134-ton freighter *Fort Yale* on the 23rd and the 5,712-ton freighter *Orminister* on the 25th. She escaped unscathed from all the resulting counter-attacks, her commander, Oberleutnant Hans-Joachim Forster, attributing this to the fact that *U480* was one of the first boats to be coated with rubber (*Alberich*) to negate ASDIC echoes, as he recorded in the log:

'25th August 1944.

1508   Am being pursued by four A/S vessels [after sinking *Orminister*], two of which are operating asdics; the third, which apparently acts as depth-charge dropper, approaches at intervals of from five to ten minutes and drops charges; the fourth can be heard to be running her engines at very low speed. Listening conditions are particularly good.

2140   Beginning of dusk. Pursuit lasts until 2200, during which time we have covered five miles over the ground. I have stopped the gyro and refrain from using the hydrophones. I maintain my depth by shifting the crew. One of the A/S vessels frequently lies directly above us with her engines just ticking over, and the least sound aboard her is clearly audible and asdic impulses are extremely loud. In these circumstances, any U-boat with a mechanical fault which causes the smallest noise must, at all costs, locate and rectify it. The depth-charge dropper, which has lately been lying stopped, approaches and drops five or six depth-charges at intervals. These cause such trivial damage that I am convinced that the enemy is unable to locate us by asdic and so is without an accurate range. He has merely a hydrophone contact which, because of the absence of noise in the boat, is bound to be vague. I attribute the enemy's failure to locate me, mainly to the protection afforded by *Alberich* ... '[14]

The last successes in the Channel were achieved when *U989* damaged the 7,176-ton US liberty ship *Louis Kossuth* on 23 August and sank the 1,791-ton British freighter *Ashmun J. Clough* on the 26th. By the end of August all the surviving boats from the second wave sent had either returned to the Biscay bases or were clearing the western Channel on the return passage. Thus ended the second and final phase of U-boat operations against the Allied maritime invasion forces. The fourteen ships sunk – eight freighters, two corvettes, one minesweeper, one infantry landing ship, one infantry landing craft and one tank landing ship – was exactly double the number sunk in the first phase. But the grand total of 21 ships sunk in both phases (five of which were warships) had made no perceptible difference to the success of 'Overlord' and had cost the Germans nineteen U-boats and some 1,000 officers and men (of whom 238 had been rescued by the enemy). The results, which were not entirely negative, were summed-up in an appreciation written by Dönitz on 15 September 1944:

'Our U-boat effort in the Channel is thereby terminated, and the old fighting spirit of the U-boat arm has again magnificently stood the test. A comprehensive survey of operations shows that, contrary to our initial misgivings and the doubts that assailed us during the course of the operations, we were right in employing the U-boats. Considering the extremely difficult operating conditions, the results achieved were good and losses tolerable, though heavy. Despite the fact that our blow at the enemy's supplies was indecisive, it was certainly severe and helped to relieve pressure on our troops ashore [*sic*]. Besides achieving tangible results, we also gained experience and knowledge of continuously submerged U-boat warfare which will be of great value, particularly for the

---

Main Types of Torpedo used by the Kriegsmarine

G7a — Weight 3,391lb; length 23½ feet; diameter 21in; warhead charge 617lb; max. speed 40 knots; max. range 47 nautical miles. This, the basic type, was developed between the wars. It was propelled by a 4-cylinder internal combustion engine, driven by a mixture of fuel, compressed air and water to create a small amount of steam. Its main disadvantage was that exhaust gasses and oil floated to the surface, leaving a tell-tale wake which made them unsuitable for daylight attacks.

G7e — Weight 3,545lb; length 23½ feet; diameter 21in; warhead charge 617lb; max. speed 40 knots; max. range 31 nautical miles. An improved G7a, being propelled by two small electric batteries which did not leave such a pronounced wake.

T5 Zaunkönig — Weight 3,296lb; length 23½ feet; diameter 21in; warhead charge 545lb; max. speed 21 knots; max. range 50 nautical miles. Also known as 'Gnat' this was an electrically driven acoustic torpedo, designed as an anti-convoy escort weapon, which entered service in October 1943. It was designed to home in on the noise of a ship's engines and propellers, and only had to be aimed in the general direction of a target. To prevent it being diverted by noise-emitting 'foxers' towed behind ships, the homing system restricted the torpedo's 'hearing' to an area 30 degrees each side of its forward path. It is estimated that of some 700 T5 torpedoes fired in action, only 77 scored definite hits.

FAT (*Federapparat Torpedo*) — Weight 3,880lb; length 23½ feet; diameter 21in; warhead charge 617lb; max. speed 30 knots; Max. range 47 nautical miles. This spring-loaded electrically driven torpedo was designed for use against convoys. It travelled in a straight line for a predetermined distance and then zig-zagged to the right or left, depending on the setting.

LUT (*Lagenunabhängiger Torpedo*) — Weight 3,880lb; length 23½ feet; diameter 21in; warhead charge 617lb; max. speed 30 knots; max. range 47 nautical miles. This electrically driven torpedo was designed to be fired from depths down to 165 feet, the periscope being unnecessary because of the *S-Anlage* homing device. It entered service in February 1944.

T3d DACKEL — Weight 4,851lb; length 43 feet; diameter 21in; warhead charge 617lb; max. speed 9 knots; max. range 50 nautical miles. This was a long-range torpedo designed to be fired by S-boats or shore installations against shipping anchored close to the shore. It could be set to run straight for sixteen miles and then, depending on the setting, either circle or zig-zag for a further eighteen miles.

new-type [Electro-] boats. We also tied down considerable sea and air escort forces, which would otherwise have been available for purposes such as the disruption of our supply traffic off the Dutch and Norwegian coasts, as well as for intensive air attacks on our lines of communication on the Western Front. Results would have been better and losses certainly lighter, had the boats been possessed of higher sub-merged speed and a greater endurance; the fact that these very qualities have been highly developed in the new-type boats gives us good hope for the future. The snorkel was, in effect, decisive, and operations in the Channel would have been out of the question without it. No one would have believed a few months ago that a U-boat could proceed submerged for 42 days without surfacing. It is the snorkel alone, which now enables us again to operate close in to the British coast, and to continue using the older boats until the new-type are ready ...'[15]

The most perceptive remark in Dönitz's appreciation was the reference that 'the snorkel was, in effect, decisive', for, during the Channel operations the snorkel mast had proved to be very difficult to spot from aircraft and surface vessels with the eye or even by radar. The dangerous significance of this development, which threatened to restore to the Germans the initiative they had been forced to surrender in the early spring of 1943, was not lost on the Allies. Four years of continuous struggle had taught them that by far the most effective counter-measure to the U-boats was to employ radar and Leigh Light-fitted aircraft in conjunction with radar and ASDIC-fitted surface escorts -the aircraft to carry out widespread searches, the ships to hold contact and attack until the enemy was destroyed. By reducing the effectiveness of airborne radar, the snorkel struck a heavy blow at Allied A/S tactics. Taken in conjunction with the construction of the Electro-boats, it had become plain that unless victory could be gained before the two developments came into general use, the Allies would find themselves struggling against an enemy once more possessed of the inestimable benefit of the initiative.

Chapter 5

DEFEAT IN THE WEST

THE K-VERBAND FIASCO

The Germans had intended to employ 'Small Battle Units' (*Kleinkampfverbande*) as soon as the Allied invasion materialized, but delays in production and difficulties in training the crews of the various craft prevented them from deploying any of the units until the end of June.

The first *K-Verband* craft to arrive in the invasion area consisted of a flotilla of *Linsen* radio-controlled motor boats, comprising ten control boats and 24 explosive-boats with 660-800lb charges packed in their sterns. Under command of Korvettenkapitän Kolbe, this flotilla arrived at Honfleur (a few miles south of Le Havre) on 21 June and launched its first attack on the invasion shipping in Seine Bay four nights later. From the outset the operation was dogged with problems, mainly because of the inadequate training of the *Linsen* pilots. On the evening of the 25th, as the pilots were priming the detonation mechanisms of the explosive charges, one of them blew up, sinking an adjacent R-boat (*R46*) and two of the control boats. Despite this mishap the operation proceeded, the remaining boats being towed from Honfleur to the mouth of the River Orne by R-boats. But the seas in the Orne estuary were so rough that all but six of the *Linsen* were either swamped and sank or lost their tows and were driven ashore. The surviving boats, after slipping their tows, failed to find any targets as a result of the high seas and appalling visibility, and they all ran aground when they attempted to re-enter the Orne. Two further sorties during the last week of June resulted in similar farces, and on the 30th Kapitän zur See Bohme, who had been appointed to command all the *K-Verband* craft in the west, reported that no further *Linsen* operations were possible because none of the surviving craft was serviceable.

The second *K-Verband* contingent to arrive in Normandy was a 40-strong flotilla of *Neger* (manned torpedoes). They had left Germany on 13 June and been transported by road to an assembly area in the Favrol Woods near Villers-sur-Mer (a few miles along the coast to the west of Honfleur), where a labour battalion had constructed camouflaged runways down which the trolley-borne *Neger* could be run out into deep water.

The flotilla arrived in the Favrol Woods on 28 June, but it was not until 2300 on 5 July, the first occasion on which the weather favoured a sortie, that 26 of the 40 *Neger* were launched to run down on the ebb-tide for an attack on the invasion shipping. Two were forced to return to the launch point with mechanical problems, fifteen were lost to navigational hazards, attacks by MTBs and gunfire from anchored landing-craft. The surviving nine made exaggerated claims on their return, insisting that they had sunk six vessels and damaged five others. In fact, they had accounted for two RN minesweepers – *Magic* and *Cato* – sunk at 0353 and 0511 respectively.

A second attack by 21 *Neger* was launched at 2300 on 7 July. One of them, piloted by Fähnrich zur See Potthast, evaded the Allied patrols and torpedoed the old 4,850-ton Free Polish cruiser *Dragon* at 0428 next day. According to Potthast's account, he closed to within 300 yards before firing his underslung torpedo which blew the cruiser's stern off. Too badly damaged to be worth repair, *Dragon* was later scuttled to form part of the 'Gooseberry' breakwater off the invasion beachhead. Potthast managed to clear the scene, but at 0737 his *Neger* was spotted by the RN minesweeper *Orestes* which raked it with machine-gun fire. Badly wounded, Potthast was taken prisoner before his craft foundered. The only other kill scored by the *Neger* that night was the minesweeper HMS *Pylades* torpedoed at 0500 while laying at anchor off 'Sword' Beach. Because the *Neger* could only travel and attack in a surfaced awash condition, and the night of 7/8 July was clear and moonlit, all 21 were sighted and sunk by gunfire from surface vessels or the cannon of aircraft (Seafires of No. 26 Squadron claimed to have attacked seven of them).

Although the cryptanalysts at Bletchley Park had broken the KdK 'Eichendorff' Enigma key (which the Admiralty code-named 'Bonito'), delays of from two to fourteen days in reading this cipher meant that the Allies gained very little intelligence of operational value. Moreover, the KdK signals never included the exact time or destination of an attack or other last-minute details, the nature of the operations being such that these decisions were left to the commander on the spot. All that the Allies gained from the 'Eichendorff' decrypts were general warnings that an attack was planned.

The loss of so many *Neger* during their two nights of operations prompted KdK to postpone further attacks until reinforcements arrived from Germany. These came in the form of 58 *Marder* (improved, slightly larger versions of *Neger*) and K-Flotilla 211, commanded by Korvettenkapitän Bastian, comprising 48 *Linsen* (sixteen control, 32 explosive-boats). All 58 *Marder*, sixteen control and 28 of the 32 explosive-*Linsen*, carried out a mass attack on the night of 2/3 August. Their target was the congestion of shipping off Courseulles-sur-Mer, the area off the British and Canadian 'Sword' and 'Juno' Beaches.

The force was launched at 2300 from Houlgate, a small port some fifteen miles north-east of Caen and some seventeen miles east of the attack area. The KdK hoped that an attack by the *Marder* on the northern end of the Allied defence line would divert a sufficient number of warships to allow the *Linsen* to break through in the centre and attack the transports.

The attack began at 0200 when a *Marder* torpedoed the light cruiser HMS *Durban*, which had already been hulked by the Allies to form part of the 'Gooseberry' breakwater. This initiated a fierce action during which destroyers and smaller craft plastered the attack area with depth-charges while manoeuvring at high speed to dodge the torpedoes fired by the *Marder*. Star-shells and bright moonlight illuminated the Perspex cupolas (observation domes) of the half-awash *Marder*, making them clear targets for a hail of gunfire of all calibres from the Allied warships and merchantmen. Some twenty *Marder* were sunk in the mêlée, but they had managed to torpedo and sink the 907-ton RN destroyer *Quorn* (at 0251), the minesweeping trawler HMS *Gairsay*, and the 7,219-ton liberty ship *Samlong*; they also badly damaged the 7,131-ton transport *Fort Lac la Ronge*.

Aided by this diversion, the *Linsen* began their attack at 0350. The first wave was sighted in the glare of star-shell from the minesweeping trawler HMS *Gateshead* and the motor launch *ML 185*. Gunfire from these two warships detonated the explosives in four of the *Linsen* almost simultaneously, and fourteen *Linsen* from successive waves were destroyed in like manner. Their only success was the destruction of the 370-ton gun landing craft *LCG 764*, rammed simultaneously by two explosive *Linsen*; it is not known for certain whether the pilots ditched before impact or died with their boats. Only ten of the control *Linsen* survived to withdraw under cover of smoke-floats as dawn was breaking.

The *Marder* were hunted mercilessly during their withdrawal. The machine-guns of MTBs sank five, other warships accounted for ten and Spitfires sank six with cannon fire. The destroyer HMS *Blencathra* was slightly damaged when she tried to winch an abandoned *Marder* aboard and the scuttling charges exploded. Of the 58 *Marder* committed, only seventeen returned to base from this *Opferkampfer* (sacrificial mission).

While waiting for more reinforcements to arrive by road from Germany, KdK launched all the *Linsen* at his disposal against shipping off Courseulles-sur-Mer on the night of 8/9 August. This attack was carried out by twelve control and sixteen explosive-boats, of which only eight control boats survived. No Allied ships were lost or damaged.

Six days later K-Flotilla 363, comprising 53 *Marder*, arrived at Houlgate, and attempted its first sortie on the night of 15/16 August. The KdK had planned to launch all 53, but, as a result of a violent thunder-storm, torrential rain and the inexperience of the launching parties, only eleven set out. Seven soon returned because of the rough seas and appalling visibility, and the remaining four accomplished nothing.

On the following night there took place what proved to he the last *Marder* operation in the Normandy area, when 42 of them put out from Houlgate. A major objective of this attack was the old, 23,189-ton French battleship *Courbet*. The Germans were convinced that this battleship, which was flying two battle ensigns, the Tricolore and the Free French Croix de Lorraine, was riding at anchor and in full fighting condition. In fact she was an empty hulk, resting on the bottom as part of the 'Gooseberry' breakwater. The Allies had reinforced the Germans' delusion by carrying out shore bombardments from warships on her seaward side. Throughout the landings the Germans wasted a great deal of effort and ammunition by attempting to 'sink' the hulk with shore batteries and aircraft attacks. The Nazi propaganda machine, therefore, claimed a great victory when two *Marder* torpedoed *Courbet*, but the damage inflicted made no difference to her efficiency as a blockship.

The only real success achieved by the *Marder* that night was the sinking of the small, 757-ton barrage balloon vessel HMS *Fratton*, and a 415-ton landing-craft fitted with AA guns. They also torpedoed the already damaged and beached transport *Iddesleigh*. Twenty-six of the manned-torpedoes were lost during this operation: destroyed by gunfire, depth-charges and the cannon fire of Spitfires which harried them from the air. One was sighted at 0645 by the support landing-craft *LCS 251*, which opened fire with her 6-pounder and 20mm guns at a range of some 400 yards, shattering the cupola and killing the pilot before he could launch his torpedo. After a 4-hour struggle with winches and hawsers, the LCS succeeded in lashing the *Marder* alongside and delivering the prize to Portsmouth for examination.

The final KdK operation in the invasion area involved the 24 6½-ton *Biber* midget submarines of K-Flotilla 261, under command of Fregattenkapitän Bartels, which had arrived in Fécamp, twenty miles north-east of Le Havre, on 27 August. Three nights later (30/31st), 22 of them were lifted into the water by cranes, but a strong gale and high seas forced all but two to abort their mission and return to Fécamp. The two *Biber* that did reach Seine Bay claimed to have sunk a 7,000-ton liberty ship and a large landing ship, but these claims are not substantiated by Allied records. Both *Biber* returned safely to port.

This marked the end of KdK operations against the invasion shipping, for although further *Marder*, *Linsen* and *Biber* were *en route* from Germany, they had to be halted because of the Allied break-out from the Normandy bridgehead and the rapid advance of the Anglo-American armies which quickly overran the ports within striking distance of Seine Bay.

SCHNELLBOOTE RESURGENT

Schnellboote strength in the west had been reduced to ten operational boats by the end of June 1944. Reinforced by 6th S-Boat Flotilla from the Baltic, newly commissioned boats from Germany and boats repaired in French Channel ports, the number available for operations against the invasion shipping had increased to twenty by the first week of July. They were disposed as follows:

Le Havre	6 boats of 2nd Flotilla	
	3 boats of 8th Flotilla	
Dieppe	2 boats of 8th Flotilla	Frequent re-dispositions
	2 boats of 9th Flotilla	took place between
Boulogne	2 boats of 2nd Flotilla	these ports during July.
	1 boat of 9th Flotilla	
	4 boats of 6th Flotilla	

The S-boats operated on nineteen nights during July, making sorties in their customary small groups of three to six boats, either laying mines or attempting to break through the Allied patrols to attack the shipping off the invasion beaches with torpedoes.

This series of operations got off to a bad start when, on Wednesday 5 July, 41 torpedoes blew up in the torpedo maintenance room in the S-boat bunker at Le Havre. The explosion also ignited the small-arms ammunition stored in the bunker and explosions continued for three hours. No S-boats were in the bunker at the time, but the bunker was so badly damaged that only six boats could be berthed inside thereafter.

The attempts to attack shipping in Seine Bay was a failure. In his mid-July report to Marinegruppe West, FdS complained that the stronger flank defence in the invasion area had brought S-boat operations almost to a standstill, and that only in a few instances had the boats succeeded in breaking through into the anchorage. Extracts from the FdS War Diary illustrate what the S-boats were up against:

'NIGHT OF JULY 3RD/4TH 1944.
2nd and 8th S-boat Flotillas left Le Havre on torpedo and minelaying operations. 8th Flotilla left Le Havre with 3 boats. At 2400 they encountered 3 MTBs approaching from the north-east whilst proceeding west-

wards. During the engagement with the MTBs 12 mines were laid in about 16 fathoms of water. Buoys to the westward. Position approx. 49° 43' N, 00° 30' W. Two destroyers were sighted to the south on an easterly course, the S-boats prepared to fire torpedoes but were attacked with bombs by fighter-bombers, the bombs dropped between the boats. Attack therefore detected by destroyers, and the S-boats made off to the north-east in order to break through the patrol lines near Cap d'Antifer, and make attacks on the destroyers up moon. Breakthrough made under destroyer gunfire. Destroyers 3,000 to 4,000 yards astern, and 4 MTBs on the bow. The S-boats made off to the north-east at 33 knots. MTBs proceeded along the coast. Two further MTBs approached on a converging course from the north. Destroyer to the eastward [HMS *Thornborough*] engaged in a running fight. Range about 300 to 1,000 yards. Hits observed on the destroyer. Slight splinter damage to the S-boats. All boats arrived Dieppe 0410.

2nd Flotilla left Le Havre in two groups of three boats each. First group to carry out torpedo attack, and second group to lay mines in the middle of the Seine Bay.

1st Group. At 0029 stopped. Two destroyers sighted at high speed head on, range about 8,650 yards bearing 140°. The S-boats made off to the south-east, followed by 3 MTBs from the north. MTBs steered to the east of Le Havre in order to drive the S-boats towards the destroyers. The S-boats retired to the south and for a short time engaged the MTBs at 1,200 yards. MTBs shaken off with the help of a smoke float. 0050 stopped. S-boats exchanged recognition signals with a patrol group in the south. Boats approached patrol group on all three engines and were fired on by the patrol vessels which had given the recognition signals. *S181* hit in three places, and owing to accidental firing of its own twin machine-gun suffered damage to the compass and to the 4cm gun, which was put out of action. One man killed and one wounded. *S181* escorted to Le Havre at 0240. *S177* and *S180* made a new thrust to the north, but met a fog bank and turned to the westward. A destroyer was sighted to the south-west. 0248 stopped. 0321 proceeded westward and entered Le Havre at 0415.

2nd Group. Proceeded from Le Havre on a general north-westerly course. Twelve mines were laid in the path of a destroyer on a southerly course. At 0220, a torpedo salvo was fired against a destroyer group to the west. Enemy turned towards the S-boats and combed torpedoes. 2nd Group joined 1st Group and entered Le Havre.

Night of 7th/8th July.
1st Group of 2nd S-Boat Flotilla (3 boats) left Le Havre to carry out torpedo attacks in company with 9th Flotilla (3 boats). Left Le Havre at

2351. Engaged and chased by 2 MTBS. During the chase, 3 other MTBs were sighted to the southward on an easterly course. *S182* developed a rudder defect and as both *S132* and *S177* found that their 4cm guns were out of action they commenced the return to harbour at 0210. The S-boats approached a large target detected by FuMB [radar interception gear]. At 0321 two destroyers were sighted [they were in fact frigates] and torpedoes were fired at them. One hit claimed as a black column of smoke, flash and a white column of steam at least 330 feet high was sighted. Destroyer probably sunk [they had in fact torpedoed and severely damaged the frigate HMS *Trollope*]. The S-boats were heavily engaged with well directed fire. 0415, 1st Group 2nd Flotilla arrived in Le Havre. 2nd Group 2nd Flotilla (3 boats) left Le Havre at 2345 to carry out torpedo attack. They were shadowed by 2 MTBs which were shaken off under smoke and by a turn to the southward. Two more MTBs were sighted to the westward and 2 destroyers to the north-east. The S-boats ran between the two groups at 15 knots. At 0145 the S-boats turned about owing to the mist. All quiet on the convoy route and to the west of it. Torpedoes were fired at two destroyers to the south-east but they all missed. Destroyers appeared travelling at high speed across the path of the S-boats to the east. The destroyers turned to give chase. One of *S180*'s engines broke down. Well directed destroyer fire. The S-boats could not shake off the destroyers chasing at 25 knots on a northerly course. Two MTBs from the north joined the destroyers in the chase. Action fought at 200 to 1,000 yards range. One MTB was hit by 2cm quadruple machine-gun fire at 200 yards range and set on fire [*MTB 447* was badly damaged]. While at high speed the second MTB rammed the leader on the starboard side [*MTB 451* was badly damaged in this collision]. MTBs did not return further S-boats fire. The S-boats disengaged because of the destroyers and the defective engine in *S180* which made it impossible to press home the attack on the anchorage. Broke through the enemy patrols at 25 knots and entered Le Havre at 0330. One badly and 2 slightly wounded. All S-boats hit, but will be operational by 8th July.

 9th Flotilla (3 boats) joined 1st Group of 2nd Flotilla, after being fired on by unspecified vessels. Entered Dieppe at 0350.'[1]

The failure to break through the Allied patrols to attack the shipping in Seine Bay, prompted FdS to shift the weight of the attack against the convoys running along the South Coast of England in the Straits of Dover.

 The first attack took place on the night of 26/27 July, when eight boats of the recently reinforced 6th Flotilla sailed from Boulogne in the early hours, and attacked a west-bound convoy off Dungeness.

One group (*S97, S114, S90, S91*) torpedoed and damaged two 7,000-ton British freighters (*Fort Perrot* and *Empire Beatrice*). During the ensuing running action with MTBs and the destroyers *Obedient, Savage* and *Opportune*, one S-boat was slightly damaged. On the same night five boats of 2nd Flotilla attempted to break through into Seine Bay, and were engaged by a group of MTBs. As a result of several collisions during a close action fought in poor visibility, two Allied boats, *MTBs 412* and *430*, foundered and *S182* was rammed and had to be scuttled.

Four nights later (30/31 July) three boats of 6th Flotilla (*S97, S114, S91*) left Dieppe at 2300, with orders to attack an east-bound convoy of eleven merchant ships off Beachy Head. The details of the attack were recorded in the FdS War Diary:

'At 0108 the flotilla was known to have been detected by British radar, and therefore was ordered to change course to the northward by the FdS. At 0117 silhouettes were sighted one mile inside the convoy route. Between 0121 and 0122 6 FAT torpedoes were fired with an initial run of 3,000 to 3,500 metres, set on a long looping right-hand course. Four hits were claimed on three different ships all of 3,000 to 4,000 tons [Allied records show that they sank the 7,219-ton freighter *Samwake*, and damaged the 7,000-ton freighters *Ocean Courier, Fort Dearborn, Fort Kaskaskia* and *Ocean Volga*]. The S-boats disengaged on a course of 130° at slow speed. At 0125 the S-boats were engaged by a destroyer bearing 250° at a range of approximately 2,700 yards. The S-boats made off at full speed, the destroyer following in their wake. Three MTBs appeared on the port quarter at 0159. Firing stopped. Destroyer bearing 160° engaged the S-boats and fired accurate torpedo salvo. The S-boats tried to get away to the westward but failed as 3 MTBs were lying in that direction. Destroyer continued to engage until 0310. The S-boats entered Dieppe over a German minefield, but destroyer would not follow. Entered Dieppe at 0410. Six torpedoes were fired in all, and four hits were claimed. No particular damage to the S-boats.'[2]

In an attempt to prevent further attacks on the South Coast convoys, the Allies mounted further bombing raids on Le Havre. On the night of 31 July, 152 Lancasters and five Mosquitos dropped 330 tons of bombs on the port, but because most of the S-boats had already put to sea only three boats were slightly damaged. Two nights later (2/3 August), in a follow-up raid which was launched before the boats put to sea, 154 Lancasters dropped 384 tons of bombs which destroyed two S-boats (*S39, S114*) of 6th Flotilla and damaged two others.

These raids reduced the strength of the S-boats in the west to fifteen operational boats. The 2nd and 6th Flotillas had six operational and four non-operational boats distributed between Boulogne and Le Havre; 8th Flotilla and the newly worked-up 10th Flotilla, based at Ijmuiden, Ostend and Boulogne, had a total of nine operational boats between them. A further three boats were refitting at Rotterdam and Amsterdam, and the three boats of 9th Flotilla had been withdrawn from service to have their engines renewed.

It was during the first week of August that FdS changed his strategy again. This came about through the delivery to Le Havre of the first of the newly developed T3d *Dackel* long-range torpedoes. The *Dackel* had a speed of only 9 knots, but could be set to run straight for sixteen miles and then either circle or zig-zag for a further eighteen miles, for a total of 3½ hours.

On eight nights, between 4/5 and 17/18 August, the S-boats of 2nd and 6th Flotillas fired a total of 91 *Dackel*, from a position some fifteen miles west of Le Havre, on a compass bearing directed towards the Allied invasion beaches off Courseulles-sur-Mer. The Germans expected great results from this weapon, but the effects were disappointing. Only four found targets: damaging the 5,208-ton transport *Iddesleigh*, which had to be beached (in this state she was torpedoed again, by a *Marder* on the night of 16/17 August – see above), and damaging the elderly cruiser HMS *Frobisher*, the repair ship HMS *Albatross* and the minesweeper HMS *Vestal*. *Dackel* operations came to an end on 18 August when stocks ran out, and FdS expressed great scepticism about their usefulness.

Meanwhile 8th and 10th Flotillas carried out minelaying sorties in the Thames estuary and torpedo attacks on South Coast convoys in the Straits of Dover. These sorties were even less successful than the *Dackel* operations. Entries in the FdS War Diary tell the tale:

'NIGHT OF 13TH/14TH AUGUST.
10th Flotilla (6 boats) planned to lay mines [including Oyster mines] off Margate. Engaged by destroyers and MTBs during approach to operational area. Hits observed on MTBs during the engagement. Four S-boats hit, one non-operational on return. Owing to loss of time caused by these attacks only one mine was laid before the boats had to return to harbour before daylight. 8th Flotilla with 6 newly commissioned boats, moved from Ostend to Boulogne. Attacked by one aircraft [of No. 855 Squadron] off Dunkirk, one S-boat damaged and required docking on arrival.

NIGHT OF 15TH/16TH AUGUST.
10th Flotilla (6 boats) to lay mines on convoy route between Queen's Channel and Dumpton Buoy. Twenty [Oyster] mines with magnetic

acoustic non-contact detonating mechanisms were laid, but not in the correct position.

NIGHT OF 17TH/18TH AUGUST.
10th Flotilla (5 boats) to carry out minelaying operation off Margate. Two boats returned to harbour with mechanical problems, and the other three were engaged by destroyers and MTBs. Two mines were hit and had to be jettisoned. Operation broken off. S-boats bombed off Ostend [by two aircraft from Nos. 524 and 143 Squadrons] but no damage.
8th Flotilla (6 boats) made an attack on a west-bound convoy off Dungeness. 1st Group fired a torpedo at a destroyer, but boats were beaten off by the destroyer and result of the torpedo fired not observed. S-boats shook off two destroyers and an MTB group and proceeded to D-buoy. Attacked by fighter-bombers off Dunkirk. No damage. 2nd Group unsuccessfully fired T5 and G7a torpedoes at a destroyer. Action with 4 MTBs during which several hits were scored on the leading MTBs at about 100 yards.

NIGHT OF 20TH/21ST AUGUST.
8th and 10th Flotilla (8 boats) to make a torpedo attack from Boulogne on an east-bound convoy in the Channel. S-boats were attacked by fighter-bombers, and two boats returned to Boulogne. Owing to further air attacks it was too late to attack the convoy. Three boats returned to Boulogne and three to Dieppe.
2nd Flotilla (5 boats) from Le Havre to make a torpedo attack on an east-bound convoy off Hastings. S-boats attacked by destroyers and MTB groups: also attacked by aircraft. Operation broken off.

NIGHT OF 24TH/25TH AUGUST.
6th Flotilla (4 boats) moved from Le Havre to Dieppe. Attacked by MTBs off Cap d'Antifer. S91 heavily hit, out of control. The remaining boats were chased off by destroyers, but later returned and scuttled the wreck of S91.
8th Flotilla (4 boats) attempted to intercept a convoy off Beachy Head. Heavily engaged by destroyers. S701 hit and set on fire. S196 collided with S701 - both boats returned to Dieppe. No contact with convoy. British "spoof" messages detected for the first time on German VHF channel.

NIGHT OF 25TH/26TH AUGUST.
10th Flotilla (7 boats) attempted to intercept convoy in the Straits of Dover. One boat damaged in a heavy bombing attack [by eight aircraft of No. 819 Squadron].'[3]

This marked the end of the *Schnellboote* operations against the invasion shipping. The Allied breakout from the Normandy beach-head and subsequent advance forced the Germans to abandon Le Havre (which surrendered on 12 September) and all the French and Belgian Channel ports: Boulogne, Calais, Dunkirk and Ostend, were invested between 6 and 15 September.

The evacuation of Le Havre began on the night of 23/24 August, after which there was a progressive move north-eastward by small convoys of coasters escorted by S-boats and other light craft. During the last week of August these convoys were attacked on 43 occasions by aircraft and MTBs, at various points along the stretch of coast between Le Havre and the Hook of Holland. The convoys were decimated, although only three of the escorting German warships were sunk (two minesweepers and one R-boat).

The final evacuation of Le Havre and Dieppe was carried out on the night of 30/31 August; 2nd, 6th and 8th Flotillas laying 60 mines in the entrance to each of the devastated harbours as they departed. As they retired up the coast the S-boats were constantly harried by aircraft, but the only loss occurred as they were passing through the Straits of Dover, when *S184* was hit by a shell from the long-range batteries at Dover and had to be scuttled. By 4 September, all the operational S-boats in the west had been withdrawn to Dutch ports, only two non-operational boats, *S145* and *S112*, being left behind; they remained trapped at Brest until the end of the war.

THE COLLAPSE OF MARINEGRUPPE WEST

The inadequate surface forces available to Vizeadmiral Krancke, and the paucity of snorkel-fitted U-boats available to BdU, meant that the Kriegsmarine's attempts to defeat the Allies were doomed from the outset. 'The truth was that in the face of the enemy air [and naval] mastery the Kriegsmarine was impotent to do much more than show it knew how to make heroic sacrifices.'[4] By the end of August German warships and *K-Verband* units had sunk a total of 28 merchant ships and 24 warships (and damaged twelve merchant ships and six warships). These 52 vessels represented 47 per cent of the 110 Allied ships lost during the 87 days from 6 June to 31 August (mines, aircraft and long-range shore batteries had accounted for the rest): the Kriegsmarine's share being a mere 0.8 per cent of the 6,500 Allied ships deployed for the invasion. During this period the Allied ships transported 2,052,299 troops, 438,471 vehicles and 3,098,259 tons of stores safely across the Channel to Normandy. This enormous, and for all intents and purposes uninterrupted, build-up in the Normandy bridgehead resulted in the defeat of the German Army in the west. On 25 July, the American armies on the left flank of the 80-mile-long bridgehead broke out into open country. Part of General Patton's US Third Army swung west and quickly overran the Brittany peninsula, cutting off the German forces in this area who retreated into the fortified ports on the Biscay coast. By the end of the first week of August, some 45,000 garrison troops and the remnant of four divisions had been pressed into defensive perimeters at St-Malo, Brest, Lorient and St-Nazaire. To avoid unnecessary loss of life, the Allies decided that, rather then capture St-Malo, Lorient and St-Nazaire by frontal assault, it would be better to invest these ports and leave the trapped German forces to wither on the vine. Only Brest, which was required as a port of entry for supplies and reinforcements shipped directly from the United States, was subjected to a heavy land, sea and air assault which opened on 25 August. The German forces, which included 15,000 naval garrison troops and other naval personnel pressed into service, resisted stubbornly until 18 September when the port was finally overrun.

Meanwhile the rest of Patton's Third Army had swept around behind the rear of the German front line in Normandy, and pressed south-east to Orléans on the Loire and then due east towards the Seine south of Paris. By the 23rd the Seine was reached and two days later Paris was liberated. By this time the German Seventh Army, and all the divisions that had been sent to reinforce it, had been torn to shreds and the survivors were hastily retreating over the lower Seine. The Canadian First Army, hugging the Channel coast, and British Second Army advanced 200 miles in four days from the lower Seine, past the battle fields of 1914-18 and 1940, into Belgium. Brussels fell on 3 September and Antwerp on the 4th. To the south of the British-Canadian forces, US First Army advanced with equal speed into south-eastern Belgium, while Patton's Third Army took Verdun, surrounded Metz, reached the River Moselle and linked up in the Belfort gap with the Franco-American Seventh Army which had landed on the French Riviera coast on 15th August (see below) and had advanced rapidly up the Rhone valley. By 15 September the Allied armies had reached the Dutch and German frontiers, and had invested the Channel ports of Boulogne (surrendered 27 September), Calais (3 September) and Dunkirk (1 October).

The spectacular speed of the Allied advance caught the Kriegsmarine in the west unprepared. When Patton's Third Army began to advance into the Brittany peninsula during the first week of August, BdU's first concern was to ensure that the U-boats in the threatened ports of Brest, Lorient and St-Nazaire were evacuated in good time. By 6 August, Allied spearheads had penetrated to within twenty miles of Angers, where the HQs of both 'U-boat Command West' and Marinegruppe West's 'Atlantic Coast' Command were situated. Both commands were forced to evacuate to La Rochelle from where the following order was promulgated:

'1.   All possible efforts are to be made to fit every U-boat in Brittany ports with a snorkel.

2.   Those boats unable to be fitted with snorkel in Brest, Lorient and St. Nazaire are to transfer as soon as possible to La Pallice and Bordeaux, and are to take with them spare U-boat crews, skilled dockyard workers and essential material such as T5 torpedo testing gear and non-ferrous metals.

3.   All snorkel parts not needed in the northern ports are to be transferred to La Pallice and Bordeaux.

4.   U-boats which, owing to lack of complete snorkels in La Pallice and Bordeaux, cannot be adapted are to be paid off and the crews, after filling any vacancies in operational boats, must be sent home to Germany as far as the land battle permits.

5.   All trained U-boat personnel not absolutely necessary on the spot must be sent home to Germany.

6.   Before transferring to the south, all U-boats are to fill to capacity with fuel.'[5]

In the Brittany ports at this stage there were 41 U-boats of which 31 were seaworthy. Commencing on 7 August, they began the exodus from Brest, Lorient and St-Nazaire bound for La Pallice and Bordeaux. Four left on the 7th, one on the 8th, three on the 9th, one on the 10th, three on the 11th, two on the 13th and one on 16 August.

The Allies had been forewarned of this exodus through Enigma decrypts, and six groups of destroyers and three cruisers, with aircraft of Coastal Command's No. 19 Group reinforced by two squadrons of Beaufighters from No. 16 Group, were dispatched to the Bay of Biscay to patrol all the coastal waters from Brest to the Gironde, with the object of destroying both the U-boats and German surface craft expected to be involved in evacuation of the Brittany ports. To add to the Germans discomfiture RAF Bomber Command and US Eighth Air Force carried out a dozen raids on the bases between Brest and Bordeaux, more than half of these raids involving attacks with Tallboy bombs on the U-boat pens.

In an attack on Bordeaux by 53 Lancasters on 11 August, the U-boat bunker received 26 direct hits from 12,000lb armour-piercing bombs, but only superficial damage was caused to the roof, which consisted of two thicknesses of reinforced concrete, one of 20 feet beneath a 'burster course' of 11½ feet. Next day, during an attack by 68

Lancasters on Brest, the 18-foot-thick concrete roof of the U-boat bunker, which had no burster course, was partially penetrated in three places by 12,000lb bombs. One of these breaches was 33 feet in diameter, but the U-boats in the bunker were unaffected. When specialists from the Todt Organization inspected the damage, they came to the conclusion that given a 11½-foot 'burster course' the roof of the bunker would have withstood the heaviest bombs known to exist. This inspection yielded valuable information which was applied to the design of U-boat and dockyard bunkers under construction in Germany.

No U-boats were sunk or even damaged during the bombing raids, but from 4 to 27 August the Allied air and sea forces operating in and over the Bay of Biscay sank eleven large merchant ships (58,835 tons), 53 coasters, minesweepers, patrol vessels and miscellaneous craft, two destroyers (*Z23*, *Z24*) and one torpedo-boat (*T24*).

The transfer of U-boats from the three northern bases to La Pallice and Bordeaux proved to be extremely hazardous. With enemy air and surface forces ever present, navigational accuracy suffered, and commanding officers were frequently unable immediately to find the escort vessels detailed to await their arrival off their port of destination to guide them through the defensive minefields and provide Flak cover. Consequently, and in view of the fact that the escorts were unwilling to dally at the rendezvous points for any length of time, the U-boats had a choice of either ensuring that they arrived early so that the approach of the escort vessels might be picked up by hydrophone, or take the risk of proceeding into port unescorted. The danger experienced from aircraft and mines in the near approach channels is illustrated in an extract from the log of *U309*:

'12TH AUGUST 1944.

0345	Approaching escort rendezvous off La Pallice in company with *U981*.
0415	*U981* mined. I send the following signal: "*U981* mined. Incapable of diving. Everything out of action. Request escort at rendezvous forthwith."
0620	Lying stopped with *U981*, whose engines are still out of action. Halifax aircraft approaches, passing over us three times and dropping flares. *U981* now able to proceed on electric motors. We proceed at slow speed, steering 090 degrees, parallel with the line of buoys.
0624	Bomb attack on *U981* ... A further attack from the Halifax. The AA fire of both boats lies well on the target. A second mine detonates alongside *U981*, which is again bombed by a twin-engined aircraft. *U981*'s diesels suddenly spring to life and she sheers off course.

0643   *U981* is clearing away rubber dinghies. She starts to sink. Her crew are jumping overboard. I close her and pick up 40 survivors ... '6

The transfer of the U-boats to the southern ports was completed by 21 August. Of the fifteen boats that sailed from Brest, Lorient and St-Nazaire, eleven were sunk on passage (eight of them being non-snorkel boats). Three boats (*U621*, *U984*, *U445*) were sunk by surface craft; three (*U385*, *U618*, *U608*) by surface craft and aircraft in concert; two (*U270*, *U107*) by aircraft; two boats (*U180*, *U667*) by mines; one boat (*U981*) was sunk as a result of hitting mines and then being attacked by aircraft. Such was the intensity of the air and surface patrols between Brest and the Gironde, that the boats were taking eight or nine days to complete the 100–200-mile southward passage.

In the event the transfer to the southern ports was totally unnecessary, for on 18 August, three days after the Allied landings in the South of France, Hitler ordered the evacuation of the whole of southern and south-western France, except for the ports of Brest, Lorient, St-Nazaire, La Pallice, La Rochelle and a fortified area at the mouth of the Gironde, and all serviceable U-boats were ordered to leave these ports. By the 21st, there were still 30 U-boats in Biscay ports, which were disposed as follows:

Brest	2 operational boats	
Lorient	4 operational boats	+ 2 paid off
St-Nazaire	4 operational boats	+ 1 paid off
La Pallice	7 operational boats	+ 1 paid off
Bordeaux	7 operational boats	+ 2 paid off

In response to Hitler's order, BdU ordered sixteen seaworthy U-boats to proceed directly to Norwegian ports, while eight fully battleworthy boats were to sail as quickly as possible and take up inshore billets in the North Channel (*U963*, *U309*, *U985*, *U953*) and Bristol Channel (*U262*, *U758*, *U714*, *U247*), where they were to operate for 10–14 days, with the object of diverting the attention of the Allied A/S forces from the exodus of U-boats from the Biscay ports *en route* for Norway. To this end BdU also dispatched seven snorkel boats from Group Mitte in Norway to the North Channel, North Minch and Moray Firth.

Only two of the six boats paid off and under repair could be made ready with make-shift snorkels in time to join the exodus to Norway: the last boat, *U267*, leaving Bordeaux on 25 August. The other four – *U123* and *U129* at Lorient, *U178* and *U188* at Bordeaux – could not be made seaworthy because there were no new batteries available, and they were eventually scuttled.

After the last U-boat had left Bordeaux the naval personnel at this base were dispersed. Some were sent to reinforce the garrison at La Rochelle; the remainder, some 20,000 naval personnel and dockyard workmen, formed a battalion that was detailed to return overland to Germany. In the event only a small number managed to fight their way through to German lines: the majority being either killed or captured by Allied troops and the Maquis. In the other Biscay bases, which Hitler had declared to be 'fortresses', quite a number of German dockyard technicians and specialist naval officers took passage in the departing U-boats, and the 27,000 naval personnel and dockyard men left behind were recruited into the land defences 'where they distinguished themselves by their toughness and courage.'[7]

Of the 26 U-boats that got away from the Biscay bases, four were sunk; the remainder, together with nine boats that had been operating in the Channel, began arriving in Norwegian ports on 18 September. That so many of these escaped damage or destruction must be credited mainly to snorkel, although the boats sent to British inshore waters had succeeded in diverting Allied attention from the northern transit route to Norway.

By 31 August 1944, Marinegruppe West had ceased to exist. Of the 516 surface warships under Vizeadmiral Krancke's command on the eve of D-Day, 221, or 43 per cent, had been destroyed by shells, mines and bombs by the end of August, and sixteen had been badly damaged. The Germans had also lost 43 merchant ships grossing 35,368 tons in the coastal waters of the Channel and Biscay, together with 35 U-boats sunk and sixteen damaged. In short, the Kriegsmarine in the west had been as roundly defeated as the German Army.

It was by now quite obvious that Germany had lost the war. On the Western Front the Allied armies were poised to advance into Germany; in the east the Russian summer offensives, which began on 10 June, had unrolled one after another, and carried the Red Army to the East Prussian border and the gates of Warsaw. In the south, Roumania had been overrun and with it the Ploesti oil fields, the only major source of natural oil for the German armed forces, while Bulgaria had formally withdrawn from the war. In the north, Finland had signed an armistice with the Russians, and had turned on the German troops who refused to evacuate Finish territory.

Against the enormous weight of British, American and Russian power, and with no allies left, Germany could not hope to reverse the inexorable tide of defeat running against her, yet she continued to fight, like a punch-drunk boxer, blind and stupid with pain. After the war, Dönitz, on the instructions of his British captors, wrote an account of why Germany continued to resist against such impossible odds:

111

'In the autumn of 1944 the situation was extremely grave. After losing the greatest part of the territories we had previously occupied in the west, south and east, "Fortress Europe" had been reduced to "Fortress Germany", with the exception of Norway, Denmark and Holland which we still firmly held.

'In the east and west the opposing armies stood on the frontiers of the Reich or had in places actually crossed them. The ever-increasing air offensive of the Western Powers on the German homeland had already seriously reduced the industrial and economic resources both by direct destruction and by cutting our communications ... The Luftwaffe had failed to bring Allied bombing to a standstill. Thus the prospect of success for Germany appeared very slender. All thought of an early end to the war was, however, destroyed by our enemies. Leading figures of the opposing side repeatedly declared that only unconditional surrender was acceptable. Enemy propaganda painted a gloomy picture of the intended treatment of Germany after defeat. For this reason our leaders had no alternative but to continue resistance as long as possible in order to exploit every opportunity of saving the German people from the fate painted in such fearful colours by the enemy press. The German people themselves, through the continual air attacks and the numerous restrictions on their daily life, had become here and there somewhat weary, but for the most part they stuck to their task faithfully and with admirable determination. The terror raids on open towns which had no military or even industrial significance brought horror and misery to all, but they only stiffened the will to resist of the defenceless population of women, children and old folk. Men and women carried on grimly and obstinately with their work, bringing unbelievable energy to the mainte-nance of production.'[8]

This explanation, written when Dönitz was a prisoner of war and awaiting trial for war crimes, differs markedly in its tenor from the speech he made to his flag officers on 24 August 1944, in which he insisted that the Kriegsmarine must remain obedient to the will of the Führer:

'It is dishonourable for an officer, who receives his position and derives his honour from the State, and who in good times serves will-ingly, to vacillate in evil times when hard and unswerving fighting is required ... our duty and our fate is to fight fanatically ... for each of us to stand fanatically behind the National Socialist State and to instil this sense of duty in the fighting men ... It is necessary to understand the sit-uation clearly and realize that in this most bitterly serious battle of des-tiny we must give fanatical adherence to Hitler and the National Socialist State. Any deviation from this is a laxness and a crime. I would rather eat dirt than allow my grandson to be brought up and become poisoned in the filth of Jewish culture, and that the purity of today's public art, culture and education, which we now all regard as obvious ... should fall into Jewish hands again.'[9]

Here is revealed the real reason why Dönitz dismissed all thoughts of surrender – blind adherence to the will of a madman. For Hitler was no longer fighting for Germany, or even for the preservation of the Nazi regime, but to save his own skin for as long as possible. Yet to the very end Dönitz 'cleaved straight, scorning any deviation from the course set by the Führer, seemingly intent only to prove that when the waters finally closed over the tortured ruins of the Third Reich the ensign of the Kriegsmarine would still be flying.'[10]

Chapter 6

TWILIGHT IN THE MIDDLE SEA

THE SUPPLY PROBLEM

During the last year of the war, the Kriegsmarine's operations in the Mediterranean were largely confined to the defence of convoys in three areas. In the Ligurian Sea, off the north-western Italian seaboard, numerous convoys plied between the French and Italian Rivieras and ports on the west coast of Italy, ferrying large quantities of munitions, fuel, supplies and stores to the German front line in Italy. This sea-lift was necessary because rail and road traffic to the front was continuously interdicted by Allied air attacks.

In the Adriatic, German convoys sailed from ports on the north-eastern Italian seaboard and Istria to supply the German forces in Yugoslavia, the Balkans and the islands on the Dalmatian coast; while convoys sailing from Greek Aegean harbours ferried supplies to the German garrisons on Corfu, Cephalonia and Zante in the Ionian Sea, and to Crete, Rhodes and the smaller islands of the Dodecanese and Cyclades groups. The size of the sea-lift can be gauged from the tonnage of cargo carried by the German convoys during April 1944:

Ligurian Sea	Adriatic	Aegean
32,500 tons	50,684 tons	21,315 tons

But in all three areas the German convoys were constantly harried by Allied submarines, coastal forces (mainly MTBs) and aircraft, and the ports of embarkation and disembarkation were constantly bombed so that the consequent losses and disruption meant that the tonnage of cargo actually delivered fell far short of the recipients' needs. To compound the problem, the amount of shipping required was never available because the programmes for the repair of damaged merchant vessels and new construction, especially of naval ferries and freight barges, were constantly disrupted by Allied bombing raids.

During the April, May, June 1944, a total of 135 German merchant ships grossing 197,917 tons was sunk in the Mediterranean, the majority succumbing to Allied bombing raids on ports. During this period Allied aircraft flew 5,610 sorties against German-held ports, sinking 51 warships, eighteen merchant ships of more than 500 tons and 33 smaller merchant vessels (including caiques); and 5,792 sorties against convoys at sea, sinking 45 warships and a number of small merchant vessels of which only two were of more than 500 tons displacement. Most of the German warships sunk were small vessels such as R-boats, *U-bootsjagelboote* (A/S vessels, the equivalent of small corvettes), auxiliary minesweepers and naval ferry barges (small barges of 150-250 tons armed with AA guns, used to carry troops or cargo as well as act as escort vessels), but a U-boat (*U421*) and seven ex-Italian torpedo-boats of between 800 and 2,000 tons displacement were also lost.

Ironically, the largest air raid mounted during this period produced the smallest result. On 29 April, 178 Flying Fortresses and 310 Liberators, operating from bases in southern Italy, dropped 2,623 1,000lb bombs on Toulon, but the results were not commensurate with so great an effort. Only *U421*, the merchant ship *Chisone* (6,618 tons) and the hopper-barge *Andromede II* (1,232 tons) were sunk by this great weight of bombs, although a great deal of damage was done to the port and the naval arsenal.

Attacks on convoys by Allied coastal forces and submarines accounted for a mere 19 per cent (11 ships) of the 135 German merchant ships sunk during April, May and June. Mines accounted for five ships, and 58 ships grossing 97,314 tons were scuttled in ports on the west and east coasts of Italy as the German Army was forced to retreat northwards.

The effect on the German island garrisons of the interdiction of the supply convoys, can be determined by taking the attempt to replenish Crete in May 1944 as an example. By the end of May the German forces on Crete had been reduced to a desperate state, because only 639 tons of the 6,000 tons of the supplies requested had reached the island during the course of the month. In an attempt to alleviate the situation the Germans loaded three merchant ships with 7,000 tons of cargo, and they sailed for Heraklion from Piraeus at midnight on 31 May. The three ships, *Gertrud* (1,960 tons), *Sabine* (2,252 tons) and *Tanais* (1,545 tons), were escorted by four ex-Italian torpedo-boats, three *U-bootsjagelboote* and a small number of aircraft. Twenty minutes after leaving port, the convoy was spotted by a patrolling Wellington bomber. Thereafter it was constantly shadowed by Allied aircraft until 1900 on 1 June when 52 bombers (Marauders, Baltimores and Beaufighters) arrived on the scene and launched an attack. *Sabine* was hit several times and set on fire; *Gertrud* was hit in the engine room, set on fire and rendered unmanageable; two of the three *U-bootsjagelboote*, *UJ2101* and *UJ2105*, were sunk and the torpedo-boat *TA16* was badly damaged but managed to remain afloat. Although one of the escorts managed to tow *Gertrud* into Heraklion, the effort was in vain because

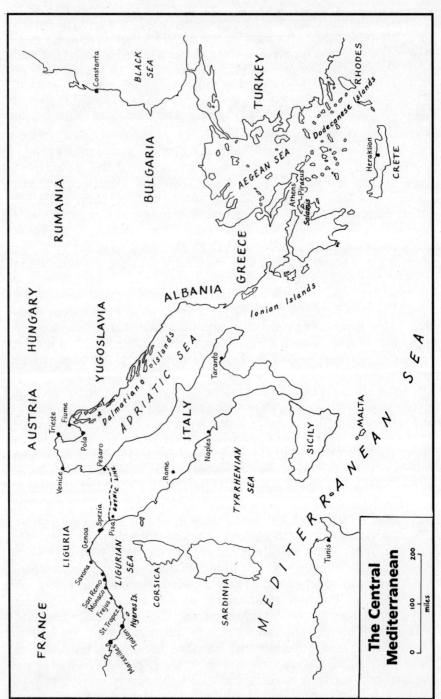

The Central
Mediterranean

at 1920 on 1 June she was hit again during a bombing raid on the port and blew up and sank; the explosion was so violent that it also sank the damaged *TA16* which was lying near by. *Sabine*, burning furiously, also managed to limp into the outer harbour of Heraklion, but she ran aground and was eventually gutted, together with her precious cargo, by the fires which could not be brought under control. Only *Tanais* reached Heraklion unscathed to unload her 2,000 tons of cargo, but on her return passage to Piraeus her luck ran out and she was torpedoed and sunk by the RN submarine *Vivid* on 9 June.

This fiasco led the Germans to conclude that it was impracticable to use fairly large merchant ships to supply the island garrisons because the Allies always put a big effort into finding and sinking merchant ships of even moderate tonnage, so local sailing vessels and naval ferry barges would be better suited to the purpose. But as there was a shortage of these craft the supply situation of the island garrisons became more and more critical as Allied pressure on German convoys increased month by month. From July until December 1944, 324 German merchant ships grossing 576,019 tons were sunk (including vessels scuttled by the Germans as they evacuated French, Greek and Italian ports). The situation is summed-up by Stephen Roskill: '... the steady pressure of [Allied], submarines, surface vessels and aircraft began to drive home the old lesson that an attempt to maintain overseas garrisons across waters which could not be adequately controlled was bound to end in disaster.'[1]

THE SWAMPING OF THE U-BOATS

In comparison with the slaughter to which German merchant shipping was being subjected, the Kriegsmarine's attack on Allied shipping in the Mediterranean was decidedly feeble, their offensive operations being almost totally dependent on sixteen U-boats which were based at Toulon in the western basin and Pola in the Adriatic. Their main targets were the large Allied convoys passing east-bound through the Straits of Gibraltar carrying supplies and reinforcements to the Allied forces in Italy, Malta and North Africa. During April, May and June 1944, 900 Allied merchant ships entered the Mediterranean in these convoys, 350 ships passing on through the Suez Canal bound for ports in India.

The U-boats concentrated their attacks on these convoys in the 100-mile-wide straits between Cape Bon on the Tunisian coast and Sicily, but the strength of the convoy escorts and Allied air superiority was such that the sixteen non-snorkel boats only succeeded in sinking one merchantman (the 7,147-ton British freighter *Fort Missanabie*) and damaging a tanker, a freighter and four warships (all during May).

Fort Missanabie proved to be the last Allied ship to be sunk by a U-boat in the Mediterranean, for by June 1944 a method of combined search and attack by surface warships and aircraft had been perfected by the Allies to the extent that it effectively put an end to U-boat operations in the Mediterranean. This method, known as 'Swamp', involved packing the area where a U-boat was known or suspected to be operating with aircraft and A/S vessels which searched systematically and continually. This forced the U-boat to remain submerged until it had no choice but to surface to recharge its exhausted batteries and ventilate the boat, or until its captain decided to try and escape at high speed on the surface under cover of darkness. Either alternative usually proved fatal because numerous aircraft and surface vessels were waiting for just such an eventuality.

The first U-boat to be sunk in May 1944 by the 'Swamp' method was *U371*. She was lying in wait for a convoy off Djidjelli on the Algerian coast, and on the night of 2/3 May, when she surfaced to top up her batteries, she was immediately detected by a patrolling Wellington and a 'Swamp' hunt began. Aircraft from three squadrons, and the destroyers HMSS *Blankney* and *Campbell*, US destroyers *Menges* and *Pride*, and the US minesweeper *Sustain* with the French destroyer *Sénégalais*, were all involved in a relentless pursuit of *U371*, which ended on the morning of 4 May when, her batteries exhausted, she was forced to surface and was sunk by gunfire, but not before her commander Oberleutnant Horst-Arno Fensk, had managed to torpedo and damage *Menges* and *Sénégalais* .

On 14 May another 'Swamp' took place when *U616* attacked a convoy north-east of Cape Tenes and damaged two merchant ships with torpedoes (the 10,627-ton US tanker *G. S. Walden* and the 7,127-ton British freighter *Fort Fidler*). Aircraft from five squadrons and eight American destroyers joined in the hunt at various stages as *U616* was chased across the Mediterranean to a position south of Alicante on the eastern Spanish seaboard, where she was finally sunk by depth-charges from the US destroyer *Hambleton* on the 17th.

Some five hours after *U616* was sunk, *U960* attacked and missed the US destroyer *Ellyson* off Oran (the destroyer had prisoners rescued from *U616* on board). A 'Swamp' was immediately instituted by the forces that had been involved in the pursuit of *U616*, and although rough weather hindered them *U960* was finally forced to surface off Cape Tenes on 19 May, and was sunk by cannon fire and depth-charges from an RAF Ventura from No. 500 Squadron.

On the same day, but far to the east, *U453* attacked a convoy *en route* from Taranto to Augusta and sank *Fort Missanabie*. Aircraft from Malta and some Italian seaplanes began the hunt by air, and the RN destroyers *Termagant*, *Tenacious* and *Liddesdale* and some Italian escort vessels joined in. The hunt went on until midnight on 20/21 May when *U453* was finally forced to surface to the north of Sardinia, and was sunk within twenty minutes by gunfire from the three destroyers.

One other U-boat, *U731*, was sunk after being depth-charged by a sloop, a trawler and a US Navy aircraft, off Tangier on 15 May, although this was not a 'Swamp' operation. The loss of these five U-boats reduced the number in the Mediterranean to eleven, none of which was destined to score a single kill and all of which would he destroyed by the end of September.

STRATEGIC IMPOTENCE

In July the German Intelligence agencies became aware that the Allies were planning a major seaborne landing in the Mediterranean theatre. Three main possibilities were mooted. A landing in Istria in the north-eastern Adriatic, was deemed to offer strategic enticements of a high order, providing not only a short and direct route for an advance on Vienna, but also the means of cutting off the German forces in the Balkans. Alternatively, a landing on the north-western seaboard of Italy would cut the lines of communication to the German front line forces defending the 'Gothic Line' – a defensive position running across the width of the Italian mainland from just north of Pisa on the west coast to Pesaro on the Adriatic coast. The third possibility, which the German Naval Staff held to be the most likely option, was an invasion of south-ern France with the object of capturing the major ports of Toulon and Marseilles, prior to an advance up the Rhone valley to link up with the Allied armies in northern France. In the event, the Naval Staff assess-ment accurately forecast Allied intentions – the landing of seven French and three American divisions on the French Riviera coast in Operation 'Dragoon'.

As a preliminary to 'Dragoon' Allied bombing raids increased in intensity throughout July up to the eve of the landing which took place on 15 August. The bombing pattern was designed to conceal Allied intentions and the raids were equally distributed along the coasts of southern France, the north-western Italian seaboard and the head of the Adriatic. The heaviest raids were aimed at German naval resources at Toulon, Genoa and Trieste, in which 98 German warships (mainly small vessels) and 44 merchant ships grossing 104,162 tons were sunk.

It was during these raids that five of the eleven remaining U-boats in the Mediterranean were destroyed. On 5 July, 233 American Liberators, operating from bases in southern Italy, bombed Toulon, destroying *U586* and damaging *U466*, *U471*, *U642*, *U952*, *U967* and *U969*. Only *U230* escaped unscathed. A month later, on 6 August, the Liberators made another big attack on Toulon, destroying four of the damaged boats, *U471*, *U642*, *U952* and *U969*, and further damaging

U466 and *U967*. Once again *U230* emerged unscathed, to become the sole operational U-boat available when 'Dragoon' materialized (the other three were in the eastern Mediterranean).

This destruction reduced the forces available to Konteradmiral Scheurzen, commanding the naval forces on the French Mediterranean coastline, to one operational U-boat (*U230*), two ex-French torpedo-boats, 32 *U-bootsjagelboote*, 29 minesweepers, 29 artillery-barges and 70 armed fishing vessels and miscellaneous defence craft.

In the early hours of 15 August, 2,251 transports, landing ships, landing-craft and warships (including five battleships, nine escort-carriers and 117 destroyers) were detected approaching the French Riviera coast to the east of Toulon in the area Fréjus–St-Tropez. In the face of such opposition, Scheurzen's scant forces were powerless to intervene; the four *U-bootsjagelboote* that attempted to attack detached units on the flanks of the main invasion force were quickly sunk by gunfire from US destroyers and RN gunboats.

The only other response by the Kriegsmarine was to order *U230* to put to sea from Toulon on the morning of 17 August, to attack the mass of shipping off the landing-beaches. Having no snorkel and being unable to dive deep in the coastal waters, it is not surprising that her sortie was ineffectual. Although none of the Allied patrols detected her, she met her end four days later when she grounded while charging her batteries close inshore in the Gulf of Hyères, and was blown up by her crew to prevent capture. The last of the Toulon U-boats, the severely damaged *U466* and *U967*, were also blow up by their crews to prevent capture when French troops reached the outskirts of the port.

Having been impotent to prevent the Aliies landing 324,069 French and American troops, 68,419 vehicles and 815,867 tons of stores, the German Naval Staff rather belatedly decided to resort to *K-Verband* operations.

By the end of August KdK had set up an operational command at San Remo under the title of 'K-Staff Italy'. The Allies were aware of this development through decrypts of the KdK 'Bonito' Enigma key, and they responded by instituting strong surface patrols off Monaco and Villefranche to intercept the *K-Verband* units on their approach to the landing-beaches.

Early in September K-Flotilla 364, consisting of 30 *Marder* arrived at Menton, a few miles east of Monte-Carlo. The first sortie took place on the morning of 5 September. Five *Marder* set out to attack the 'Dragoon' support ships, but at 0810 they ran into the French destroyer *Le Malin* and the US destroyer *Ludlow* patrolling off Cap Ferrat. Four of the half-awash craft were sunk by gunfire and depth-charges; the the fifth scurried back to base. Five nights later a second attempt by ten

Marder was launched from Ventimiglia, a few miles east of Menton. All ten were sunk only a few miles from their launch site by the US destroyers *Hilary P. Jones* and *Madison* and two PT-boats that were patrolling off Menton. Later that same day the two destroyers were joined by the old French battleship *Lorraine*, and the three ships bombarded the *Marders'* launch site at Ventimiglia, destroying or damaging all the remaining craft.

A last desperate attempt to salvage something from this fiasco was carried out by the *Molch* midget submarines of K-Flotilla 411, which arrived at San Remo on 20 September. Their first and only sortie, on the night of 25/26 September, was no more successful, ten of the twelve *Molch* being sunk by Allied patrols; the two survivors were destroyed in a subsequent bombardment of San Remo by Allied warships. This marked the end of the *K-Verband* operations against the 'Dragoon' shipping.

DEMISE OF THE U-BOATS

The losses suffered by the U-boats prior to and during Operation 'Dragoon' left only three U-boats in the whole of the Mediterranean. These three, all recently fitted with snorkel at Pola, operated in the eastern basin during August and September, but none of them scored a single kill.

On the afternoon of 18 September, the Polish-manned destroyer HMS *Garland*, which was part of a powerful squadron of escort-carriers, cruisers and destroyers on its way to carry out an offensive sweep in the Aegean, sighted a wisp of smoke in the Anti-Kithera Channel to the north of Crete at the remarkable range of eight miles. The alertness of *Garland*'s look-outs was rewarded when, on closing the position, the source of the smoke was identified as the exhaust from a snorkel mast. In company with the RN destroyers *Troubridge* and *Terpsichore*, after a grim 10-hour pursuit *Garland* depth-charged and sank the U-boat (*U407*) north of Crete early next morning. This was the last German U-boat to be sunk at sea in the Mediterranean; five days later, on the 24th, both *U565* and *U596* were destroyed in a bombing raid carried out by American Liberators on the Greek port of Salamis (ten miles to the west of Athens).

During August and September, all the German U-boats operating in the Black Sea, which had access to the Mediterranean through the Bosporus and Dardanelles, were also eliminated. Between October 1942 and June 1943 the Germans had, by a remarkable feat of improvisation and organization, transported six 279-ton, 140-foot-long, Type IIB U-boats, disassembled into sections, from the German Baltic coast to Galatz on the Danube where they were re-assembled and then floated down river to Constanza on the Roumanian Black Sea coast to operate against Russian shipping.

Although these six small coastal U-boats sank only six Russian merchantmen grossing 28,303 tons, they had imposed considerable restrictions on Russian seaborne movements in the Black Sea. But on 20 August 1944, a heavy Russian air raid on Constanza sank *U9* and damaged *U18* and *U24* so severely that the Germans decided to scuttle them. Three weeks later the remaining three boats, *U19*, *U20* and *U23*, were scuttled by their crews off the Turkish coast on 10 September, by which time the advance of the Russian armies had trapped them beyond hope of escape.

The destruction of the last of the Mediterranean U-boats, and the removal of the threat of the Black Sea boats entering the eastern basin via the Dardanelles, was such a relief to the Allies that the British Mediterranean C-in-C, Admiral Sir John Cunningham, noted in his War Diary that 'for the first time in five years merchantmen are now permitted to burn navigation lights in certain areas.'[2] So ended the tyranny of the U-boats in the Middle Sea which, since the first boat entered the Mediterranean through the Straits of Gibraltar almost three years before, had sunk 95 Allied merchant ships totalling 449,206 tons; 24 major RN warships, including the battleship *Barham*, the aircraft carriers *Ark Royal* and *Eagle*, four cruisers and twelve destroyers, although this was achieved at a cost of 63 U-boats.

DEFIANT TO THE END

By the end of August the problem of supplying the German island garrisons had changed to one of evacuating them from most of the Dalmatian, Ionian, Aegean and Dodecanese islands. The defections of Roumania and Bulgaria from the Axis in August critically affected the situation of the German forces in Greece and the Aegean islands. On 27 August Hitler, realizing that these forces were in danger of being cut off by the Russian advance, authorized a gradual withdrawal to the central Balkans. At first the Germans hoped to stand on a line running from Corfu north-east across Greece, but the threat of a Russian incursion southwards from Bulgaria forced them into complete evacuation of Greece, Crete and the Aegean islands.

To effect this withdrawal, which began on 5 September, the Germans assembled 52 merchant ships of large and medium tonnage, as well as numerous small warships, naval auxiliaries, landing-craft and about 200 caiques. From the beginning of September until the end of October, the Kriegsmarine and Luftwaffe succeeded in removing more than 67,000 troops from Crete and the Aegean islands to the Greek mainland, where they joined the retreat on a 1,000-mile march from the torrid heat of the eastern Mediterranean up the length of Yugoslavia to the mid-winter snows of the Croatian mountains. The Kriegsmarine's share of the total evacuated was 37,000 men, 400 guns and 2,000 vehicles, for the loss of 29 of the 52 merchant ships, five torpedo-boats, a minelayer, an R-boat and three *U-bootsjagelboote.*

The collapse of Roumania and Bulgaria also forced the Germans in Yugoslavia to pull back their forces from the Dalmatian coast into the interior to build a defence line facing east against the Russians. The withdrawal from the coast necessitated the evacuation of the garrisons occupying the Ionian and Dalmatian islands, which were being invaded by British forces and Yugoslav partisans.

The evacuations from the Adriatic and Ionian islands were severely handled by the Allied naval and air forces, and heavy losses were suffered on almost every occasion the Germans attempted movement by sea. From September until the end of December the Germans lost 68 warships (23 being of more than 500 tons displacement).

By the time that 1944 drew to a close, the entire coastlines of Albania and Yugoslavia up to the entrance to the Gulf of Fiume in the northern Adriatic, together with all the Ionian and Dalmatian Islands were firmly in Allied hands. The only areas of the Mediterranean in which the Kriegsmarine was still able to exert a measure of control were confined to the Ligurian Sea between the Franco-Italian frontier and the port of La Spezia, and the northern Adriatic. Although German garrisons totalling some 26,000 troops had been left behind on Rhodes, Cos, Leros, Milos and a number of the smaller Aegean islands, it was impossible to keep them supplied and they became almost completely ineffectual; for this reason the Allies by-passed them, allowing them to wither on the vine.

By this time the Kriegsmarine's strength in the Mediterranean was derisory compared to the scale of the Allied forces in those waters. In the Ligurian Sea, the Germans could only deploy one destroyer, two torpedo-boats (all ex-Italian), four small escort vessels, some 35 naval ferry barges, two minelayers, five *U-bootsjagelboote* and ten R-boats; in the northern Adriatic the forces had been reduced to one destroyer, four torpedo-boats (all ex-Italian), eighteen S-boats, 22 R-boats, one minelayer and a large number of small Flak-armed landing-craft. The position regarding merchant shipping was even more parlous (104 merchantmen grossing 80,930 tons were lost from January to May 1945), yet with dogged determination and ingenuity, the Germans improvised what they did not possess and by a variety of measures, including the transport of small craft overland and by river and canal, they managed to maintain a reasonably efficient coastal convoy service almost to the end. For although the Allies greatly reduced the tonnage of seaborne supplies delivered to the German front line troops in Italy, they never succeeded in completely stopping the traffic.

In the Ligurian Sea, the German convoys generally ran between Savona or Genoa and La Spezia carrying some 1,500 to 2,000 tons of supplies a month. In the Adriatic, the Germans employed the few surviving merchant ships of medium tonnage to carry some 2,500 to 4,000 tons per month of supplies from Trieste to Venice, whence large numbers of barges transferred the cargoes to the ports at the mouth of the River Po. The German forces in Yugoslavia were supplied mainly by ferry barges, landing-craft and other small vessels which crept down the coast from the Istrian ports of Fiume and Pola.

During the last six months of the war, offensive operations in the Ligurian Sea and the northern Adriatic were undertaken solely by *K-Verband* units. During the late autumn of 1944, K-Flotillas 213 and 611, composed of *Linsen* arrived at San Remo, but from the moment they arrived they suffered such severe losses from regular Allied bombardments and air raids on the port that only ten feeble sorties against the bombarding ships were launched up to the time that San Remo was evacuated on 24 April 1945. Their only success was to inflict minor damage on the French destroyer *Trombe* on 17 April.

Two flotillas of *Marder* also operated from San Remo during the closing months of the war, suffering crippling casualties during their clashes with Allied light forces in the Ligurian Sea without scoring a single success. Their final operation, a last-ditch act of suicidal defiance, was launched against Allied shipping off Livorno. Seventeen *Marder* set out from San Remo on 24 April 1945, and although they pressed home their attack with great determination they caused no damage of any kind, and fifteen of their number were destroyed by warships, aircraft and shore guns. Roskill attributes the failure of the 'Small Battle Units' to the following factors:

'Apart from the lack of training from which the crews undoubtedly suffered, and the unsuitability of many of the devices used, the failure of the whole genus can confidently be attributed to the skilful employment by the Allies of the more conventional instruments of maritime power ... Against an enemy possessed of almost complete maritime control, and whose forces never relaxed their vigilance, the chances of gaining any important success were remote. The Germans themselves had been late in developing such weapons ... and by the time the small battle units were ready for service the conditions for their successful employment had almost entirely vanished.'[3]

By the time that their armies in Italy surrendered unconditionally on 2 May 1945, the Germans had lost virtually all their merchant shipping in the Mediterranean and practically all their warships. From the beginning of January 1945 up to the day of surrender, 112 warships and 118 small auxiliary vessels had been destroyed, more than half of these being scuttled to prevent capture. The final balance sheet was appalling. During five years of conflict the azure waters of the Mediterranean had engulfed the shattered and burning wrecks of 3,082 Axis merchant ships, 1,390 warships and naval auxiliaries (the majority flying the Swastika battle ensign of the Kriegsmarine), 62 U-boats and 65 Italian submarines. It had been a terrible price to pay for the destruction of 413 Allied merchantmen and 169 warships.

Chapter 7

DEATH OF A GIANT

THE QUEEN OF THE NORTH

Less than two months after the Germans invaded the Soviet Union on 22 June 1941, Britain began shipping *matériel* to Russia via the Arctic route to the northern Russian ports of Archangel and Murmansk. From August 1941, when the first Arctic convoy sailed, and April 1944, 1,038 merchant ships sailed to and from Russia in 32 east-bound and 26 west-bound convoys. In the endeavour to stem the flow of supplies reaching the hard-pressed Russians, the Germans attacked the convoys with U-boats and aircraft based in northern Norway, sinking 79 merchant ships (34 of these being accounted for by U-boats).

Because of the need to amass a huge number of warships for the D-Day landings, the Allies suspended the sailings of the Arctic convoys in April 1944 and did not resume them until 15 August, when the 33 ships of Convoy JW.59 sailed from Loch Ewe, bound for the Kola Inlet. Apart from the U-boats and the Luftwaffe, a major threat to the convoys was posed by the powerful, 52,700-ton battleship *Tirpitz*.

Tirpitz had arrived in the northern Norwegian fiords in January 1942, and her constant presence close to the flank of the Arctic convoy route exerted an enormous influence on Allied maritime strategy. Indeed, Roskill concludes that 'one may doubt whether a single ship *in being* ever exerted such a great influence on maritime strategy.'[1] As long

---

Principal Characteristics of Tirpitz

Builder:	Wilhelmshaven Naval Yard
Laid down:	2 Nov 1936; launched: 1 April 1939; commissioned 25 Feb 1941
Displacement:	41,700 tons standard; 52,700 tons deep load
Dimensions:	length 792 feet wl; 814 feet overall; beam 118 feet
Armour:	12½in main belt; 14in turrets; 8in deck
Machinery:	3-shaft Brown-Boveri geared turbines; twelve Wagner boilers = 63,000shp
Maximum speed:	30 knots
Endurance:	10,200nm @ 16 knots; 3,740nm @ 30 knots
Armament:	eight 15in; twelve 5.9in; sixteen 4.1in AA; sixteen 37mm AA; sixteen 20mm AA; eight 21in torpedo tubes
Complement:	2,400

---

as *Tirpitz* was based in northern Norway she could choose her own moment for a sortie against any of the Arctic convoys, and as no single British ship was able to engage this powerful ship on equal terms the Admiralty was forced to keep a powerful combination of aircraft carriers, battleships and lesser vessels ready in the offing to providing distant cover to every convoy.[2]

During the two years and ten months that she was stationed in Norway, *Tirpitz* exerted this influence largely by lying at anchor in the fiords. Only on three occasions did she carry out offensive sorties. During March 1942 she attempted to attack PQ.12, but failed to find the convoy in the appalling weather and perpetual darkness of the Arctic latitudes (the sun never rose more than 12° below the horizon in the winter months). Four months later, a brief sortie of only 4½ hours' duration, caused the Admiralty to panic and order the ships of PQ.17 to scatter with disastrous consequences (the convoy was practically wiped out by U-boats and aircraft). Her final sortie was carried out in company with the battlecruiser *Scharnhorst* in September 1943, when both ships bombarded an Anglo-Norwegian weather reporting station on Spitzbergen (the only occasion on which *Tirpitz* fired her eight 15in guns in action other than in an AA role).

Apart from her strategic influence on Allied dispositions, *Tirpitz* forced the British to expend a very great naval and air effort in trying to damage or destroy her. From 28 January to 29 April 1942, she was subjected to five bombing attacks (four by RAF Bomber Command and one by Russian aircraft) while berthed in Aasfiord and Fottenfiord near Trondheim, but no hits were scored. Further bombing raids by the RAF were rendered impracticable when *Tirpitz* moved north to Kaafiord, a side-water of Altenfiord, in July 1942, which put her beyond the range of Bomber Command aircraft. On 22 September 1943, however, a daring raid by six RN X-craft (midget submarines), caused such serious damage to the battleship's propulsion machinery and gunnery control system that she was out of action for six months.

Tirpitz was not seaworthy again until the end of March 1944. When the Admiralty learned, through Enigma decrypts, that her repairs were nearing completion, they launched a carrier-borne strike in an attempt to sink, or at least put out of action, this menace lurking on the flank of their convoy route. The attack, which was timed to coincide with the running of the east-bound convoy JW.57 and the west-bound RA.57, took place at dawn on 3 April 1944, and was launched from two fleet carriers and four escort-carriers from a position 120 miles northwest of Altenfiord.

At first light on the 3rd, *Tirpitz* was preparing to leave Kaafiord to run trials in the broad waters of the adjoining Altenfiord. It was a

127

clear spring morning and everything seemed still in Kaafiord. The only signs of life were the tugs opening the torpedo nets that surrounded the battleship in the narrow body of water, specially selected as a berth because the high, steep mountains on both sides of the long fiord made air attack difficult, especially for torpedo-bombers, which would be unable to swoop low enough to drop their torpedoes from a low altitude.

Tirpitz was in the process of weighing anchor when the fiord began to echo with the sound of scores of aircraft engines. Taken completely by surprise, the battleship suffered fourteen hits (four 1,600lb armour-piercing bombs, five 500lb semi-armour-piercing bombs, five 500lb medium-case high-explosive bombs). Her decks were ripped up, bulkheads were shattered, and the ship was filled with smoke, the cries of the wounded and the noise of escaping steam. Some of the bombs had burst on the thickly armoured turret tops and only scratched their surface, but some of the heavy armour-piercing bombs had penetrated the upper armoured deck and, bursting below, had caused substantial damage, particularly to the complex fire-control system. None, however, penetrated the lower, 8in armoured, deck so the ship's vitals remained unaffected. None the less, the damage to the upper decks and superstructure put *Tirpitz* out of action for a further three months (122 men were killed and 316 wounded).

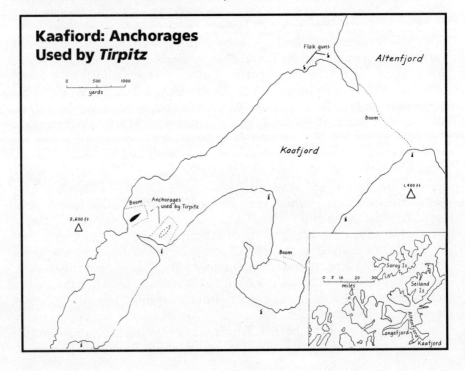

Above: A pre-war photograph of the 924-ton torpedo-boat *Greif* which was fitted for minelaying. She was bombed and sunk by a Coastal Command Albacore north-west of Ouistreham in the early hours of 24 May 1944.

Below: A wartime photograph of the torpedo-boat *Möwe*, one of the four boats of 5th Torpedo-boat Flotilla which sallied forth from Le Havre on the morning of D-Day to attack the 1,213 warships of the Allied invasion fleet.

Above: Seamen painting a recognition sign on the roof of *Tirpitz*'s 'Caesar' turret. Astern is the pocket-battleship *Admiral Scheer* followed by two light cruisers.

Below: The 52,700-ton battleship *Tirpitz*. As no single British warship was capable of engaging her on equal terms, her presence in the Norwegian fiords tied down a powerful force of enemy capital ships in case she sortied against the Arctic convoys.

Above: Sunset over Kaarfiord silhouetting *Tirpitz*'s port side 4.1in heavy guns. Between January 1942 and November 1944 *Tirpitz* was attacked on fifteen occasions by Allied aircraft while lying in Norwegian fiords.

Below: One of *Tirpitz*'s quadruple 20mm 'Rhinemetall' C/38 AA mountings. Note the range-finder behind the mounting.

Above: The 2,527- ton destroyers *Z35* and *Z36* photographed in the Bay of Biscay during the spring of 1944. Both ships sank after striking mines in the Gulf of Finland on 12 December 1944.

Above: Three 2,200-ton *Leberecht Mass*-class destroyers providing an A/S screen for the battleship *Tirpitz* in Norwegian waters. Completed between 1937 and 1938, these were the oldest German-built destroyers in *Kriegsmarine* service. Of the sixteen destroyers of this class, only six survived the war.

Left: An S-boat of the 112-ton *S38-S53* class, seen surrendering at Felixstowe on 13 May 1945. This was the first German surface craft to surrender in a UK port at the end of the war.

Right: The 1,628-ton destroyer ZH1, originally the Dutch Gerard Callenburgh, which was captured by the Germans and commissioned into the Kriegsmarine in the summer of 1940. She was battered into a blazing wreck by British destroyers during the action fought north-east of Ushant on the night of 8/9 June 1944, and was scuttled to prevent capture.

Below: The 2,600-ton destroyer Z32, flagship of 8th Destroyer Flotilla, which was scuttled on the rocks of the Ile de Batz off the Brittany Coast on the morning of 9 June 1944 while being pursued by Canadian destroyers.

Below: The wreck of the destroyer *Z23* which was bombed by Allied aircraft on 21 August 1944 while undergoing a refit in a dock in the French Biscay port of La Pallice.

Above: *Tirpitz*'s 4.1in heavy flak guns firing during a practice shoot. During an attack by Fleet Air Arm aircraft on 17 July 1944, they fired 1,973 rounds in 33 minutes.

Right: A salvo from *Tirpitz*'s 15in guns of 'Anton' turret. During her entire career *Tirpitz* never fired her main armament at an enemy warship, although they were employed in an AA role during the numerous air attacks on the battleship.

Above: Vizeadmiral Otto Ciliax, C-in-C German naval forces in Norway, inspecting members of *Tirpitz*'s ship's company.

Left: *U2326*, a Type XXIII Electro-boat, which surrendered at Dundee, after carrying out a sortie between Aberdeen and St. Abb's Head in the final week of the war.

Left: Type XXIII coastal Electro-boats damaged by bombing in a floating dock at Kiel, May 1945.

Below: Uncompleted Type XXIs on the builder's slips, Hamburg, May 1945.

Opposite page, top: The Type XXIII coastal Electro-boat *U2332* running constructor's trial off the Germania Werft yard at Kiel, October 1944.

Above: The Type XXIII Electro-boat *U2361* fitting out at Deutsche Werft, Hamburg, February 1944.

Left: The launch of *U3001* (Type XXI) at A. G. Weser's yard, Bremen, on 30 May 1944.

Above: 0950, 12 November 1944. The massive explosion of *Tirpitz*'s 'Caesar' turret, which blew up while the battleship was capsizing to port off the south coast of Haakoy Island. Note the explosion from a near miss by one of the 12,000lb Tallboy bombs to the left of the smoke-covered ship.

Below: The capsized wreck of *Tirpitz* heeled at 130 degrees, her superstructure and turrets embedded in the mud in the shallow water off Haakoy. The steel tomb of 1,204 German sailors.

Above: Prefabricated central sections of a Type XXI ocean-going Electro-boat on the quay-side at Hamburg. 25 feet long and weighing 140 tons, this section contained the control room and galley. The pipe-like structures on the top housed the snorkel and periscope masts.

Below: A Type XXI Electro-boat scuttled in shallow water in the entrance to a bombed U-boat pen at Howaldts Werke, Hamburg, May 1945.

Above: The wreck of *U2542*, which was bombed during a US Eighth Air Force raid on Kiel on 3 April 1945.

Below: The Type XVII Wa201 'Walter' experimental boat *U793* undergoing trials off Hamburg in April 1943.

Above: The after section of an uncompleted *Seehund* midget-submarine. Note the plethora of internal pipe and electrical fittings.

Right: The light cruisers *Nürnberg* and *Köln* (distant) photographed off the port quarter of *Tirpitz*.

Below: The old (1908) 13,000-ton battleship *Schleswig-Holstein* on ice-breaking duties in the Baltic during the final winter of the war. Bombed and burnt-out during an RAF raid on Gdynia in December 1944, the wreck of the battleship was scuttled on 21 March 1945 to prevent capture.

Below: The desolate, abandoned wreck of the light cruiser *Emden* in Kiel Bay; she had been badly damaged during an air raid in April 1945. Note the damaged Type XXI U-boat alongside the starboard quarter.

Above: A *Biber* 6.5-ton midget-submarine on its transportation trailer, abandoned in Northern France after being damaged during an air attack.

Opposite page, top: *Seehunde* 14.7-ton two-man midget-submarines at Kiel. *Seehunde* proved to be the most successful of the K-Verband craft.

Right: The 11,700-ton pocket battleship *Lützow* in the Baltic, April 1945. To prevent capture by the Russians, she was scuttled in shallow water in Swinemünde harbour during the last week of the war.

Above: A *Marder* manned-torpedo on its transport and launching trolley, being inspected by British and Danish officers at Copenhagen, May 1945. Note the Plexiglass cockpit on the carrier-body and the underslung 21in torpedo.

Right: *Molch* one-man midget submarines at Copenhagen at the end of the war. Displacing 11 tons, 35 feet long on a beam of 6 feet, the *Molch* resembled enlarged torpedoes.

Above: A *Molch*, minus its underslung torpedoes, on its transportation and launching trolley at the Deschimag *Molch* production plant at Bremen.

Left: The wreck of the light cruiser *Köln* resting on the bottom of the dock in Wilhelmshaven, after being bombed on 30 April 1945.

Far left: The capsized hull of the pocket-battleship *Admiral Scheer* framed by the ruins of a bombed-out U-boat assembly yard at Kiel.

Below The wreck of the 13,900-ton heavy cruiser *Admiral Hipper* settled on the bottom of a dock in Kiel after being hit in the last Bomber Command raid on Germany on 3 May 1945. *Hipper* was painted in black and brick-red camouflage so that her outline would merge with the dock-side buildings.

Left: The Type XXI Electro-boats *U2506* (nearest), *U2511* and *U3514* at Bergen during the last week of the war. Note the Kriegsmarine's battle ensign flying on the conning towers.

Above: *U2322* (Type XXIII coastal Electro-boat) undergoing trials after being taken over by the Royal Navy.

Below: Three Type XXI Electro-boats scuttled in Kiel harbour, May 1945. In the background is the wreck of the 22,337-ton German liner *New York*, which was sunk during a bomber raid on 4 April 1945.

Above: The aftermath of defeat. German submarine crews lined up near their barracks in Kiel to give their names and numbers to German personnel under the supervision of Royal Navy officers.

Opposite page, top: Generaladmiral Hans-Georg von Friedeburg, who was promoted C-in-C of the Kriegsmarine on 2 May 1945, followed by Vizeadmiral Kummetz, C-in-C of German naval forces in the Baltic, leaving the liner *Patricia*, which had been requisitioned by the Allied Control Commission in Flensburg, 22 May 1945. Friedeburg committed suicide by poison shortly after this photograph was taken.

Right: *U2502* (Type XXI) and *U2326* (Type XXIII) alongside the Royal Navy depot ship *Al-Rawdah* after the surrender. This photograph graphically illustrates the difference in size between the two types of Electro-boats.

Above: British officers of the occupation forces inspecting the wreck of *Admiral Hipper* amidst the ruins of Kiel harbour.

Right: The 1,084-ton Type VIIC U-boat *U1305* surrendering to a Royal Navy warship off Loch Eriboll, May 1945.

Above: The 1,120-ton Type IXC U-boat *U516* surrendering to the destroyer HMS *Cavendish*, May 1945.

Above: Grossadmiral Karl Dönitz (1891–1980), C-in-C of the Kriegsmarine from January 1943 to 2 May 1945, when he was appointed Hitler's successor as president of the Third Reich, Minister of War and Supreme Commander of the Armed Forces. In 1946 he was sentenced to ten years' imprisonment by the International Military Tribunal in Nuremberg.

Unaware of the extent of the damage, the Admiralty mounted three more carrier strikes between 24 April and 28 May 1944, but all were aborted because of bad weather. It was not until the first week of July, when intelligence reports indicated that *Tirpitz*'s repairs had been completed and that she was undergoing trials in Altenfiord, that the Admiralty decided on another carrier strike, timed for the night of 16/17 July, prior to the resumption of the Arctic convoys which had been suspended in April because of the Normandy landings.

In the meantime the Germans, to prevent being taken by surprise again, had installed a number of radar warning stations on the approach routes to Altenfiord, and had increased the number of AA guns and smoke-generating facilities in and around Kaafiord. In addition, in an attempt to intercept a British carrier force *en route* or on the return passage from the waters off Altenfiord, a U-boat patrol line running from north-west to south-west of Jan Mayen Island was maintained. When the British strike force of three fleet carriers, *Formidable*, *Indefatigable* and *Furious*, supported by the battleship *Duke of York*, four cruisers and twelve destroyers, sailed from Scapa Flow on 14 July, the twelve U-boats of Group Trutz (*U716, U992, U365, U965, U636, U956, U361, U921, U347, U995, U742 U387*) were on patrol off Jan Mayen. In addition there were a further sixteen U-boats at short notice for sea, disposed between the northern Norwegian ports of Bodo, Narvik, Tromso and Hammerfest; another four boats were refitting at Trondheim and Bergen. However, none of the boats in Group Trutz sighted the British strike force on passage to the flying-off position north-west of Altenfiord, and the attack on *Tirpitz* was launched at 0135 on 17 July.

At 0200 the German radar warning stations sited around Altenfiord detected the incoming strike of 44 Barracuda bombers, and their fighter and Flak-suppression escort of 50 Corsairs, Fireflies and Hellcats, when they were 43 miles from Kaafiord. This gave Kapitän zur See Wolf Jünge, *Tirpitz*'s commanding officer, fifteen minutes in which to sound action stations, close up the gun crews, and activate the smoke-generators ashore and on the battleship's upper deck. Within a few minutes, smoke had covered the ship and it steadily thickened to the extent that by the time the aircraft reached their attack position at 0219, a dense and effective smoke-screen had risen to nearly 1,000 feet over Kaafiord. When the aircraft appeared over the mountains, *Tirpitz* fired blind through the veiling smoke with all her eight 15in, twelve 5.9in, sixteen 4.1in, sixteen 37mm and fifty-eight 20mm AA guns.

As a result of the dense smoke-screen, only two fighters and two Barracudas actually sighted *Tirpitz*; the rest of the Barracudas bombed individually over a period of some 25 minutes, using the flashes from the battleship's guns as aiming points. No hits were scored, but seven near misses were felt aboard the ship, which was severely shaken.

Extracts from *Tirpitz*'s log gives the German view of the attack:

'Wind SW 1–2 [strength 6-9 feet per second], cloudy. Ceiling 2,000–3,000 metres [6,000 to 9,000 feet]. Visibility good.

0204	Signal received from Alta [at the mouth of Altenfiord]: "60 aircraft observed at 0200, 43 miles, to NE on NW course." Subsequent signal: "90 aircraft at 43 or 38 miles on NNW course E."
0208	Both Flak watches at action stations. Ammunition hoist started.
0209–0210	Further signals from Alta confirming earlier signals.
0213	Smoke-screen started at stern and smoke candles on upper deck lit.
0214	Smoke-screen from shore reached the stern of ship.
0215	Order to engine-room: "Make smoke as soon as ready."
0217	Water-tight doors closed.
0219	Opened fire (Barrage and/or Target).
0220	[Aircraft] approach from starboard fore and aft. Ship well-covered by smoke-screen, with the exception of the super-structure on the starboard side and the mast-heads.
0221	KR signal sent: "Air attack on Tirpitz". At the same time a violent vibration was felt in the control position. Shortly afterwards a message was received from the Engineer Officer: "Damage control leader IV reports heavy vibrations in the immediate vicinity." [On investigation, no damage was found; evidently it had been a near miss.]
0225	Aircraft passed overhead [no further observations because, apart from an occasional slight clearing, the ship was effectively wrapped in thick smoke until the end of the attack.]
0230	Black smoke from funnel.
0240	Message to 1st Flak officer: "Flak must on no account run out of ammunition."
0244	Signal from Flak Group Command: "New approach of 10 aircraft from NW."
0247	KR signal sent: "Attack continuing, so far no hits."
0250	Signal from Main Aerial observation Post at Alta: "Nothing further to report."
0252	Ceased firing. Ship undamaged except for a barrel in right-hand gun of starboard IV 4.1in gun mounting, damaged due to a premature detonation of a shell. One man was slightly injured. Observation from the deck showed 4 near misses

on the starboard side and 3 on the port side of the ship. 5 men in the forward 5.9in turrets suffering from smoke and gas poisoning.

0314.   W/T signal Sent: "Aircraft from the first wave ended with no hits. The exact number of aircraft was not observed clearly. Further reports to follow through Battle Group Command."

0425   KR signal received from Patrol Boat NH 01: "0230 40 aircraft, English twin-engined carrier planes flown off on course W. Attack by ten planes, 2 observed to be shot down. No damage."

0541   From FDK: "Air Raid Alarm ended." Increased Readiness.'[3]

Ammunition expended by *Tirpitz* during the attack, which lasted 33 minutes, was:

Main armament	15in	39 rounds
Medium armament	5.9in	359 rounds
Heavy Flak	4.1in	1,973 rounds
Light Flak	37mm AA	3,967 rounds
Light Flak	20mm AA	28,550 rounds

In his post-action report Kapitän Jünge concluded:

'The failure of the attack was due to the fact that *Tirpitz* had 15 minutes' warning which gave her sufficient time to man her guns, clear the ship for action, and put the various smoke-screen apparatus into action. The weather conditions were particularly suitable for the use of smoke-screen. The concentrated barrage from guns of all calibres screened the ship with such success as to ward off the attacker, whose task was made more difficult by this smoke-screen.'[4]

During the attack, one Barracuda bombed a Flak battery on the shore, another attacked a destroyer in Langfiord, and a third narrowly missed the tanker *Nordmark* with a 1,600lb bomb. The fighters straffed Flak positions up and down Altenfiord, and caused the 510-ton patrol-boat *Vp 6307* to run aground while taking avoiding action.

GROUP TRUTZ OPERATIONS

While the attack on *Tirpitz* was in progress, the senior officer 'U-Boote Norwegen' ordered Group Trutz to shift the axis of its patrol line to the south-east of Jan Mayen Island, in the belief that their present positions were too far north to intercept the British carrier force on its return passage to Scapa. To counter such an eventuality, the Admiralty had ordered long-range aircraft from Coastal Command's No. 18 Group to carry out sweeps and patrols across the homeward track of the carrier force, and this homed them on to Group Trutz.

At 2148 on 17 July, *U361* was caught on the surface by a Liberator of No. 86 Squadron which sank her with depth-charges. Six survivors were seen struggling in the icy water after *U361* foundered, but none was rescued. Eight minutes later, and some miles to the north, *U347* was sighted on the surface by a Catalina of No. 210 Squadron. During the run-in to attack, the Catalina was repeatedly hit by *U347*'s Flak which killed the navigator and badly wounded the captain, Flying officer J. A. Cruickshank, and wounded three other members of the crew. Despite his wounds, Cruickshank pressed home the attack and managed to straddle and sink *U347* with depth-charges. The second pilot was then obliged to take over the controls and fly the badly damaged aircraft back to base where Cruickshank, notwithstanding severe loss of blood and weakness, insisted on taking over the controls so that he could put down safely and beach the extensively holed flying-boat. For his gallantry Cruickshank was awarded the Victoria Cross.

During the night of 17/18 July, the British carrier force steamed unnoticed through the gap in Group Trutz caused by the loss of *U361* and *U347* a few hours previously. Next morning a German meteorological aircraft, on routine patrol, sighted and reported the position of the British force, but either the pilot was confused as to the course of the British ships, which were zig-zagging, or his report was garbled in transmission, because *Marineoberkommando Norwegen* (Naval Command Norway) believed that the enemy force sighted was steering north-east and this would indicate another carrier-borne strike on *Tirpitz* or merchant shipping in the Norwegian leads. As a result Group Trutz was ordered to shift the axis of its patrol line to a more northerly position, and four boats were dispatched from Narvik to take up positions guarding the sea approaches to Alten and Vest fiords.

On the evening of the 18th, *U968*, one of the boats from Narvik, which was making for her patrol billet at high speed on the surface, was sighted by a Liberator. She dived to safety before the aircraft could attack, but three hours later she was sighted again by the same Liberator, and this time *U968*'s commander chose to fight it out on the surface. While evading damage from two depth-charge attacks by violent manoeuvring, the U-boat shot up the Liberator with accurate Flak, forcing it to ditch in the sea (six survivors were rescued by a Catalina three days later). At 1145 next day *U968* was again sighted on the surface and attacked by a Liberator. This time her Flak was countered by accurate shooting from the Liberator, and in the course of three attacks the U-boat was seriously damaged by near misses from depth-charges and seven of her crew were wounded by machine-gun bullets. In spite of the damage she sustained, however, she managed to dive and was able to limp back to Narvik.

A similar action was fought at 1915 that evening when *U716* of Group Trutz was attacked by a Liberator. Her Flak was rendered inaccurate by the well-directed machine-gun fire from the aircraft, and she suffered serious damage in the depth-charge attack and was obliged to make for Hammerfest. She was sighted again at 2100 but was able to dive before an attack could be made. Just over two hours later, *U387*, which was returning to Narvik from the patrol line to refuel, was taken by surprise by a Sunderland which attacked out of a bank of low cloud only half-a-mile from the surfaced U-boat. The Sunderland obtained a perfect straddle, the middle depth-charge of the pattern landed square on the U-boat's deck but bounced off without exploding. The rest of the pattern exploded just outside lethal distance from the boat but were close enough to cause serious damage, although *U387* managed to reach Narvik two days later.

Three more boats, *U636*, *U921* and *U965*, were subjected to air attacks on 20 July, and although only *U921* suffered minor damage, the senior officer '*U-Boote Norwegen*' decided to dissolve Group Trutz rather than expose the boats to further attacks. If the Trutz boats had been snorkel-fitted they would have been far more difficult to locate, but as it was, all the boats except *U921*, *U995*, *U425* and *U668* were ordered to return to base, while the four boats retained at sea were re-deployed in single widely spaced billets in more northerly latitudes, beyond the reach of Coastal Command aircraft.

The final attack on the returning Trutz boats occurred on 23 July when *U992*, which was approaching Vestfiord, was attacked by a Sunderland of No. 330 Squadron. The aircraft obtained a perfect straddle, the middle depth-charge of the pattern falling plumb on the U-boat's bridge where it burst open without exploding, smothering everyone on the bridge in a cloud of blinding Torpex dust. The other charges did no serious damage and *U992* escaped by crash-diving. Altogether fifteen air attacks had been made on eleven boats of Group Trutz, resulting in the loss of three and damage to four for the loss of one aircraft.

STRIKES FROM THE SEA

Although the Admiralty was made aware from PR and Enigma decrypts that *Tirpitz* had escaped damage during the Fleet Air Arm attack on 17 July, no further attacks were launched until the resumption of the Arctic convoys, when the east-bound JW.59 of 33 merchant ships sailed from Loch Ewe bound for the Kola Inlet on 15 August.

The first of four carrier strikes, launched from three fleet and two escort-carriers powerfully screened by *Duke of York*, three cruisers, fourteen destroyers and a group of frigates, took place on 22

August, being timed to cover the passage of JW.59 past Bear Island. In total, 32 Barracudas, 24 Corsairs, eleven Fireflies, nine Hellcat fighter-bombers and eight Seafires took off from the five carriers, commencing at 1150. When the strike aircraft reached the coast they found the hills surrounding Altenfiord shrouded in dense cloud at 1,500 feet. As this would prevent accurate bombing from high altitude the Barracudas and Corsairs returned to the carriers, but the Fireflies and Hellcats, descending below the cloud base, followed a road over the mountains to Kaafiord.

The radar warning stations surrounding Altenfiord were late in detecting and warning the battleship of the approaching aircraft and the smoke-screen was incomplete when the Fireflies began their Flak-suppression runs at 1249, two minutes before the nine Hellcats attacked, each dropping a 500lb semi-armour-piercing bomb. No hits were scored, although there were several near misses. Twenty men aboard *Tirpitz* suffered smoke-gas poisoning from the main armament. Meanwhile the Seafires, in diversionary attacks, badly damaged *U965* at Hammerfest, and destroyed two of *Tirpitz*'s seaplanes which were in the harbour at Bukta. Three aircraft were shot down.

A second attack by six Hellcats and eight Fireflies was launched that evening and achieved complete surprise; it was not until the Fireflies began their anti-Flak run at 1916 that the smoke-generators were activated. The Hellcats scored several near misses but once again *Tirpitz* emerged unscathed apart from one killed and ten wounded by the fighters' cannon fire. During the withdrawal all the fighters attacked shipping and radar stations, damaging the tankers *Jeverland* and *Nordmark*, the supply ship *Neumark* and the patrol vessel *Vp 6504*. *Tirpitz* expended 75 rounds of 15in, 487 of 5.9in, 2,000 of 4.1in, 4,000 of 37mm and 30,000 rounds of 20mm AA during the two attacks.

The third attack took place on 24 August by 33 Barracudas (armed with 1,600lb bombs), 24 Corsairs (five carrying one 1,000lb armour-piercing bomb), ten Hellcats, ten Fireflies and eight Seafires. In an endeavour to achieve surprise, the launch was made from a position farther to the south, and the aircraft flew parallel to the coast to make a landfall for an approach from the south of Kaafiord, but their approach was detected by the radar station at Alta which alerted *Tirpitz* at 1541 to a 'large number of planes 63 miles WNW flying low'.

The smoke-screen was well developed, although still insufficient fully to cover the forward and starboard sections of the battleship, by the time the Hellcats and Fireflies began their attack at 1600, five minutes ahead of the Barracudas and Corsairs.

One 500lb semi-armour-piercing bomb dropped by a Hellcat exploded on the roof of 'B' turret, destroying the quadruple 20mm Flak sited there, damaging the range-finder and dishing the turret roof plating to a depth of eight inches. By the time the Barracudas and Corsairs attacked, *Tirpitz* was completely shrouded in smoke, and they had to bomb blind from 4,000-5,000 feet. One 1,600lb bomb hit on the port side of the bridge superstructure, penetrated five decks of a total thickness of 5.8 inches, and came to rest in No. 4 Switchboard Room on the lower platform deck, but failed to explode. When the Germans dismantled and inspected the bomb, they found that not only had the detonation fuze failed to function, but that the bomb had only been partially filled: instead of 215 pounds of explosive it contained only 100 pounds – a convincing example of how a failure in manufacture can prejudice an operation of war. Two Corsairs were shot down, which was a poor reward for the 72 rounds of 15in, 510 5.9in and 40 per cent of the remaining automatic Flak ammunition expended. Eight men, including one dockyard employee, were killed, three were severely wounded, ten were slightly wounded, and five suffered smoke-gas poisoning, but *Tirpitz* had, once again, escaped serious damage. In his post-action report Kapitän Jünge concluded that:

'The attack on the 24.8.1944 was undoubtedly the heaviest and most determined so far experienced. The English showed great skill and dexterity in flying. For the first time they dived with heavy bombs. During the dive-bombing, fighter planes attacked the land Flak batteries which, in comparison with earlier attacks, suffered heavy losses. The fact that the armour-piercing bomb of more than 1,540 pounds did not explode must be considered an exceptional stroke of luck, as the effects of that explosion would have been immeasurable. Even incomplete smoke-screening upsets the correctness of the enemy's aim, and it has been decided from now on to use smoke in wind strengths up to 9 metres per second, irrespective of possible gaps. It has also been ordered that the time of notice for smoke (at present 10 minutes) is to be reduced to 7 minutes.'[5]

During the attack, the Fireflies and Seafires, in strafing runs, severely damaged two patrol boats, a minesweeper and a radar station. They also blew up a naval Flak ammunition dump and destroyed three guns of a heavy Flak battery.

The fourth and final strike by the Fleet Air Arm was launched on the afternoon of 29 August. At 1640 the radar stations detected the 26 Barracudas, seventeen Corsairs, ten Fireflies, seven Hellcats and seven Seafires flying at high altitude 54 miles WNW of Alta. On receipt of this report the air raid warning was sounded aboard *Tirpitz* and the smoke-generators were activated. By the time the aircraft reached Kaafiord *Tirpitz* was completely veiled by dense smoke and they were forced to bomb blind. The Germans had installed a look-out post on a high mountain overlooking the fiord under the direction of an officer from *Tirpitz*, and he communicated with the battleship by VHF radio, giving the positions of the aircraft and the bearings on which they were flying. This gave some direction to *Tirpitz*'s Flak, and she shot down one Firefly and one Corsair, expending 54 rounds of 15in, 161 of 5.9in and some 20 per cent of her remaining, depleted stocks of light-calibre ammunition. The aircraft approached Kaafiord from the west in four waves, and launched their attacks from the north, west and south, commencing at 1702. No bombs hit *Tirpitz*, but she was shaken by several near misses and six men were wounded by bomb splinters.

All four attacks, in which 52 tons of bombs had been dropped and eight aircraft lost, had failed to damage let alone immobilize the battleship, but her luck was fast running out.

DISASTER OFF HAAKOY

Towards the end of August 1944, the Allied Joint Planning Staff, disappointed by the failure of the carrier strikes, discussed ways and means of ending the impasse whereby the presence of *Tirpitz* in Altenfiord was tying down strong forces in the north, and so frustrating the Admiralty's desire to build up British naval strength in eastern waters. They suggested that Mosquito bombers, each carrying a 2,000lb armour-piercing bomb, be used to overcome the problem of the slow Barracudas giving the enemy ample time to enshroud the target with smoke. When the proposal was put to C-in-C, Bomber Command, Air Chief Marshal Sir Arthur 'Bomber' Harris, he argued against the use of Mosquitos because he considered their bomb load quite insufficient to cripple let alone sink such a heavily armoured ship. He suggested that a relatively small number of Lancasters, armed with the largest bombs available, fly from a Scottish base and, after attacking the battleship, land in Russia to refuel for the homeward leg.

In its final details the plan called for the Lancasters, armed with 12,000lb Tallboy bombs and the newly developed Johnnie Walker 400lb mine-bombs, to take-off from airfields in the north of Scotland during the evening of 11 September, attack *Tirpitz* just before dawn next morning, and then land at Yagodnik airfield (twenty miles south-east of Archangel). However, during the forenoon of the 11th, bad weather closed in and Harris decided that the attack would have a far better chance of success if it were launched from the Russian end; and that if the force were not got away immediately the operation might have to be postponed indefinitely in view of an approaching bad weather system. Accordingly, the 38 Lancasters (of No. 9 Squadron and No. 617 'Dam Buster' Squadron), one PR Mosquito and two Liberators carrying supplies, took off from Lossiemouth during the evening of the 11th and landed in very poor weather at Yagodnik and neighbouring airfields early next morning. The landings were made with 10/10 cloud at 350 feet in driving rain on primitive wood-boarding or muddy runways, and ten of the Lancasters so bent or collapsed their undercarriages that they were of no further use.

Bad weather prevented an attack being mounted until 15 September when 28 Lancasters (21 carrying Tallboys, six carrying Johnnie Walkers and one a film unit) took-off for Kaafiord shortly after dawn. Warned of the approaching bombers by the radar stations, the Germans activated the smoke-screen generators eight minutes before the Lancasters reached Kaafiord at 1100. Although the smoke-screen was well developed by this time, the leading aircraft caught a glimpse of *Tirpitz's* masts sticking out of the thick fog, and this was enough to confirm that the battleship was lying in her usual boom-protected anchorage close to the shore on the eastern side of the fiord.

The Lancasters attacked in groups of five to seven aircraft from an altitude of 6,500-10,000 feet. Only the first group, led by the squadron's leader, Wing Commander J. B. Tait, bombed accurately. The following groups were incommoded by the ever-thickening smoke-screen, and the heavy Flak from *Tirpitz* and the shore batteries (134 guns in all). A total of seventeen Tallboys and 72 Johnnie Walker mine-bombs (designed to strike the water short of the target, and rise to explode against the unprotected bottom of the ship) were dropped, but only one hit was scored. But this single hit by a 12,000lb Tallboy had a devastating effect.

The bomb hit the bow section, just forward of the anchor cable hawsepipes. Passing out through the flare of the starboard side it detonated below the keel about 35 feet aft of the bow, and blew open a great hole, 32 feet wide and 48 feet long, in the side, 'so large a motor boat could go in' as a Norwegian agent reported. It wrecked the ship's structure below the armoured deck as far aft as the transverse armoured bulkhead (below 'A' turret), 118 feet from the stem. Both the armoured and the upper deck in this area were bulged upwards to a maximum height of three feet, and the forward sections were completely flooded with some 1,000 tons of sea-water, causing the bows to settle eight feet below the normal draught. To compensate, the damage control officer counter-flooded the port and starboard wing sections in the stern with 500 tons of sea-water, and oil fuel was pumped from the forward to the rear tanks, putting the ship on an even trim but increasing the mean draught from 33 to 36.3 feet. Four other Tallboys burst inside the rectangular boom which was 1,110 feet long by 500 feet. One exploded close alongside the port quarter of the ship; one a little farther forward and slightly further away from the port quarter; one just within the boom at a point opposite the port bow; and one just aft of the stern. The shock from these near misses sheared the main engine foundations and shattered many of the fire-control optical instruments. It was considered that vibration damage from the near misses would have been far greater but for the fact that much of the shock was absorbed by two Dutch tugs lying alongside *Tirpitz* which were blown into small pieces. Casualties aboard the battleship were surprisingly light: one man killed and five wounded. The unfortunate who lost his life was a man in the cells, situated in the flooded forward section, who was under sentence of death for desertion.

Despite the heavy Flak, only three aircraft sustained minor damage, and the 27 attacking aircraft returned safely to Yagodnik; the Lancaster carrying the film unit flying back direct to Lossiemouth.

After examining the damage, German engineers came to the conclusion that it would take at least nine months to rebuild the bow section, and that repairs of such a major nature were impossible to accomplish unless the ship returned to a dockyard in Germany. Unable to make the long and dangerous passage in her damaged state, *Tirpitz* was effectively finished as a seagoing fighting unit, but Dönitz believed that she could still play a role as a floating fortress in the defence of the Norwegian coast against the expected Allied invasion. As the Germans were planning to withdraw from northern Finland, and in so doing they would probably have to abandon Altenfiord, Dönitz decided to move *Tirpitz* to Tromso, some 200 miles south-west of Altenfiord. Accordingly, at midday on 15 October, by which time her damaged engines had been repaired, *Tirpitz* steamed slowly out of Kaafiord, escorted by five destroyers, two Flak cruisers and four minesweepers. The entire damaged bow section was 'hinged' on the port side, and temporary stringers were welded across the gaping hole in the starboard side, stiffening the structure sufficiently to allow the ship to proceed at a maximum speed of 8 knots.

Tirpitz arrived next morning at her new berth, off the south coast of Haakoy Island, some three miles to the west of Tromso. A few days later Kapitän Jünge left the ship, handing over command to Kapitän zur See Robert Weber. The berth she now occupied had been recommended by her navigating officer, Korvettenkapitän Brutzer, because according to the available charts the depth of water under the ship would be a constant 40 feet at all states of the tide, providing security against the ship's sinking or capsizing. Moreover, by berthing the ship in a north-easterly direction in this position, the arcs of fire covered the seaward approaches to Tromso. But as soon as the ship had made fast, the water around her was sounded and it was discovered that the charts were in error, the depth of water being found to be 56 feet, too deep to provide security against a capsize. As the position of the ship could not be changed without seriously interfering with the favourable arcs of fire, it was decided to reduce the depth of water by dumping rubble on the sea bed under and around the ship. It was estimated that one million cubic feet of rubble would be required. But before the necessary dredgers and hoppers could be found to undertake the work, Bomber Command struck again.

The move to the Haakoy anchorage placed the battleship just within range of Bomber Command airfields in Scotland. Aware of *Tirpitz*'s new position from PR flights, but not the extent of the damage sustained during the last bombing attack, a further strike by Nos. 9 and 617 Squadrons was ordered. For the aircraft to make the 2,250-mile round trip from Lossiemouth and back, the selected Lancasters had their 1,460hp Merlin engines replaced by 1,620hp Merlins, and they were fitted with extra 300-gallon fuel tanks. To compensate the extra weight, the mid-upper turrets, the front guns, 3,000 rounds of ammunition from the rear turrets, the pilots' armoured plate protection and all the oxygen and nitrogen bottles were removed.

Prevailing medium-level cloud over Tromso did not dissipate until the wind changed on 28 October, and on the strength of a forecast of clear weather over the target the strike force of 38 Lancasters, all armed with Tallboy bombs, and one Lancaster carrying a film unit, took off just before dawn on the 29th. Although good visibility was experienced right up to the Norwegian coast, a sudden change in the wind carried low cloud over Tromso, which made accurate bombing difficult. Thirty-two Tallboys were dropped but no hits were scored and the nearest bomb detonated some fifty feet off the battleship's port quarter. But shock waves from this bomb split the hull plating on the port quarter, damaged and distorted the port rudder and propeller shaft, and caused flooding of the port shaft passage to a length of 115 feet, sufficient to give the ship a one degree list to port. The bent shaft, coupled with the existing damage to the bows, virtually immobilized *Tirpitz*, to the extent that she was thereafter referred to in official reports as *'Die Schwimmende Batterie'* – 'the floating battery'.

Work on dumping rubble under the ship began on 2 November, but only some 14,000 cubic feet had been dumped when the bombers returned for the last time, on 12 November.

Shortly after midnight 11/12 November 1944, 29 Lancasters of Nos. 9 and 617 Squadrons took-off from Lossiemouth to deliver their third attack on *Tirpitz*. The outward passage was not flown in formation in order that the aircraft could make individual landfalls on the Norwegian coast to the south of Tromso to take advantage of known gaps in the air warning radar cover. Despite this tactic, *Tirpitz* received early warning of the approaching bombers, as a contemporaneous account of the attack compiled by one of her officers, Oberleutnant zur See Fassbender, recounts:

'12/11/44. Clear, cloudless, very good visibility. Wind SW 1-2. Sunrise 0930. High Water 1100.

0800   W/T signal reporting penetration of one Lancaster in Bodo area. As penetrations of four-engined bombers are likely to have special significance, a clarification of this report was requested from the main observer post.

0815   Penetration of 3 Lancasters reported near Mosjoen, course east (tactical time 0738). On account of this report an attack by four-engined formations similar to that on 29th October, is anticipated, as the circumstances are similar – time of day, weather and approach. Telephonic consultation between AA gunnery officer and officer-in-charge of main observer post [Oberleutnant Hamschmidt] for the purpose of clarifying the air situation and securing fighter protection.

0825   Another 4 Lancasters reported, course NE in Mosjoen area. It therefore strengthened our suspicions that the enemy intended to attack. Consultation between First AA officer,

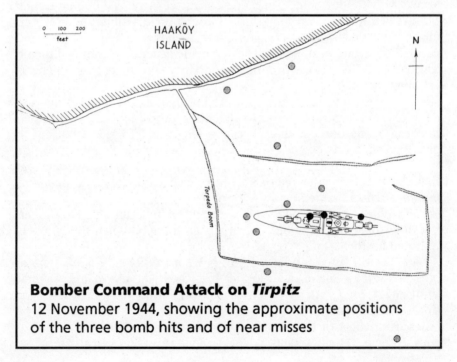

Bomber Command Attack on *Tirpitz*
12 November 1944, showing the approximate positions of the three bomb hits and of near misses

Oberleutnant Herer, and main observer post. Fighter protection requested from divisional control at Bardufoss. Inquiry made regarding strength and course of formation. Fighter protection not yet granted up to the present. Up to 0840 no further report on air situation. AA alarm given as a precaution.

0854   Report from main observer post: "7 monoplanes [one-engined] 50 km [31 miles] NE." Simultaneous carrier attack suspected and air raid alert given.

0855   Air raid alert. Also for Tromso. As report of 7 monoplanes originated from an auxiliary observer post at an Army coastal battery, and as no further reports on the subject were received, the report appears to have been false. In spite of this, the alert remains, as special significance must be attached to the four-engined bomber formation approaching from the south.

0902   Ship made ready for action. Stand to.

0903   Signal from main observer post: "Situation still not clear. No more reports available."

0905   Open formation of about 20 to 25 aircraft sighted 120 km [75 miles] to the south. From now on intentions of attack on *Tirpitz* are obvious. All eyes keep watch on the formation. First its course is NE, then it turns at a distance of about 70 km [44 miles], to make a direct approach. From the time of the first sighting, fighter protection has been requested continuously via the main observer post. About 0912 a second formation is sighted in the south and simultaneously reported by the main observer post. The formations are flying at a height of about 2,500 to 3,000 metres [8,200 to 9,800 feet]. Upon repeated requests for fighter protection a signal is received about 0915, as follows: "Enemy formation over Bardufoss, therefore impossible for fighters to take off."

0915   Captain [broadcasting to ship's company]: "Fighters have been requested."

0925   One fighter reported to have taken-off; shortly afterwards more fighters. [Nothing was seen of these fighters because the Luftwaffe base commander was unaware that *Tirpitz* had moved to Tromso, with the result that the fighters flew to Kaafiord!]

0927   Captain to all: "We are expecting a heavy air attack and the ship's company of *Tirpitz* will again fulfil its duty and prepare a hot reception for the four-engined bombers."

0927 Smoke flares sighted from first formation at about 40 km [25 miles] distance. The formation forms up into groups each of 4 to 5 machines flying at great height and prepare for the attack. Meanwhile the second formation has thinned out. Contrary to previous experience, the attack commences not in the fore-and-aft direction but athwartships from the starboard side on a bearing of 060 to 070 degrees. [For some reason the smoke-generators on board *Tirpitz* were not activated, and the smoke from the shore generators was ineffective, failing to provide any cover for the battleship.]

0938 Captain to Senior Gunnery Officer: "Permission to fire when bomber formation within range."

0940 Forward main armament opens fire at about 210hm [13½ miles]. At about 150hm [9½ miles] range secondary armament and heavy anti-aircraft armament also open fire. The bursts of the first main armament salvo were low, the range was good. In spite of well-directed secondary armament and main anti-aircraft fire, the aircraft proceed steadily on their course of attack. The medium and light anti-aircraft guns came into operation mostly only after the bombs had been dropped. On the approach of the formation, one was observed to be shot down [no Lancasters were lost in the attack].

0942 A stick of bombs of the heaviest calibre fall in close proximity, mostly inside the net enclosure. Two direct hits are observed on the port side, one on the aircraft catapult [port side amidships] and one beside 'B' turret. The ship is drenched by high water columns, and a few seconds later lists heavily (15 to 20 degrees) to port. [The main mast snapped as the ship heeled.] From the effect of the first hit there is a marked decrease in defensive fire, due to casualties in *matériel* and personnel. In spite of the increasing list the fire from the heavy and light anti-aircraft guns is kept up until shortly before the capsizing. Shortly after the first bomb-hits the order was given by the repair party control to correct the trim by flooding. [The bomb that hit the ship port side amidships entered through the catapult track and exploded as it passed through the armoured deck over the port boiler room. The explosion tore a 45-foot-long hole in the ship's side, extending in width from the bilge keel to the upper-deck, causing Port No. 1 Boiler Room, Centre Boiler Room, and Port Engine Room spaces to flood. This great inrush of sea-water caused the ship to heel 15 to 20 degrees to port. The effects of the hit on the port side of 'B' turret are not known, but in conjunction with a near miss off the bows, must have added substantially to the existing damage in the forward sections.]

0945   Ship listing about 30 to 40 degrees to port. Order from Captain: "Abandon lower deck." Shortly afterwards, Captain to Gunnery officer: "Fire everything possible." [A third bomb hit the ship on the port side abreast the after 5.9in turret, and this explosion in conjunction with a near miss in the area of the midships 5.9in turret ripped another hole in the hull, causing Port No. 2 Boiler Room, two 5.9in magazines and shell rooms, the gyro compartment and a fan room, to flood. The port side midships section was now flooded over a length of 220 feet from the double bottoms to the water-line, which had reached the upper deck as the ship continued to roll over to port.]

0950   Ship listing 60 to 70 degrees to port. "C" turret blows up with a tongue of fire. Cause unknown. At this time there were still three aircraft over the ship. Bomb-hits near "C" turret were not observed. It is supposed that the explosion was caused by the ammunition catching fire. List increasing quickly. [A fire had apparently been started by the hit near the after 5.9in turret, and this reached 'C' turret magazine. The resulting huge explosion blew the 15in turret out of its barbette and hurled it overboard.]

0952   The ship capsizes to port [having been flooded with 17,000 tons of sea-water] and is lying at an angle of about 135 degrees. A small number of the crew were able to remain on the capsizing ship. The rest of the men on the upper deck tried to reach land by swimming or with the assistance of floats or objects drifting around. After about 15 minutes the first rescue vessels arrived.

After the ship capsized no more bombs were dropped. One aircraft circled once more at a height of about 2,000m [6,500 feet] over the anchorage [this was the Lancaster carrying the film unit] ... Two direct hits were certain and several near misses were observed. The effect of the bombs could be estimated from the bomb craters on the island of Haakoy: the bombs had fallen in massive rocks and the craters had a diameter of 30m [100 feet] and a depth of 10m [33 feet].'[6]

Tirpitz came to rest, heeled to 130 degrees, with her superstructure and turrets embedded in the mud, the starboard side of her bilge keel sticking out of the water like a smooth, rounded rock in a near vertical position, the highest point being 26.5 feet above water at low tide. Of her complement of 1,900 officers and men, 1,204 lost their lives, including Kapitän Weber, the majority being trapped below decks when the ship rolled over. After the order to vacate the lower decks had been given, by which time the ship was already heeling 40 degrees to port, she capsized so quickly that the men on the lower decks were unable to reach the upper deck. The fortunate members of the crew already on the upper deck and in the gun turrets, were able to save themselves by swimming to the nearby shore of Haakoy or by clinging to the floats of the net barrage. Those who swam were greatly hampered by fuel oil on the surface of the water, patches of which were ablaze, and when 'C' turret blew up some of those in the water were killed by the blast or by steel splinters. A few survivors did not even get their feet wet. As the decks inclined, they stepped on to the side of the ship, by then nearly horizontal, and from there ran up the hull as it continued to roll until they were standing on the bottom of the keel, from where they rescued by small craft.

Eighty-five of the survivors owed their lives to the quick thinking of the Senior Engineer. He was ashore when the attack began, and when he saw what had happened he collected all the blow torches he could find in Tromso, either from the Wehrmacht or from civilians. When his team clambered on to the upturned hull they heard the hammering of men who had made their way up through the inverted hull to the inner bottom, and cut through the shell plating to free them from the steel tomb. The first group of five were freed at 1700, some seven hours after the ship capsized. The work went on all night, the last man to be freed alive being got out at 0800 next day.

At the end of the war, enterprising Norwegians began modest salvage work on the wreck, removing valuable pieces of metal sufficiently small to be easily handled. This 'pilfering' went on until 1948, when a Norwegian-German consortium of ship-breakers purchased the wreck and began dismantling the 52,000-ton steel grave of 1,204 German sailors. The work took nine years to complete, and it was not until 1957 that the last vestiges of the 'Lonely Queen of the North' was finally removed from the shallow waters south of Haakoy Island.

So ended *Tirpitz* which for so long had haunted Allied strategy on the broad oceans she never sailed. Given a determination on the part of her commanders commensurate with her great fighting strength, she might have accomplished more, even if in the end she were cornered and sunk like *Bismarck* and *Scharnhorst* before her. At least she would have died in battle, most probably having first taken a heavy toll of Allied ships; instead, she was battered into immobility and finally destroyed while skulking in a Norwegian fiord.

Chapter 8

THE SETTING OF THE MIDNIGHT SUN

A NEW-FOUND OPTIMISM

From November 1943 until April 1944, when the Admiralty suspended the convoys to Russia for the summer months, the Arctic-based U-boats sank only four merchant ships and two escorts during attacks on the eight east-bound and six west-bound convoys that traversed the Barents Sea to and from the Kola Inlet. The sum total of Allied A/S measures, which had defeated the U-boats in the Atlantic, had proved equally effective in Arctic waters; especially the provision of adequate escorts including at least one small escort-carrier per convoy.

When the Allies resumed the convoys to Russia in August 1944, however, the U-boat crews returned to the attack with their wilted morale partially restored by faith in the potential of the Gnat acoustic homing torpedo. The Gnat had first been issued to U-boats based in northern Norway early in 1944, but in small numbers, and the Arctic convoys had been suspended before this new weapon had been brought to bear in significant strength.

By the time that the first of the new series of convoys sailed, none of the 29 Arctic U-boats had received snorkels. At the polar bases the fitting of the device did not begin until the second week in September, and thereafter the work proceeded at such a slow pace that only 50 per cent of the boats had been fitted by March 1945.

The success of a new campaign depended, therefore, on the Gnat (T5 *Zaunkönig*) torpedo whose sensitive hydrophone homed in on the noise of a ship's propellers and steered it to the source of the sound. Its great advantage was that it only had to be fired roughly in the direction of its target for the homing mechanism to guide it to the selected ship. This did away with the often fatal necessity of exposing the periscope for a relatively lengthy period of time in order to take aim. Nor was it necessary for the commander to determine the course and speed of a zig-zagging target, as was the case with conventional torpedoes.

The U-boat men's faith in Gnat was misplaced, however, because in practice it had serious limitations. Not being very fast (21 knots maximum), it could not catch up with a ship making 25 knots or more. Furthermore, the homing device was only attracted to cavitating

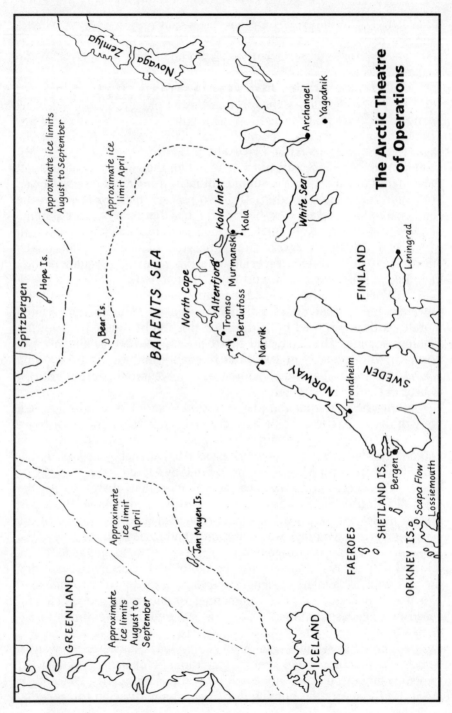

propellers (biting hard into the water), which only happened when a ship was being driven at high speed or when accelerating. Consequently a ship steaming at slow speed was as immune from a Gnat as a ship making 25 knots.

Gnat also suffered from an over-sensitive detonator, and was apt to explode on meeting the disturbed water of a ship's wake, causing many commanders erroneously to claim 'kills'. Gnat's effectiveness was further compromised by a counter-measure, quickly developed by the Allies, in the form of a noise-box which, towed astern of a ship, provided a stronger lure to the homing device than the sound of the ship's propellers. This was available in two forms: a pair of noise-boxes towed one on each quarter, known as a 'Foxer', or a single noise-box towed directly astern, known as a 'Cat'. Both proved effective, but they had the drawback of distracting ASDIC operators and so reducing their efficiency in detecting submerged U-boats.

Largely unaware of the Gnat's shortcomings, the U-boat crews set out in August 1944, with misplaced confidence in its potential, and, buoyed up with optimism that snorkel would in due course give them back the lost initiative, believing that they were about to stage a great comeback against the Arctic convoys. They were to be quickly disillusioned. Despite the fact that the Arctic U-boat Command's Enigma key had been changed from the Home Waters' 'Triton' key in May 1944, to a new 4-wheel setting code-named 'Niobe' ('Narwhal' by the Allies), this cipher was broken by the cryptanalysts at Bletchley Park in September, providing the Admiralty with 'comprehensive intelligence about the strength and location of the U-boat patrol lines in the Barents Sea, and disclosed the orders issued to them when convoys were sighted'.[1]

This decided advantage enabled the convoys to evade the U-boat patrol lines on a number of occasions, and inaugurate the tactic whereby the escorts and aircraft from the carriers were commonly sent ahead of the convoy to attack the U-boats in the positions revealed through the Enigma decrypts. As had happened in the Battle of the Atlantic, it was the breaking of the Enigma ciphers, that was to prove decisive in defeating the Arctic U-boats.

THE FREEZING STING OF REALITY

The first of the new series of Allied Arctic convoys, JW.59, which consisted of 33 merchant ships, sailed from Loch Ewe on 15 August 1944, bound for that most hazardous and terrible of all operational areas – pack ice; fog; ferocious storms; perpetual darkness in winter; perpetual day in summer when the sun was still high in the sky at midnight; compasses rendered unreliable because of the high latitudes, which made navigation a nightmare; and always the merciless sub-zero temperatures.

JW.59 was strongly protected by two escort-carriers, a cruiser, seven destroyers, four sloops, two frigates and five corvettes, but it sailed without the benefit of prior warning of U-boat dispositions because the cryptanalysts at Bletchley were still, at this stage, struggling to break the 'Niobe' Enigma key settings.

At 0820 on the 20th, the convoy was sighted by a German reconnaissance aircraft to the east of Jan Mayen Island. Next day it crossed a patrol line hastily formed by the four U-boats of Group Trutz (*U921*, *U995*, *U425*, *U668*) which had remained at sea in billets to the northeast of Jan Mayen Island when the rest of the Group were recalled to harbour. These four boats had been reinforced by *U344* which, at 0600 on the 21st, unsuccessfully attacked the convoy with a spread of Gnat torpedoes, but managed to hit and sink the sloop *Kite* with a salvo of FAT pattern-running torpedoes. Thereafter all five boats were forced to remain submerged by aircraft; the two escort-carriers were able to work their aircraft almost continuously for the remainder of the passage thanks to unusually favourable weather, and this prevented the five boats from overhauling the convoy. During the chase *U344*, having surfaced to recharge her exhausted batteries, was sighted by a Swordfish from the carrier *Vindex*. Although she managed to crash-dive before the Swordfish could attack, she was subjected to a 12-hour hunt by the destroyer *Keppel*, the frigate *Loch Dunvegan* and the sloops *Mermaid* and *Peacock*, which were directed to the area by the aircraft. Finally, when the air in the boat was exhausted, *U344*'s commander, Ulrich Pietsch, was forced to surface, but unluckily for him, he came up a mere 5,000 yards from *Loch Dunvegan*. All four warships closed in on the U-boat, which crashed-dived again, and were able to hold ASDIC contact and send down a hail of depth-charges on the luckless *U344*. 'We can only imagine the scene below as each attack brought further damage, leaks developing and lights going out as the boat rocked and shuddered to the blast of the explosions. Then on the sixth attack the end came, for in the warships a violent underwater explosion was heard and felt after which oil came welling to the surface.'[2]

During the early hours of the 24th, the convoy ran into a second patrol line of four boats, *U997*, *U363*, *U354* and *U711*, deployed to the east of Bear Island. *U997* and *U363* attacked the convoy, and each commander, Hans Lehmann of *U997* and Werner Nees of *U363*, claimed to have sunk two merchant ships – claims based on hearing end-of-run detonations; in fact all four Gnats exploded harmlessly in the wakes of the 'Cat'-towing warships. At 0300 next day, *U354* revealed her position while carrying out an unsuccessful attack on the sloop *Mermaid*, and was herself sunk by a Swordfish from *Vindex*. Later in the day all 33 merchantmen of JW.59 reached the Kola Inlet and safety.

The return convoy, RA.59A of nine merchantmen, sailed from Kola on 28 August, under the protection of the same warships that had escorted JW.59, and enjoyed an unopposed passage. Only *U394* made contact and she was damaged by a patrolling aircraft from *Vindex*, and then hunted to extinction by the destroyers *Keppel* and *Whitehall* and the frigate *Affleck*. On this occasion, after a hunt of six hours, the warships had the grim satisfaction of seeing wreckage from *U394* came to the surface together with gruesome human remains. All the ships of the convoy reached Loch Ewe safely on 6 September.

The next pair of convoys, the Russia-bound JW.60 and the homeward-bound RA.60, both of 30 merchant ships, also had comparatively uneventful voyages. They were protected by two escort-carriers, a cruiser and twelve escort vessels. JW.60 sailed from Loch Ewe on 15 September. By this time the Bletchley Park cryptanalysts had broken the Niobe Enigma key, and the Admiralty was able to re-route the convoy clear of the six U-boats of Group Grimm which had been deployed to the south-west of Bear Island; the convoy arrived intact in the Kola Inlet on 23 September.

The return convoy, RA.60, left Kola on 28 September, and although the Admiralty was once again able to route it clear of Group Grimm, it overran one of the six boats of the newly formed Group Zörn, which had gathered to the north of the Kola Inlet and whose existence had not been revealed through Enigma decrypts. At 1625 on the day the convoy sailed, Oberleutnant Wolfgang Ley, commander of *U310*, fired a spread of Gnats which hit and sank two merchantmen: the 7,176-ton American liberty ship *Edward H. Crockett* and the 7,219-ton British freighter *Samsova*. *U310* escaped the resulting counter-attack by the convoy escorts, but *U921*, which tried to approach the convoy on the following morning was not so lucky, being sighted, depth-charged and sunk by Swordfish from the escort-carrier *Campania*. No further attacks were made and the 28 surviving ships of the convoy reached Loch Ewe on 5 October.

One sloop and two merchantmen sunk, for the cost of four U-boats, was an inauspicious start to the campaign, but Arctic U-boat Command requested the commanders 'not to be shaken by this further failure against the convoys, promising to make as many snorkel-fitted U-boats as possible effective in time for the next convoy'.[3]

CAT AND MOUSE

Disturbed by the meagre results, Arctic U-boat Command decided on new tactics. As more snorkel boats were becoming available, it was decided to station them outside the entrance to the Kola Inlet where, it was confidently assumed, they could not fail to intercept the convoys passing in and out, and would have opportunities to attack single ships while they were forming up. Group Panther – nineteen boats, the majority being snorkel-fitted – was deployed off the Kola Inlet during the third week of October.

The Admiralty were made aware of this development through Enigma decrypts, and appropriate counter-measures were devised. When convoy JW.61 of 29 freighters sailed from Loch Ewe on 20 October, it was provided with exceptionally strong air and surface protection: three escort-carriers, a cruiser and 24 escort vessels. When the convoy reached a position to the east of Bear Island, having encountered no opposition, escorts were sent ahead in strength to search the approaches to the Kola Inlet. Ironically, given the large number of U-boats in the area, ASDIC conditions were so bad that no contacts were made. On the other hand, the U-boats were equally handicapped by the strength of the forces arrayed against them, and although four of the nineteen U-boats of Group Panther made torpedo attacks on the warships searching for them (between 2330 on the 26th and 1415 on the 27th), the Gnats either detonated prematurely or exploded in the wakes of the warships, and all the ships of JW.61 passed safely into the Inlet.

Similar tactics were adopted prior to the sailing of the returning RA.61 of 33 freighters on 2 November. Although the boats of Group Panther tried hard to get at the convoy as it emerged from the Inlet into the open sea, the escort forces proved too strong, and all that was achieved was damage to the frigate *Mounsey* by a Gnat fired from *U295*, and a near miss on a merchant ship by a Gnat fired from *U711* whose commander, Kapitänleutnant Hans-Günther Lange, heard an end-of-run detonation after 11 minutes 8 seconds and so claimed a kill. The convoy reached Loch Ewe without loss on 9 November.

The seventeen boats of Groups Stock and Grübe, deployed off the Kola Inlet, were no more successful in their attacks on convoys JW.61A, JW.62 and RA.62. The first of these, JW.61A, left the Clyde on 29 October, and consisted of only two vessels: troopships carrying 11,000 Russian ex-prisoners of war who had been liberated from German camps during the Allied advance across western Europe. This convoy, and the 30 freighters of the heavily escorted JW.62, which sailed from Loch Ewe on 29 November, reached Kola without being attacked. This was achieved by exploiting the known propensity of U-boats' mistaking single ships, or doubtful hydrophone effects, for convoys. The U-boats of both groups were duped on these occasions by a few escorts making as much din as possible with their 'Foxers' and 'Cats', a ploy which succeeded in enticing all seventeen boats to pursue ghost convoys, while JW.61A and JW.62 passed safely into the Kola Inlet.

To clear the waters off the Inlet for the returning RA.62 of 28 freighters, which sailed on 10 December, hunting groups of British and Russian escorts scoured the entrance on the preceding day. While this was in progress, *U997* fired a Gnat at the Soviet destroyer *Zhivuchi* and missed, only narrowly escaping destruction during the ensuing depth-charge attack by *Zhivuchi* and the destroyer *Razumny*. The frigate *Bamborough Castle* had better luck when she detected *U387* with her ASDIC and promptly destroyed the U-boat with a well-placed pattern of depth-charges.

By the time RA.62 sailed, the U-boats of Groups Stock and Grübe had been so scattered by the hunting groups that only *U365* was able to make contact. During the early hours of the 11th she fired a spread of Gnats, one of which exploded harmlessly in the wake of the merchantmen, but another blew off the bows of the destroyer *Cassandra*, stationed on the outer screen of the convoy. After a great struggle, which entailed a notable feat of seamanship and endurance, the destroyer was finally towed back to Kola for repairs. Two days later, *U365*, which had pursued the convoy tenaciously, was sighted on the surface off Jan Mayen Island by Swordfish from the escort-carrier *Campania* which sunk her with depth-charges.

In an endeavour to achieve better results against the next two convoys, JW.63 of 35 merchantmen and RA.63 of 30 ships, which sailed on 30 December 1944 and 11 January 1945 respectively, Group Stier was deployed south-east of Bear Island, but the Admiralty knew the U-boats' whereabouts through Enigma decrypts and both convoys were successfully re-routed around them.

The attempt by the 26 merchantmen of JW.64 to evade the twelve U-boats of Group Rasmus, whose position south of Bear Island was revealed by Enigma, was foiled by reconnaissance aircraft which first sighted the convoy north-east of the Faeroes on 4 February and thereafter shadowed it almost continuously. But appalling weather, with visibility reduced to a maximum of five miles, and the strength of the escort (two carriers, one cruiser and seventeen escort vessels) robbed Group Rasmus of the chance to capitalize on the reconnaissance reports, and they moved south-east to join the seven boats that had gathered off the Kola Inlet. Heavy snowstorms, which reduced visibility to a few thousand yards, veiled the convoy as it entered the Inlet, but shortly after midnight on 12/13 February, as the last freighter passed safely through the entrance, *U992* managed to torpedo the corvette *Denbeigh Castle*. The strenuous efforts of her ship's company kept the corvette afloat, but although she was towed into harbour by the corvette *Bluebell*, she had to be beached to prevent her from sinking and was eventually declared a total constructional loss.

Group Rasmus's disappointment was tempered on the morning of 14 February, when they encountered a small Soviet-escorted convoy of Allied merchantmen approaching Kola from the White Sea to join up with RA.64. The convoy was attacked by three U-boats: *U711*, which sank the 7,200-ton freighter *Horace Gray* at 1039; *U968*, which sank the 8,129-ton tanker *Norfjell* at 1230, and claimed three other ships sunk as a result of hearing end-of-run Gnat detonations; and *U992*, which unsuccessfully attacked one 7,000-ton freighter.

Prior to the departure of the 34 merchantmen of RA.64 on 17 February 1945, escorts in strength swamped the area of the Kola Inlet in an attempt to scatter the waiting Group Rasmus. Working in pairs, the escorts quartered back and forth in driving snowstorms, searching for the invisible enemy with ASDIC – a task made the more difficult by the relatively shallow water that produced a confusion of echoes on the sets. Through the eerie 'sea-smoke', the low-lying drifting mist which is a common feature in Arctic waters, the snow-covered escorts weaved and zig-zagged, 'Foxers' and 'Cats' rattling astern to exorcize the Gnats. Their efforts were rewarded when, at 0100 on the 17th, after 24 hours of hunting, an ASDIC operator in the sloop *Lark* made a definite contact. In conjunction with the frigate *Alnwick Castle*, which forced *U425* to surface after damaging her with four bombs from a 'Squid' (mortar), *Lark* sank the U-boat with gunfire.

Despite the efforts to clear the entrance of the Kola Inlet, nine U-boats of Group Rasmus remained in the area, and when RA.64 began clearing the harbour *U968* avenged *U425* by torpedoing *Lark* at 1024 with a Gnat which blew off the sloop's stern. By skilful damage control, *Lark*'s crew managed to keep their ship afloat and she was eventually towed back into the Kola Inlet and beached. She was never salvaged by the British, who later transferred the beached wreck to the Soviets who scrapped her after the war. Thirty minutes later, *U968* torpedoed and sank the 7,176-ton American liberty ship *Thomas Scott*. *U968*'s commander, Oberleutnant Otto Westphalen, capped his success later that day when he torpedoed the corvette *Bluebell* at 1523. Hit in the magazine, *Bluebell* blew up, leaving only one survivor to be snatched from the icy sea.

On the way home RA.64 encountered a fierce gale which caused a number of the merchant ships to straggle miles behind the main body. Although U-boats from Group Rasmus pursued and managed to maintain contact with the convoy, the escorts prevented them from getting into attack positions, and none of the stragglers was spotted. But the 7,176-ton liberty ship *Henry Bacon*, which had fallen fifty miles astern of the main body, was sunk by a German aircraft, earning her the grim distinction of being the last Allied ship to be sunk by the

Luftwaffe during the war. The remaining 32 storm-tossed freighters of RA.64 reached the safety of the Clyde on 1 March 1945.

The next east-bound convoy, JW.65 of 24 merchantmen, protected by two escort-carriers, one cruiser and nineteen escort vessels, sailed from the Clyde on 11 March. To intercept this convoy the Germans deployed the ten snorkel-fitted U-boats of Group Hagen in two lines off the Kola Inlet. Aircraft from the two carriers, supported by Russian shore-based aircraft, patrolled the area as the convoy approached the Inlet on the morning of 20 March. But during a heavy snowstorm, which grounded the aircraft for 1½ hours, *U995*, in the first line, torpedoed and sank the Liberty ship *Horace Bushnell*. Towards midday, even though aircraft patrols had resumed, the convoy ran into further trouble while passing over the second line of U-boats; *U716* torpedoed and sank the sloop *Lapwing* and *U968* sank the 7,210-ton American freighter *Thomas Donaldson*.

These losses caused the escort commander to devise a new ruse to outwit Group Hagen. It was decided to sail the homeward bound RA.65 at midnight on 23/24 March, in three columns instead of the usual two, so that the ships would clear the entrance more quickly. In addition, instead of sending the hunting groups out on the preceding day in an attempt to scatter the waiting U-boats, they were held back until two hours before the convoy weighed anchor, in the hope of catching the Germans off guard. Then four destroyers were sent out along the old standard route at high speed, dropping depth-charges and firing starshell, to convince the Germans that they were following the normal procedure of scouring the entrance 24 hours before the convoy emerged. While this was going on the convoy cleared the Kola Inlet through a newly swept channel. This stratagem proved highly successful, and by the time the boats of Group Hagen became aware of the ruse the convoy was well clear and away to sea, reaching the Clyde unscathed on 1 April.

A similar stratagem was employed by the last east-bound convoy to make the Kola run before the war ended; the 22 freighters of JW.66 managing to evade the sixteen boats of Group Faust which had concentrated on the old approach channels. But the Germans did not fall for the ruse a third time, and when the last of the returning convoys, RA.66 of 24 freighters, sailed on 29 April, a simulated sailing by a ghost convoy along the old route, did not deflect Group Faust's concentration across the new channel. The first indication that the trick had not worked came when the screening frigate *Alnwick Castle* was shaken by two Gnat torpedoes (fired by *U968*) exploding in her wake. A little while later the frigate *Loch Insh* picked up *U307* on her ASDIC and forced her to the surface with a perfectly placed pattern of mortar-bombs from her 'Squid', and then sank her with a torrent of gunfire. The score was evened when *U968* torpedoed the frigate *Goodall*, which was rent apart by a devastating blast as the Gnat detonated against her forward magazine.

During the night *U427* unsuccessfully attacked the Canadian destroyers *Haida* and *Iroquois*, which then hunted the U-boat for several hours, dropping a total of 678 depth-charges, but miraculously *U427* managed to escape. The last attempted attack on RA.66, and indeed the final attempt to attack an Arctic convoy, was made by *U286* during the night of 29/30 April. She was sunk by depth-charges from the frigates *Loch Shin*, *Anguilla* and *Cotton*, before she could fire a single torpedo, earning the grim accolade of being the last U-boat to be sunk in Arctic waters. When RA.66 reached the Clyde on 8 May 1945, the Midnight Sun had finally set on the Arctic convoys.

THE BALANCE SHEET

The U-boats had managed to sink only two of the 231 merchant vessels in the nine east-bound convoys that sailed between August 1944 and April 1945. These two freighters took down to the depths 15,000 tons of cargo with them – a mere 0.11 per cent of the 1.3 million tons dispatched from British ports. The three merchantmen sunk in the returning convoys and the two sunk while joining up had empty holds, so that the total losses (seven merchant ships and six escorts) scarcely affected the issue at all, and the crews of the nine U-boats sunk died in vain. The result of the Kriegsmarine's failure to interdict the Arctic convoys is summed up by Vizeadmiral Friedrich Ruge:

'Between August 1944 and April 1945, the 231 ships on the Arctic run carried over a million tons of war material. The weapons, equipment and vehicles delivered allowed the Russians to equip a further sixty motorized divisions which gave them not only numerical but also material superiority at focal points of the battles [on the Eastern Front]. Thus Anglo-American sea-power also exerted a decisive influence on the land operations in eastern Europe.'[4]

More than double this number of ships reached North Russia during the period August 1941 to April 1944; indeed the amount of supplies convoyed on the Kola Run during the war totalled four million tons (including 5,000 tanks, more than 7,000 aircraft and 743 million shells. Of this huge quantity dispatched, only some 300,000 tons (7.5 per cent) went down in the holds of 58 fully laden east-bound ships (a further 31 unladen ships were sunk in the returning convoys). This cost the Kriegsmarine 32 U-boats, three destroyers, the battlecruiser *Scharnhorst* and the battleship *Tirpitz*, all of which found watery graves under the tumultuous waves of the Arctic wastes.

Chapter 9

NIL DESPERANDUM

THE INSHORE CAMPAIGN: THE FIRST WAVE

When the U-boats began evacuating the Biscay bases in August 1944, BdU ordered eight fully battleworthy boats from these bases to take up billets in the North Channel and the Bristol Channel, with the object of diverting the attention of the Allied A/S forces away from the other sixteen Biscay boats making for Norwegian ports. To this end BdU also dispatched seven snorkel boats from Group Mitte in Norway to the North Channel, North Minch and Moray Firth. These fifteen boats, reinforced by five more from Group Mitte at the end of August and the

---

The Inshore Campaign: The First Wave

U-Boats dispatched from 14 August to 14 September 1944

Boat	Sailed	Operational Area	Returned	Ships sunk*
U680	14 Aug 44	Moray Firth	8 Sept 44	
U482	14 Aug 44	North Channel	26 Sept 44	4 (31,611) +1 corvette
U484	14 Aug 44	North Channel	Sunk	
U296	16 Aug 44	North Minch	29 Sept 44	
U248	17 Aug 44	North Channel	14 Oct 44	
U743	21 Aug 44	North Channel	Sunk	
U1004	22 Aug 44	North Channel	23 Oct 44	
U244	23 Aug 44	Off Reykjavik	10 Oct 44	
U262	23 Aug 44	Bristol Channel	1 Nov 44	
U758	23 Aug 44	Bristol Channel	10 Oct 44	
U285	24 Aug 44	North Minch	18 Sept 44	
U398	26 Aug 44	North Channel	14 Oct 44	
U247	26 Aug 44	Bristol Channel	Sunk	
U714	27 Aug 44	Bristol Channel	24 Oct 44	
U963	29 Aug 44	North Channel	7 Oct 44	
U309	29 Aug 44	North Channel	9 Oct 44	
U979	29 Aug 44	Off Reykjavik	10 Oct 44	
U985	30 Aug 44	North Channel	23 Oct 44	
U953	31 Aug 44	North Channel	11 Oct 44	
U281	4 Sept 44	North Minch	28 Oct 44	
U1199	14 Sept 44	Moray Firth	5 Nov 44	

* Expressed in number of merchant ships sunk and total tonnage.

---

beginning of September, achieved their aim of covering the withdrawal of the Biscay boats but little else.

When seventeen of the twenty boats dispatched to British inshore waters returned to the Norwegian bases (three had been sunk), only one could report having made a kill. This was *U482* which had been operating in the North Channel. Her commander, Kapitänleutnant Hartmut Graf von Matuschka, had attacked a convoy making for Liverpool on 30 August, sinking the 10,448-ton US tanker *Jacksonville*. Two days later he sank the RN corvette *Hurst Castle* and next day the 4,115-ton Norwegian *Fjordheim* during an attack on an outward-bound convoy some 70 miles north-west of Lough Swilly. Despite an intensive air search, the U-boat was sighted only once, on 3 September, when a Sunderland glimpsed her snorkel protruding about three feet above the water and emitting wisps of brown exhaust gas. The Sunderland launched an attack, but the depth-charge release mechanism failed, and *U482* escaped to lie low for a few days. But on 8 September Matuschka attacked an incoming convoy fifteen miles north-west of Lough Swilly and with one spread of Gnat torpedoes sank the 15,702-ton *Empire Heritage* and the 1,346-ton *Pinto*, each of the British freighters being hit by a single torpedo. Escaping the subsequent concentrated air and surface hunt, and having expended all her torpedoes, *U482* headed back for Norway where she arrived on 26 September, having logged 2,729 nautical miles, only 256 of which were made on the surface. Von Matuschka attributed his success to his skilful use of snorkel and to the difficult ASDIC conditions obtaining in the relatively shallow inshore waters.

Dönitz was so disgusted by the negative results reported by the other boats that he noted in his War Diary that, with the exception of

The Inshore Campaign: The Second Wave
U-Boats dispatched during October 1944

Boat	Sailed	Operational Area	Returned	Ships sunk
U1226	30 Sept 44	English Channel	Sunk	
U300	4 Oct 44	Off Reykjavik	2 Dec 44	3 (7,819)
U483	5 Oct 44	North Channel	21 Nov 44	1 frigate
U246	7 Oct 44	English Channel	11 Nov 44	
U978	9 Oct 44	English Channel	16 Dec 44	1 (7,176)
U1006	9 Oct 44	English Channel	Sunk	
U1003	11 Oct 44	North Channel	16 Dec 44	
U991	18 Oct 44	English Channel	26 Dec 44	
U1200	19 Oct 44	English Channel	Sunk	
U1061	26 Oct 44	Bristol Channel	29 Oct 44	
U1202	30 Oct 44	Bristol Channel	1 Jan 45	1 (7,176)

U482, it was plain that none of the boats had made any determined effort to penetrate the areas of densest traffic, preferring instead to lie stopped at periscope depth away from the busiest shipping lanes, hoping for chance targets and avoiding the intense A/S patrols.

However, the very fact that only three U-boats (15 per cent of the total number involved) had been sunk in the heavily patrolled waters, taken in conjunction with the positive results obtained by *U482*, convinced Dönitz that henceforth the main thrust of the U-boat campaign should be carried out in British coastal waters; reasoning, that provided the boats patrolled close inshore and the commanders acted with the same enterprise as Graf von Matuschka, rich pickings were to be had.

THE INSHORE CAMPAIGN: THE SECOND WAVE

The success of the inshore campaign was compromised from the very beginning by the loss of the Biscay bases. In an endeavour to keep the refit and replenishment periods of the Atlantic U-boats as short as possible, the Germans had, since 1941, accorded priority to the French west coast ports as regards the provision of dockyard personnel, machinery and other equipment, at the expense of U-boat repair facilities in Norway and Germany. As a consequence the repair and refit facilities at Bergen and Trondheim, the only front-line bases now available in western waters, had been fitted to meet the requirements of only thirty medium-sized U-boats. Even with an immediate increase of dockyard personnel, these bases could not cope with more than a third of the U-boats that the Biscay bases had accommodated, and it was found necessary for the rest to use German dockyards. This additional repair and refit work imposed a heavy burden on the already over-stretched German bases, and although the repair of training boats was deferred and additional labour was drafted in – mostly from the U-boat building programme – the repair and refit of *Frontboote* took protracted periods to complete, and drastically cut down the amount of operational time.

This situation was exacerbated by the long time spent by the U-boats on passage from Norway to Germany and back: a one-way trip taking an average of six to eight days, but often longer as a consequence of mines *en route*. For these reasons the *Frontboote* were inactive for more than double the time it had previously taken to refit them in the Biscay bases. Allied bombing raids on Bergen, Trondheim, Kiel and Hamburg, and increased minelaying off the Norwegian bases and in the Baltic Belts, compounded the problem. In comparative terms, whereas in August 1942, during a 100-day period the average U-boat spent 40 days in harbour and 60 at sea, of which 40 were actually spent in the operational area, during the last three months of 1944 a U-boat spent 63 days in harbour and 37 days at sea, of which only nine days were spent in the operational area.

Despite the difficulties, the Senior Officer, U-boats West, Kapitän zur See Rösing, did everything in his power to increase the capacity of the bases in Norway, and to facilitate as rapid a turn-around period as possible for the *Frontboote* involved in the inshore campaign; he expedited the construction at Trondheim and Bergen of new bomb-proof pens, and the enlargement of the existing pens, by drafting in a large number of German technicians and mobilizing local labour. He also attempted to increase the capacity for ordinary servicing by pushing ahead with the expansion of berthing facilities at Stavanger, Farsund, Christiansand and other smaller Norwegian ports. In addition, Rösing set about devising measures to simplify the problem of making rendezvous with local escorts when the U-boats returned from the operational areas. This was an urgent matter because the enemy was concentrating so many aircraft off the Norwegian coast that commanders could not take the risk of surfacing to fix their position. Moreover it was very difficult to identify recognized navigational landmarks on the rugged Norwegian coastline quickly through a periscope, and as a prolonged search along the coast not only invited air attack, but also courted the danger of running on to German defensive minefields, Rösing put in hand work to instal new and more powerful radio beacons at prominent positions on the coast.

His efforts received a setback shortly after daybreak on 4 October 1944, when 47 Lancasters and 93 Halifaxes dropped 603 tons of 1,000lb bombs on Bergen harbour. Seven bombs hit the U-boat pens, causing little structural damage because of the thickness of the concrete roofs, but the electrical wiring system in the pens was wrecked, and nearby repair yards were seriously damaged. Three vessels were sunk in the harbour and eight were damaged, but more importantly *U228* and *U993* were destroyed and *U92* and *U437* were so seriously damaged that they had to be paid off.

Another raid on the night of 28/29 October was carried out by 237 Lancasters, not all of which could bomb because of thick, low-lying cloud covering Bergen. A total of 189 tons of 1,000lb bombs were dropped, none of which hit the U-boat pens, but the dock area was devastated, which reduced repair capacity from thirty to six U-boats for a considerable time.

The inability of the Norwegian bases to deal with a large number of U-boats seriously diminished operational time and the numbers of *Frontboote* sent into British coastal waters up to the end of 1944. During the whole of October only eleven boats were dispatched, six of which were ordered into the English Channel.

U-boats from the first wave had reported a sudden dropping off in the amount of enemy merchant traffic in the North Channel during the second half of September. *B-Dienst*, the radio monitoring and cryptanalytical service, reported similar indications, observing that enemy radio transmissions to the Atlantic convoys had been switched from Liverpool to Land's End since 15 September. Furthermore, a plot was made on a chart to show DF bearings of signals from British warships at sea and it revealed that only a few were centred off the North Channel, but a broad concentration to the south-west of Ireland and in the Bristol Channel and English Channel; the old great circular route between the North Channel and Newfoundland, formerly so well defined, being no longer in evidence.

These indicators convinced BdU that the bulk of the Atlantic convoys had been re-routed from the North Channel and were approaching and leaving British waters to the south of Ireland. Dönitz also suspected that the enemy's strenuous efforts to re-open the captured French Channel ports indicated their intention to send a large amount of the supply traffic from the USA directly into the English Channel to relieve the congestion at Brest. Hence the decision to send more than half the U-boats dispatched during October into the English Channel.

Of the six boats ordered into these waters, three (*U1226, U1006, U1200*) were sunk *en route* and one (*U246*) was so badly damaged during a depth-charge attack by surface craft off the south-west of Ireland on 25 October that she was forced to return to base without reaching the operational area. The two that which reached the English Channel unmolested achieved very little.

The first, *U978* (Kapitänleutnant Günther Pulst) entered the Channel on 2 November and made her way up to her billet north of Cherbourg where she patrolled from 8 to 23 November. She achieved nothing until the end of her 3-week patrol when, on the day she began to withdraw, she attacked a convoy off Pointe de Barfleur and sank the 1,176-ton US liberty ship *William D. Burnham*.

The second boat, *U991*, reached the area on 12 November, and patrolled off Cherbourg from the 17th until the end of the month. She returned to base without having scored a kill although her commander, Kapitänleutnant Diethelm Balke, claimed to have sunk a 14,000-ton freighter on the 27th (a claim based on hearing an end-of-run Gnat detonation).

Of the other five boats dispatched in October, *U1061* was damaged *en route* to the Bristol Channel and had to return to base, but three of the remaining four boats that reached their operational areas scored kills. At 0220 on 1 November, *U483* torpedoed the RN frigate

Whitaker, which was escorting a small local convoy to the north of Lough Swilly. The Gnat detonated against her forward magazine which exploded, destroying the entire bow section forward of the bridge: 92 officers and men were killed. The frigate remained afloat and was eventually towed into Belfast, but was declared a total constructional loss. Evading the subsequent hunt, *U483* left the North Channel on the 4 November to return to Norway. On 1 November she had been joined in the North Channel by *U1003* which remained in the area until the 30th, sighting no targets and suffering no attacks during the entire month of her patrol.

U300 arrived off Reykjavik in Iceland on 22 October. Her commander, Oberleutnant Fritz Hein, sighted only small single ships and coastal fishing craft, none of which was worth a torpedo, until 10 November when he attacked a convoy and sank the 1,542-ton Icelandic freighter *Godafoss*, the 6,017-ton British freighter *Shirvan* and the 260-ton tug *Empire World*. *U300* remained in the area unmolested until the 22nd, but Hein was presented with no further targets.

U1202 rounded Cape Clear at the end of November and entered the Bristol Channel on 1 December. She patrolled off Milford Haven for ten days during which she fired torpedoes at, but missed, three independently routed merchant ships. On the 10th, as she prepared to return to base, she attacked a convoy off St. David's Head and sank the 7,176-ton US liberty ship *Dan Beard*.

STRATEGIC AND TACTICAL ASSESSMENT

From its inception in the middle of August until the second week of December, the inshore campaign had yielded only eight freighters grossing 53,522 tons, two warships and a tug, at a cost of six U-boats. Nevertheless BdU was impressed by the results, as Günther Hessler, one of BdU's staff officers, explains:

'... to our surprise a survey of operations ... showed, not only that the old-type boats were again capable of achieving results, but that losses had sharply decreased at the same time. Their effectiveness while actually in the operational area and measured in tonnage sunk per U-boat per day was exactly equal to the figure for August 1942.'[1]

But this calculation was little more than wishful thinking, for expressed another way the comparison did not bear out BdU's optimism. In the single month of August 1942, U-boats in the Atlantic theatre accounted for 105 ships grossing 540,765 tons for the loss of nine boats; in the inshore campaign, the U-boats, during a period of almost four months, had sunk only nine merchant ships grossing 53,522 tons for the loss of six boats: a ratio of 11.66 ships per U-boat lost for August 1942, compared to 1.5 merchant ships per U-boat lost for the period mid-August to mid-December 1944. BdU's confidence was also buoyed up by the fact that only six U-boats had been lost in the coastal operations:

'... it might have been expected that, with large numbers of snorkel boats working in difficult areas, losses would increase; but this was not the case. On the contrary, losses were down to the 1942 level, a fact which provided fresh and, perhaps, the most striking proof of the inestimable worth of the snorkel ... This changed situation not only gave the crews of the old-type conventional boats new faith in their weapons, but also showed that the new type Electro-boats, with their high submerged speed and endurance, had been rightly conceived and promised great achievements.'[2]

The relative immunity of the boats operating in coastal waters was not solely attributable to snorkel. By the autumn of 1944 the Germans had devised a method of fixing their radar detection aerials to the snorkel head (previously they had been fixed to the conning tower and were only effective when the boat was surfaced). When a snorkel head was exposed above water it gave the enemy a radar echo of only one-eighth of the strength produced by a surfaced U-boat, and could, therefore, only be located from the air at very short range, when the aircraft's radar emissions would also be picked up by the search receiver. Thus, with the aid of her search receiver and periscope, which had to be manned while snorkelling, a U-boat was reasonably certain of observing an attacking aircraft, by day or night, in time to dive to a safe depth before the aircraft could release its depth-charges or bombs. The combined effectiveness of snorkel plus radar search and detection aerials fitted to the snorkel head is borne out by the fact that none of the six U-boats lost in the inshore campaign had been accounted for by aircraft.

'By mid-December the U-boat campaign had gradually changed since August 1944 into a condition of stalemate in the inshore operational areas. Both sides had made technical advances which tended to cancel each other out. The U-boats had adopted the snorkel and possessed an efficient search receiver which together nullified the improved airborne radar carried by aircraft [ASV Mk III/H$_2$S] and the increased concentration on flying A/S patrols. Snorkel was, undoubtedly, the ace of trumps against visual and radar location except in flat calm weather.

'The centimetric ASV radar carried by Allied aircraft was excellent against surfaced U-boats. It gave positive and unmistakable indications at ranges up to 15 miles. There were, therefore, few suspicious or disappearing radar contacts during the first eight months of 1944. By September, however, all U-boats were becoming expert at snorkelling in seas up to State 5 or 6 on the Beaufort scale. Even in calmer weather the snorkel head gave far less definite echoes and of course at shorter ranges than any surfaced U-boat. Moreover, these contacts were indistinguishable from those coming from flotsam such as casks, crates, oil drums, etc., and the more momentary echoes off prominent wave tops, whales spouting or even porpoises leaping. Many of the echoes disappeared off the ASV reception screen, due to some of the above natural reasons, as the aircraft homed towards them, but could give rise to a suspicion that a U-boat had detected the ASV impulse and had dived. On many occasions aircraft used sono-buoys to verify suspicious contacts. These, in the hands of any but very experienced listeners, produced another crop of dubious reports on the supposed presence of submerged U-boats because the natural sea noises so often occasioned wishful thinking ...

'In fact, the aircraft had descended from its exalted position of "U-boat Killer No. 1" to the humble yet useful role of scarecrow to ensure the continual submergence of U-boats while at sea and consequent lack of mobility. Some of the above remarks applied equally to the surface craft when they were employed solely on blocking patrols and unrelated to convoys. U-boats had by the end of 1944 become almost immune from detection or attack while on passage to and from the British Isles. When they reached their inshore operating areas they could exist for lengthy periods without molestation as long as they committed no hostile act. It was only when they attacked and hit a target that surface craft were provided with a datum point for an immediate retributive hunt and counter-attack.'[3]

Another factor in the U-boats' favour was the nature of the operational area. Experience proved that when a U-boat in coastal waters was detected by surface A/S patrols, it stood a better chance of evasion by heading into shallow inshore waters than by trying to escape into the open sea. This was because the rocks and wrecks which littered the coast produced false ASDIC echoes, while the tide-rips and density layers deflected the ASDIC beam and restricted hydrophone performance. For these reasons BdU continually impressed upon the U-boat commanders the need to make for shallow water, rather than deep water, after attacking a convoy off the British coast.,

However, although the poor ASDIC and hydrophone conditions afforded considerable protection to the U-boats, they also had their disadvantages. On several occasions boats lying bottomed, or proceeding at depths of 100–130 feet, were passed over by individual ships or whole convoys whose propeller noises had not been detected by the U-boats' hydrophones until they were directly overhead, too late for an attack. When BdU was made aware of this he ordered commanders operating in coastal waters to remain at periscope depth during the day, and to refrain from going deeper unless they found a water layer in which hydrophone range was likely to exceed optical visibility through the periscope.

The Allied ability to read BdU's Enigma 'Triton' key had been a decisive factor in defeating the U-boats in the Battle of the Atlantic, but during the inshore campaign the volume of Enigma decrypts relating to U-boat movements began to decline quite markedly. The reasons are explained by Professor Hinsley:

'The accuracy of the OIC's U-boat Tracking Room [began] to decline as the tactical conditions of the offensive in inshore water and other developments brought about a change in the enemy's wireless habits, which added to the difficulties produced by his increasing experience of operating snorkel ... As well as moving to and from their patrol areas in a state of total submergence, thus greatly reducing the number of Allied sightings, the U-boats were doing so at differing speeds; and this made it impossible for the Tracking Room to judge their current whereabouts by extrapolating from such sightings as were made or from such intelligence as the decrypts had provided. On the 30th October the OIC gave this as the main reason why its plot, which was relied on for all convoy escort flying and much of the patrol flying carried out by the Allies, did not succeed at all closely in reproducing the reality. To make matters worse, the volume of Sigint [Signal Intelligence] about U-boat movements itself was declining. For a number of reasons – the fact that the U-boats were now normally operating singly; the fact that they were so often submerged, the loss of so many shore W/T stations [in France and Belgium] in Germany's retreat – the U-boat Command discontinued its long-established practice of signalling sailing orders and patrol instructions to U-boats while they were at sea. Increasingly, the signals sent to them merely supplemented or modified orders given in advance and known only to the U-boat concerned; and from early in December, in a further refinement of the process, the signals were increasingly enciphered in *Sonderschlüssel* [keys restricted to a single U-boat and unreadable to the Allies] instead of in the general U-boat Enigma key.'[4]

The settings of the *Sonderschlüssel* (lit. special key) Enigma were different for each individual U-boat, and the succinct nature and paucity of the signals sent to and by an individual boat did not provide the cryptanalysts at Bletchley Park with enough intercepted material to break the settings by analytical means. This was a severe blow to the Allies, who had derived such a wealth of vital intelligence from the 'Triton' key; for from early December 1944 until the end of the war, the indecipherable *Sonderschlüssel* carried practically all BdU's operational traffic regarding departure times and dates for U-boats involved in the inshore campaign, and the operational areas for which they were bound.

THE INSHORE CAMPAIGN: THE THIRD WAVE

The 53,522 tons of merchant shipping sunk during the inshore campaign up to the middle of December 1944, was hardly of war-winning potential, but the *raison d'être* of the campaign was not based on this criteria, as Dönitz explained:

'... every ship, laden with war *matériel* ultimately bound for France or for the Scheldt estuary, which we could sink off the English coast, lightened the burden of our struggle ashore. Furthermore, there was, still, the employment of our U-boats to tie down enemy light forces in their coastal waters and thus prevent them from becoming free to attack our own coastal shipping in the North Sea, the Skaggerak and off the long stretch of the coast of Norway ... for instance, an unbroken stream of transports carrying troops for the reinforcement of our fronts on the borders of Germany had been flowing through all these waters.'[5]

In this respect the campaign was highly successful, for to deal with the problem the Allies concentrated a large number of surface escort groups in home waters to provide every convoy approaching or leaving British ports with a powerful close escort, while one or more support groups trailed the convoys or patrolled the busiest waters continuously. By the end of 1944, 426 escort vessels of all types and 420 Coastal Command aircraft were deployed on these duties.

However, this great concentration of A/S forces dealt a severe blow to the thirteen U-boats of the third wave which put to sea from the Norwegian bases during November 1944.

Of the three boats dispatched to St. George's Channel only one survived. *U322* was sighted while snorkelling to the west of the Faeroes/Shetlands Channel on 25 November, by a Sunderland of No. 330 Squadron. The aircraft directed the RN frigate *Ascension* to the area which, at 0300, after a short hunt, destroyed *U322* with her 'Hedgehog' (a ripple-firing multiple spigot mortar which threw a spread of 24 projectiles forward over the bows).

On 17 December, while rounding Cape Clear on her way to the operational area, *U400* attacked a convoy without success and was sunk in the subsequent counter-attack by the frigate *Nyasaland*. *U979*, the only boat of this trio to survive, was prevented from making any attacks on the large amount of traffic plying the St. George's Channel by the strong A/S forces patrolling the area, and she returned to Norway on 16 January without having made a single attack.

Only one boat was sent into the North Channel. This was *U482* (Kapitänleutnant Graf von Matuschka) which arrived in her operational area on 1 December, but sighted no targets until the 16th. On the morning of that day Matuschka torpedoed and damaged the 7,429-ton Norwegian tanker *Spinanger* in the entrance to the Firth of Clyde, and shortly afterwards torpedoed the 8,300-ton escort-carrier HMS *Thane* which was towed into the Clyde but declared a constructional loss. While withdrawing to seaward after these attacks, Matuschka paid the penalty for his boldness when *U482* ran into a patrol group and was destroyed by a hail of depth-charges sent down from a frigate and four sloops.

Both boats dispatched to the North Minch area, *U296* and *U775*, which they reached on 14 and 25 November respectively, survived but achieved little. *U296* began her passage back to base on 10 December, reporting no kills and no attacks made on her. *U775* achieved nothing until daybreak on 6 December when she sighted three warships about ten miles north-east of Cape Wrath. After torpedoing and damaging the leading frigate, HMS *Bullen*, she was subjected to a counter-attack by the other two frigates of the group, *Loch Insh* and *Goodall*, which hunted her for fourteen hours before they lost ASDIC contact, allowing the U-boat to escape and return to base.

Five boats were ordered to operate in the central waters of the English Channel but only four reached the area, one being sunk *en route*. On 18 December, as the result of a navigational error, *U1209* foundered, having collided with the Wolf Rock while running submerged. Two boats, *U680* and *U485*, achieved nothing, but *U486* and *U772* scored the only kills of the thirteen boats dispatched during November.

Shortly after entering the Channel, Oberleutnant Gerhard Meyer, commander of *U486*, attacked a convoy off Falmouth on 18

The Inshore Campaign: The Third Wave
U-Boats dispatched during November 1944

Boat	Sailed	Operational Area	Returned	Ships sunk
U296	4 Nov 44	North Minch	25 Dec 44	
U979	9 Nov 44	Irish Sea	16 Jan 45	
U680	13 Nov 44	English Channel	18 Jan 45	
U322	16 Nov 44	Irish Sea	Sunk	
U482	18 Nov 44	North Channel	Sunk	1 escort-carrier
U775	18 Nov 44	North Minch	22 Dec 44	
U400	18 Nov 44	Irish Sea	Sunk	
U772	19 Nov 44	English Channel	Sunk	4 (21,053)
U1209	24 Nov 44	English Channel	Sunk	
U1020	24 Nov 44	Orkneys	Sunk	
U297	26 Nov 44	Orkneys	Sunk	
U486	28 Nov 44	English Channel	15 Jan 45	2 (17,651)
U485	29 Nov 44	English Channel	2 Feb 45	

December and sank the 6,142-ton British freighter *Silver Laurel*. After working his way up the Channel undetected, Meyer attacked another convoy off Cherbourg on Christmas Eve, sinking the 11,509-ton troop-ship *Leopoldville* which took more than 800 American soldiers down with her. Two days later Meyer capped his success by attacking a third convoy, damaging the RN frigates *Capel* and *Affleck* with one spread of torpedoes, surviving the counter-attack to reach base on 15 January.

Oberleutnant Hans Reimers, commanding *U772*, was equally enterprising. At 0943 on 23 December he sank the 1,536-ton British freighter *Slemish* off Cherbourg, and two hours later he accounted for the 5,149-ton British freighter *Dumfries* south of the Isle of Wight. Remaining undetected in the central Channel for another five days, Reimers sank the 7,177-ton transport *Empire Javelin* at 1536 on 28 December. While withdrawing from the Channel next day, Reimers struck again at a convoy off Portland Bill, sinking the 7,191-ton liberty ship *Black Hawk* and damaging the liberty ship *Arthur Sewall*. While withdrawing from this attack *U772*'s periscope was sighted by a Wellington of No. 407 Squadron which destroyed the U-boat with a well-placed stick of bombs.

Two boats from the third wave, *U297* and *U1020*, were sent to a new area of the inshore campaign. BdU had decided to take action against the British aircraft carrier forces which were continually attacking German merchant shipping off the west coast of Norway. Dönitz's intention was to intercept the carriers as they set out from or returned

The Inshore Campaign: The Fourth Wave
U-Boats dispatched during December 1944

Boat	Sailed	Operational Area	Returned	Ships sunk
U650	9 Dec 44	English Channel	Sunk	
U325	11 Dec 44	English Channel	14 Feb 45	
U905	11 Dec 44	English Channel	1 Feb 45	
U1009	11 Dec 44	North Channel	8 Feb 45	
U1055	11 Dec 44	Irish Sea	8 Feb 45	3 (11,232)
U312	13 Dec 44	Orkneys	3 Jan 45	
U285	20 Dec 44	Irish Sea	31 Jan 45	
U1172	23 Dec 44	Irish Sea	Sunk	1 (1,599)
U313	23 Dec 44	Orkneys	15 Feb 45	
U278	24 Dec 44	Orkneys	11 Feb 45	
U315	25 Dec 44	Orkneys	6 Jan 45	
U764	26 Dec 44	English Channel	10 Feb 45	
U825	29 Dec 44	Irish Sea	18 Feb 45	1 (8,262)
U1051	29 Dec 44	Irish Sea	Sunk	1 (1,152)
U1017	29 Dec 44	English Channel	28 Feb 45	1 (5,222)

to Scapa Flow. To this end *U297* and *U1020* were detailed to billets off the islands of Hoy and Ronaldsay respectively.

U297 approached Hoy from the west and had reached a position to the north-east of Cape Wrath in the early hours of 6 December, when she ran full tilt into the frigates searching for *U775*. A depth-charge attack by HMSS *Goodall* and *Loch Insh* brought a lot of oil, splintered woodwork and other wreckage to the surface, marking the end of *U297* and her entire crew.

U1020 approached the Orkneys from the east, and patrolled off the Pentland Firth from 7 December until the end of the month. Sighting nothing, she began moving south on New Year's Eve to seek targets off the Moray Firth, where she ran into a minefield and disappeared with all hands.

The loss of seven U-boats for the sinking of six freighters and an escort-carrier was not encouraging for the Germans' close investment policy, but BdU continued to persevere, pending the confidently expected readiness of the Type XXI and Type XXIII Electro-boats.

THE INSHORE CAMPAIGN: THE FOURTH WAVE

The loss rate among the U-boats dispatched during December 1944 fell back to the level of the first two waves; and the exchange rate of 2.3 ships per U-boat lost was far more sustainable than the third wave exchange rate of one ship per U-boat lost.

BdU hoped for outstanding results from the five boats sent in December to the Irish Sea, the southern sector of which was now the main transit area since the convoys had been diverted from the old North Channel route. And, although the results obtained in this area proved to be far from outstanding, four of the five boats operating achieved the only kills of the fifteen fourth-wave boats.

The first was made by *U1055* which attacked a convoy to the west-south-west of St. David's Head at 1730 on 9 January 1945 and sank the 7,198-ton American freighter *Jones Lie*, afterwards getting away to the north undetected. Two days later *U1055* struck again, sinking the 1,428-ton British freighter *Normandy Coast* and the 2,606-ton US auxiliary *Roanoke* off Holyhead at 1520 and 1536 respectively (both ships had been independently routed). At 1703 next day (12 January) a Liberator made a firm radar contact on the snorkel mast of *U1055* while she was snorkelling to the west of Holyhead. The Liberator attacked with depth-charges, but the U-boat dived in time to escape damage and lived to torpedo and damage the 8,181-ton British oil-tanker *Maja* at 1214 on 15 January, 25 miles south-west of the Isle of Man.

The next boat to reach the area was *U1051* which made her presence known by sinking the independently routed 1,152-ton Norwegian freighter *Galatea* on 20 January, some 25 miles south-west of Bardsey Island in Cardigan Bay. Seven days later, at noon on the 27th, *U1051*, in company with *U825*, attacked a convoy 27 miles south-west of Bardsey Island, and although *U1051* missed with her torpedoes, *U825* sank the 8,262-ton Norwegian oil-tanker *Solar* and damaged the US freighter *Ruben Dario*. After unsuccessful counter-attacks by the close escort, two support groups took up the hunt, severely damaging *U825*, which none the less managed to escape, and, some eight hours later, destroying *U1051* in the early hours of 28 January.

The fourth boat to reach the Irish Sea was *U1172* which on 23 January sank the 1,599-ton Norwegian freighter *Vigsnes* in Liverpool Bay, soon after she had broken away from a local convoy. *U1172* was then rash enough to attack the frigate HMS *Manners* on 26 January south-west of the Isle of Man. Although she hit and damaged the frigate, the attack invited the attention of two nearby escort groups which plastered the luckless U-boat with depth-charges and sent her to her watery doom.

Only four of the five boats ordered into the English Channel reached the area (*U650* disappeared without trace *en route*), and only one of these, *U1017*, made an attack on a convoy, damaging the 5,222-ton British freighter *Everleigh* on 6 February, south-west of the Needles. *U1017* escaped the counter-attack by the escorts and began her homeward passage.

The single boat sent into the North Channel, *U1009*, patrolled for five days off Lough Swilly but achieved nothing. The four boats ordered by BdU to attack the carrier forces based in Scapa Flow sighted nothing, and *U312* damaged her rudder after grounding while trying to enter the Flow through Hoxa Sound.

By the end of the fourth-wave operations, the inshore campaign had arrived at a stalemate. The U-boats were doing only superficial damage to Allied seaborne trade, but conversely the losses that Allied A/S forces were inflicting on the U-boats was insufficient to drive them away from British coastal waters. But Dönitz's assessment of the results remained optimistic:

'We were entitled to assume that the U-boat war would enter a new phase. Considerable successes had already been achieved by the old types of boats fitted with snorkel on operations of long duration without needing to surface at all. The strain on crews who remained submerged up to 70 days was surprisingly small. Thanks to the snorkel the air remained fresh during underwater cruising and considerably better than in former circumstances. But the most important reduction in strain came from the removal of the continual nervous tension in U-boat crews caused by the earlier danger of surprise air attack. The Type

Approx Positions of
U-boats Lost In The
Inshore Campaign
August 1944 - May 1945

XXI [Electro-boat] with its range of 22,000 miles, was capable of scouring all waters of importance to the U-boat war without once having to surface. It was obvious that this would bring about a change in the naval war. Hitherto control of the sea by the great sea powers had been exercised through surface craft supported by aircraft; a warship whose primary operational sphere lies beneath the surface renders such control of the sea largely impossible. If, in addition, such a warship has a high underwater speed, making it easier to approach the enemy, it would obviously be a very valuable instrument of war.'[6]

Dönitz's optimism was matched by Allied chagrin. An OIC appreciation warned that, 'Reliable evidence over a period of months indicates that Dönitz intends launching an all-out U-boat campaign in the near future, and in full confidence that improved radar devices, snorkel and the new types of [Electro] U-boats ... will regain the ascendency the U-boats enjoyed in 1942.'[7] This threat caused the OIC to conclude that even 'partial success will hamper the maintenance of our forces in Europe and a major success might halt our offensive indefinitely and certainly prolong the war as well as acting as a violent stimulant to German morale.'[8]

German optimism and Allied anxiety were well founded – the first of the Electro-boats were rapidly approaching full operational status.

FAR-DISTANT WATERS

Not all the U-boats operating in the autumn and winter months of 1944 were involved in the inshore campaign. A number of the large 1,200-ton Type IX boats made appearances in Atlantic waters remote from the British Isles during these months, although some of them had sailed from French, Norwegian and German bases back in May. All told, BdU dispatched 22 U-boats from 1 May to 4 October 1944, to operate in the Caribbean, off the Atlantic coastlines of Africa, Canada and the USA, and in the approaches to Gibraltar.

The amount of shipping these boats accounted for was small (eleven merchant ships grossing 51,352 tons, plus a frigate and a minesweeper), but their spasmodic appearances in far-distant Atlantic waters caused the Allies an expenditure of effort which was wholly disproportionate to their numbers.

Not only did these far-roaming U-boats force the Allies to continue to sail the vast majority of their ocean-going merchant ships in escorted convoys, but they also tied down seventeen hunter-killer groups, composed of escort-carriers, destroyers and frigates, which ranged the central Atlantic searching for the elusive marauders.

Up to December 1944, when the *Sonderschlüssel* settings were introduced, the Allies were fairly well informed from 'Triton' decrypts of the departure and return of these U-boats and, usually, the general areas in which they were to operate. But because the boats were operating individually, their positions on passage or within their operational areas was only revealed if they received new orders after sailing, and as this was a rare occurrence Enigma decrypts only contributed to the sinking of one of the three boats lost. This was *U1229* which was engaged on a mission to land German agents near Maine. A number of decrypts allowed the Allies to track this boat and bring her to book south of Newfoundland on 20 August, when she was sunk by aircraft from the US escort-carrier *Bogue*.

In addition, from 4 June to 3 November BdU sent eleven U-boats (mostly medium-sized Type VIIs) into the North Atlantic on weather reporting duties. The Germans attached considerable importance to the meteorological information transmitted by these boats, two or three of which were normally kept on station. For instance, the timing of von Rundstedt's Ardennes offensive, which began on 16 December 1944, was decided on the strength of the U-boats' reports of weather fronts moving in off the Atlantic. Despite their frequent use of

U-Boats Dispatched to Remote Atlantic Waters
From May until the end of 1944

Boat	Sailed	Operational Area	Returned	Ships sunk
U539	1 May 44	Caribbean	17 Sept 44	1 (1,517)
U516	7 May 44	Caribbean	1 Oct 44	1 (9,887)
U107	10 May 44	Off Nova Scotia	22 July 44	
U530	22 May 44	Caribbean	1 Oct 44	
U233	27 May 44	Off Nova Scotia	Sunk	
U546	25 June 44	Off West Africa	6 Nov 44	
U518	15 July 44	US seaboard	22 Oct 44	
U802	16 July 44	Off Nova Scotia	12 Nov 44	
U1229	26 July 44	US seaboard	Sunk	
U170	4 Aug 44	Off West Africa	30 Nov 44	
U541	6 Aug 44	Off Nova Scotia	6 Nov 44	1 (2,140)
U1221	20 Aug 44	Off Nova Scotia	26 Nov 44	
U1223	28 Aug 44	Off Nova Scotia	14 Dec 44	
U1227	31 Aug 44	Off Gibraltar	26 Dec 44	1 frigate
U300	4 Oct 44	Off Gibraltar	2 Dec 44	3 (7,819)
U1230	8 Oct 44	Off Newfoundland	Jan 45	1 (5,458)
U1228	12 Oct 44	Off Newfoundland	28 Dec 44	
U1231	15 Oct 44	Off Newfoundland	30 Jan 45	
U806	30 Oct 44	Off Nova Scotia	21 Feb 45	1 mine-sweeper
U1232	12 Nov 44	Off Nova Scotia	14 Feb 45	4 (24,531)
U869	8 Dec 44	Off Gibraltar	Sunk	
U1233	24 Dec 44	US seaboard	28 Mar 45	

radio, the Allies found these scattered boats difficult to locate, and only three of the eleven were sunk: *U877* by surface escorts when a convoy happened to pass over her position on 27 December. None of these 'weather' boats scored any kills.

The most successful of the U-boats dispatched to distant waters were the thirteen boats (mostly 1,600-ton *U-Kreutzer*) dispatched to the Indian Ocean from 19 February to 23 August 1944, to join up with five already based at Penang (a Japanese-held base on the west coast of Malaya). *En route* down the length of the Atlantic, four of these *U-Kreutzer* sank five merchant ships grossing 29,372 tons. Added to the twenty merchantmen grossing 126,557 tons which they subsequently sank in the Indian Ocean, this brought their total kills to 25 ships grossing 155,929 tons during the 9-month period May 1944 to January 1945. This was achieved at a cost of seven U-boats lost: an exchange ratio of 3.28 ships per U-boat lost.

SCHNELLBOOTE OPERATIONS:
SEPTEMBER-DECEMBER 1944

Contemporaneous with the U-boat campaign in inshore waters were operations carried out by *Schnellboote* in the southern sector of the North Sea. At the end of August the S-boat flotillas had been withdrawn from the French and Belgian ports to Dutch harbours where they arrived on 5 September. Next day the two remaining boats of 2nd Flotilla proceeded to Wilhelmshaven for refitting, while 6th Flotilla was transferred back to the Baltic, where its boats were handed over to the S-boat Training Division. This left thirteen operational boats in the west which were deployed in three flotillas:

Ijmuiden	8th Flotilla	5 boats
Rotterdam	9th Flotilla	3 boats
Amsterdam	10th Flotilla	5 boats

These boats put out from the Dutch ports on minelaying and torpedo-attack sorties off the coasts of Flanders and Norfolk. Undisturbed sorties to the former took place after dark on 8 and 10 September, but when ten S-boats set out on the night of 11/12 September on a combined torpedo and mining operation off Cromer, they were detected shortly after leaving harbour by Wellingtons of No. 524 Squadron and Avengers of No. 885 FAA Squadron. Although the aircraft scored no hits with their bombs, surprise was lost and the Germans abandoned the sortie.

Another attempt was carried out on the night of 16/17 September when nine S-boats from 9th and 10th Flotillas left Ijmuiden

172

to lay mines off Cromer and carry out a torpedo attack on a north-bound convoy in the area. The boats sailed in three groups, one group having to return to harbour because one boat developed a rudder defect. The other two groups laid their mines, but were attacked by aircraft and chased off by a destroyer before they could begin searching for the convoy.

These abortive attempts to attack enemy shipping with torpedoes caused *Führer der Schnellboote*, Kommodore Petersen, to complain that:

'It was my endeavour primarily, to use every opportunity offered by the weather to carry out offensive operations with torpedo and mine against the British south-east coast convoy traffic. Only once, however, did an opportunity occur, and even then the weather was against us. On this occasion it could be seen that the enemy, having his Air Force free from ties on the Atlantic and Channel coasts, uses concentrated forces to watch every movement of our ships in the Hoofden ports, from the moment they pass the pier-head. In practice, therefore, the least possibility of a surprise attack by an undetected S-boat advance into the operational area is lost to us, S-boat freedom of movement having been considerably decreased by enemy coastal and ship-borne radar, more intensive control of the coastal area, and convoy escort activity; these causes have therefore lessened our chances of success. I have been repeatedly forced to point out the necessity for the use of air co-operation over the sea; for a planned use of night-fighters against the British night reconnaissance aircraft; further support for S-boat attacks on enemy convoys by the rendering of reliable reconnaissance reports, and last but not least, offensive action over the sea by the Luftwaffe. This would force the enemy to concentrate his convoy defence *not solely against S-boats* as has long been the case, but would also bring the necessary relief to our S-boats, and an increase in the prospects of success with an augmented S-boat arm.'[9]

This was the nub of the problem that was to dog S-boat operations from the Dutch ports until the end of the war. Allied air superiority allowed them to fly constant patrols over the S-boat bases, while the hard-pressed Luftwaffe could not spare aircraft from the defence of Germany to fight off the Allied reconnaissance aircraft or co-operate in S-boat operations against British coastal traffic.

To add to FdS's problems, the landing of Allied airborne troops at Arnhem took place on 17 September, causing the *Seekriegsleitung* (Naval War Staff) to panic and order the immediate destruction of the ports of Rotterdam, Ijmuiden and Amsterdam, close on the left flank of the airborne forces, and which they feared would be quickly overrun. FdS was aghast, and his urgent representations that the destruction of these ports would mean the end of all defensive and offensive S-boat operations in the area, caused a reconsideration and finally a rescission of the order. But as a precaution FdS shifted his headquarters from Scheveningen to Dan Helder, seventy miles to the north.

The effects of enemy air patrols were felt during the next operation by the S-boats. On the night of 18/19 September, four boats successfully ran deck cargoes of stores to the besieged German garrison at Dunkirk, and returned unopposed to the Hook of Holland with General von Klug and his staff. But three other boats (*S163*, *S200*, *S702*) which covered the operation to seaward, were sighted by aircraft and brought to action 35 miles north-west of Dunkirk by the frigate HMS *Stayner* and two MTBs. All three S-boats were sunk, but 67 survivors, including the senior officer of 10th Flotilla, Kapitänleutnant Müller, were rescued from the sea by the British warships. No further S-boat operations took place during September, mainly because of bad weather.

By 1 October, S-boat strength in the Dutch ports had been reduced to nine boats, and their primary task was changed to laying mines in the West Scheldt estuary and its approaches. This strategic shift of priorities was occasioned by Allied attempts to clear German forces from the south and north banks of the Scheldt, with the object of opening Antwerp as a port of disembarkation for military supplies for the Allied offensive into western Germany.

To this end eight S-boats put out after dark on 4 October to lay mines off the Scheldt. But in bright moonlight they were quickly located by five Avengers of No. 855 Squadron, and although they escaped the attack unscathed the boats were forced to abandon the sortie.

Reinforcements to the slender S-boat force began arriving on 5 October, and by the 10th refitted boats from Germany had brought the number up to twenty. After dark on 10 October, fourteen of these boats put to sea and, thanks to low-lying cloud, managed to lay 56 mines in the Scheldt approaches undetected by Allied aircraft. Atrocious weather prevented further operations until the end of the month, by which time 4th Flotilla had been withdrawn to Germany for refitting, which reduced the total strength in Dutch ports to fifteen boats.

When the Allies took possession of the south bank of the West Scheldt during the third week of October, FdS switched his operational priority to combined minelaying and torpedo-attacks against Allied supply traffic plying the Thames-Ostend route. The first of the operations directed against this traffic took place on the night of 29/30 October when seven boats set out from Ijmuiden to lay mines off Ostend. But as they cleared the harbour entrance they ran into a 7-strong group of MTBs, and after a short engagement in which *S191* was damaged, the operation was broken off and the boats beat a hasty retreat to harbour. The next attempt, on the following night, was more successful. A moonless, stormy night veiled the departure of seven boats from Ijmuiden, and *en route* they avoided several destroyer and MTB patrols. Divided into two groups, they laid two fields of twenty and fifteen mines in the buoyed route off Ostend, which subsequently accounted for a tank landing craft (*LCT 420*).

Scarcely had the boats returned to harbour after this nocturnal sortie when they were ordered to sea again, to attack an Allied assault fleet, 181 vessels strong, which had begun landing troops at 0545 on the island of Walcheren, situated between the estuaries of the West and East Scheldt. A total of eleven S-boats put out to launch torpedo attacks on the mass of assault craft, but five of them had to return to Ijmuiden with engine defects. Four of the remaining boats managed to launch attacks, sinking a small tanker and an armed trawler with their torpedoes before they were driven off by a group of MTBs. A second attempt was carried out that night. Three boats from 9th Flotilla fired torpedoes at the battleship *Warspite* which was bombarding the German shore batteries on Walcheren. All the torpedoes missed the battleship and exploded harmlessly on the beach. Four boats from 8th Flotilla made an unsuccessful attack on a destroyer and were driven off by fighter-bombers; while three boats from 10th Flotilla were sighted and shadowed by aircraft as they cleared Ijmuiden and were driven back to port by a group of MTBs.

So few boats pitted against such a large assault fleet could not have hoped to prevent the landings on Walcheren, and the occupation of the island finally allowed the Allies to open Antwerp to supply convoys. The sweeping of the 80-mile-long West Scheldt approach to Antwerp began on 4 November, and by the beginning of December some 18,000 tons of supplies a week were passing through the port. Gales and boat maintenance prevented any further operations by the S-boats until the night of 15/16 November, when five boats laid mines off the mouth of the Humber unopposed, while six boats operated in the Scheldt approaches where they were engaged by two groups of MTBs. During the brief but violent engagement, *S168* was set on fire forward, but managed to regain port, and one MTB was damaged.

Two weeks later, on the night of 29/30 November, five boats laid eighteen mines in the Scheldt approaches; three boats laid fifteen mines off Dunkirk; while five boats carried out a torpedo attack on a convoy plying the Thames-Scheldt route, firing three Gnat acoustic-homing torpedoes and 7 FAT pattern-running torpedoes, none of which found a target. All three groups of S-boats were engaged by aircraft, destroyers and MTBs, but all the boats regained port undamaged.

Bad weather again halted operations, but when conditions began to moderate Bomber Command struck first in anticipation of the renewal of S-boat activity. On 15 December, fourteen Lancasters attacked the S-boat shelter at Ijmuiden. Two 12,000lb Tallboys penetrated the roof of the shelter, destroying *S198* and damaging six other boats. The entire S-boat maintenance arrangements were disorganized, six pens were rendered unusable, and one boat was trapped in a pen by debris. In his War Diary Kommodore Petersen lamented that:

'This event brings the bitter knowledge that the S-boat shelters in Rotterdam and Ijmuiden in their present form no longer afford protection against bombing and have accordingly lost their purpose. I have therefore decided not to fill the pens with S-boats any longer, in view of the character of these shelters as special targets. The S-boats will be, henceforth, dispersed in the harbours, even at the expense of other advantages. This measure is not an ideal solution, and may be subject to alteration under certain circumstances, according to air situations or the tactics of enemy day fighter-bombers.'[10]

To replace the damaged boats, all of which belonged to 8th Flotilla, eight boats of 2nd Flotilla were immediately transferred from Germany to Den Helder, and together with boats from the two Rotterdam flotillas (9th & 10th) they carried out minelaying sorties off the Flanders coast during the nights of 18/19, 22/23 and 24/25 December. Unsuccessful aircraft attacks were made on the boats during each of these sorties, but destroyers, frigates and MTBs summoned by shadowing aircraft on the night of the 22nd/23rd resulted in the sinking of *S185* off Dunkirk and *S192* off Ostend.

The year ended for the S-boat crews with another visit from Bomber Command. On 29 December sixteen Lancasters attacked the S-boat shelters at Rotterdam. A great deal of structural damage was done to the shelters, but, profiting from the experience at Ijmuiden, the S-boats had been well dispersed around the docks and all escaped damage.

During the last four months of 1944, the Hoofden *Schnellboote* lost six of their number, but in return they sank one tanker and an armed trawler with torpedoes, and a tank landing craft, a minelayer and one freighter of 7,000 tons came to grief on the minefields they had sown off the Flanders and Norfolk coasts and in the Scheldt estuary. An effort that did not affect the strategic situation one iota.

K-VERBAND OPERATIONS:
SEPTEMBER-DECEMBER 1944

After the K-Verband fiasco in the Normandy invasion area, there had been a lull in Small Battle Unit operations in northern Europe until early in October, when 62 *Linsen* arrived at the Dutch port of Flushing.

On the night of 5/6 October the entire flotilla set out to attack Allied minesweepers operating off the Flanders coast, but, like all previous K-Verband operations, it ended in fiasco. Two *Linsen* were sunk by German harbour-defence craft as they put to sea from Flushing, and the remainder ran into rapidly deteriorating weather and rising seas; fourteen were driven ashore and twenty foundered in the storm. Twenty-six, all badly damaged by the heavy seas, managed to struggle back to harbour, but later in the day, when they were being withdrawn to Rotterdam, two more were destroyed by fighter-bombers.

Another flotilla of 60 *Linsen* was sent to Groningen in northern Holland, where they arrived on 12 October, and were moved down to Rotterdam two days later. On the 22nd, 28 of them were transported to Flushing by barges and they set out that night to attack Allied shipping off the Flanders coast. On leaving harbour they were scattered by gunfire from an enemy battery sited near Westkapelle and fourteen explosive-boats that had lost contact with their control boats returned to base. There is no record of what happened to the other fourteen, none of which returned. Another twelve *Linsen* sailed from Flushing on the night of 26/27 October to attack Allied warships off the West Scheldt, but all twelve grounded on a sand-bank astride the approach route. Notwithstanding this farce, the operation was repeated next night. All twelve *Linsen* involved in this sortie reached the target area and four explosive-boats were released, one of which hit and sank a 300-ton lighter. The final operation by this group took place after dark on 31 October when six *Linsen* carried out an attack in the West Scheldt estuary, and claimed, erroneously, to have sunk three Allied craft.

During the first half of November additional *Linsen* were moved into Holland and a total of 96 were apportioned between Den Helder, Scheveningen and Hellevoetsluis at the mouth of the West Mass. In addition, thirty *Biber* midget submarines were sent to Poortershaven (between Rotterdam and the sea), and 59 were sent to Groningen as a reserve. But by this time the commander of the *Kleinkampfverbande*, Konteradmiral Helmut Heye, had come to the conclusion that all the *K-Verband* craft were expensive failures. Not only was it becoming increasingly difficult to get volunteers, but Heye had come to the conclusion that 'the only hope is for independent operations to be carried out by selected crews and to keep the bulk of the [K-Verband] craft in reserve to deal with possible Allied landings in northern Holland'. In response the Naval Staff decided to adapt a number of the *Linsen* and *Biber* to carry mines, and the rest of November was spent in making the necessary modifications.

When the *Linsen* returned to the attack, the usual catalogue of farcical results ensued despite the fatalistic bravery of their crews. A sortie of twelve craft from an advanced base near Hellevoetsluis on 5 December came to an abrupt end when the group was almost entirely wiped out by Allied fighter-bombers as they emerged into open sea from the Mass estuary. A sortie by 27 *Linsen* on the 17th came to grief when four of them were swamped by high seas and the remainder were forced to return to base. The surviving 23 *Linsen* put to sea again that evening to operate in the Scheldt, but thirteen ran aground off Goeree and only three reached the target area. These managed to attack a destroyer, but the two explosive-boats missed. Next evening (19 December) 21 *Linsen*

U-Boats Despatched To Remote Atlantic Waters
From January 1945 until the end of the war

Boat	Sailed	Operational Area	Returned	Ships sunk
U866	5 Feb 45	Off Nova Scotia	Sunk	
U857	8 Feb 45	US coast	Sunk	
U879	11 Feb 45	US coast	Sunk	1 (6,959)
U530	20 Feb 45	US coast	3 Mar 45	
U190	22 Feb 45	Off Nova Scotia	Surrendered in Canada	
U853	23 Feb 45	US coast	Sunk	1 corvette
U805	4 Mar 45	Group Seewolf	Surrendered in Canada	
U548	7 Mar 45	US coast	Sunk	1 (8,300)
U518	13 Mar 45	Group Seewolf	Sunk	
U805	4 Mar 45	Group Seewolf	Surrendered in Canada	
U518	13 Mar 45	Group Seewolf	Sunk	
U858	14 Mar 45	Group Seewolf	Surrendered in USA	
U880	14 Mar 45	Group Seewolf	Sunk	
U1235	20 Mar 45	Group Seewolf	Sunk	
U546	22 Mar 45	Group Seewolf	Sunk	
U873	1 April 45	Caribbean	Surrendered in USA	
U889	6 April 45	US coast	Surrendered in Canada	
U881	7 April 45	US coast	Sunk	
U541	11 April 45	Off Gibraltar	Surrendered at Gibraltar	
U1228	14 April 45	US coast	Surrendered in USA	
U1231	27 April 45	Off Gibraltar	Surrendered in UK	
U485	26 April 45	Off Gibraltar	Surrendered at Gibraltar	

U-Boats Dispatched to the Indian Ocean during the Last Year of the War

Boat	Sailed	Arrived	Ships sunk
U510	already on station		1 (7,136)
U168	already on station		
U183	already on station		1 (5,259)
U532	already on station		
U1062	already on station		
U843	19 Feb 44	11 June 44	1 (8,261)
U196	16 Mar 44	10 Aug 44	1 (5,454)
U181	16 Mar 44	8 Aug 44	5 (35,067)
U537	25 Mar 44	2 Aug 44	
U859	4 April 44	Sunk	2 (14,598)
U860	11 April 44	Sunk	
U198	20 April 44	Sunk	4 (22,912)
U861	20 April 44	22 Sept 44	4 (22,048)
U862	3 June 44	9 Sept 44	6 (35,194)
U863	26 July 44	Sunk	
U871	31 Aug 44	Sunk	
U195	20 Aug 44	28 Dec 44	
U219	23 Aug 44	11 Dec 44	

put out, but ran into fog and were forced to return: five of them ran aground on the return passage and had to be abandoned.

The first of the *Biber* midget submarine operations took place on the night of 22/23 December, when eight of them left Poortershaven in tow of R-boats, and ten put out from Hellevoetsluis in tow of Rhine patrol craft, to attack Allied shipping in the West Scheldt. The former group ran into British MTBs off the Hook of Holland and four *Biber* were lost while trying to slip their tows in a hurry. The latter group ran on to a minefield off the West Schouwen Bank, one *Biber* being sunk and another badly damaged. This left twelve *Biber* armed with torpedoes and mines to carry out the operation. None of them survived the attack on Allied shipping, but they did account for the 4,702-ton Panamanian freighter *Alan-a-Dale* which was torpedoed and sunk to the south-east of Flushing. Next night eleven *Biber* left Hellevoetsluis to operate in the Scheldt. They were towed to a position north-west of Goeree where the tows were slipped, after which one sank *en route*, another ran aground on the West Schouwen Bank, and none of the other nine returned.

Despite these catastrophic losses, three more *Biber* put to sea after dark on Christmas Eve, in company with nine *Linsen*, bound for the West Scheldt. None of the *Biber* returned, and only one *Linsen* unit (one control boat and two explosive-boats) reached the target area. This unit attacked a large ship off Zeebrugge, but one of the explosive-boats missed and the other hit a nearby wreck. The control *Linsen* returned to base on Christmas morning heavily iced up and the pilot nearly dead from cold. Finally, six *Biber* set out from Hellevoetsluis after dark on Christmas night to lay mines in the West Scheldt, but again none returned. On no occasion were any of the *Biber* or *Linsen* sighted by

Comparison of Mercantile Shipping Tonnage sunk by U-boats (all theatres) during the most successful period of the U-boat campaign (May 1942–May 1943) and during the last year of the war

Date	Number Sunk	Gross tonnage	U-boats sunk
1942			
May	129	616,835	4
June	136	636,926	3
July	96	467,051	11
Aug	117	587,245	9
Sept	96	461,794	11
Oct	89	583,690	15
Nov	126	802,160	13
Dec	64	337,618	5
1943			
Jan	44	307,196	6
Feb	67	362,081	19
Mar	110	633,731	16
April	50	287,137	15
May	45	237,182	41
Totals	1,169	6,320,646	168
6.95 ships sunk per U-boat sunk			
1944			
May	4	62,149	23
June	12	57,406	25
July	14	61,395	27
Aug	17	91,454	32
Sept	8	50,790	25
Oct	4	1,659	14
Nov	5	25,193	7
Dec	11	53,268	17
1945			
Jan	14	67,410	12
Feb	18	75,911	21
Mar	15	65,901	34
April	12	64,532	64
May	4	10,722	41
Totals	138	687,790	342
0.40 ships sunk per U-boat sunk			

Allied reconnaissance aircraft, but two *Biber* were claimed sunk off Flushing soon after daylight on Boxing Day by Typhoon fighters. Naval claims amounted to six *Biber* sunk between 23 and 26 December, leaving thirty *Biber* whose fate remains unknown. Heavy seas, poor visibility and navigational hazards probably put paid to most of them.

At daylight on 27 December, the last fourteen *Biber* at Hellevoetsluis were preparing to put to sea under cover of a smoke-screen, but while manoeuvring in the harbour two torpedoes exploded prematurely, sinking eleven of them and two harbour-defence vessels. The tidal lock gates were also damaged, and the remaining three *Biber* were left hanging by their mooring lines as the water drained out of the harbour.

The heavy loses sustained (115 *Linsen* and 52 *Biber*) caused Konteradmiral Heye to recommend that operations by these types be suspended, but Dönitz replied that the situation on the Western Front demanded immediate all-out action against the Allied supply convoys in the Scheldt area where there were ample opportunities for effective action by *Biber*. Heye commented caustically that as none of the *Biber* crews had so far ever returned it was impossible to assess the effectiveness of their operations, but Dönitz insisted that after reinforcement *Linsen* and *Biber* operations were to continue.

Meanwhile the first six *Seehunde* 2-man midget submarines had left Germany by road on 24 December, bound for Ijmuiden. They were followed by daily batches of six, and by the end of December some twenty 20 *Seehunde* were operationally ready in Dutch ports to usher in a new phase of *K-Verband* sacrificial missions.

Chapter 10

END GAME

THE FATAL DELAYS

By January 1945 the war had finally come home to Germany. The Ardennes offensive, launched on 16 December 1944, on which Hitler had staked his last reserves in men, guns and ammunition in a desperate attempt to regain the initiative in the west, had proved a costly failure. By 16 January, the German forces had lost their small gains and had been pushed back to their start-lines; after which the Anglo-American armies began their advance into western Germany on a broad front, reaching the Rhine by 8 February.

Meanwhile, on the Eastern Front the Russians had unleashed their greatest offensive of the war from north and south of Warsaw, and within weeks the tidal wave had reached the industrial area of Upper Silesia as far as Frankfurt-on-Oder, and East Prussia was engulfed.

By this time Allied bombers had reduced practically every German city and major town to spectral ruins standing in wastes of rubble; coal and oil supplies had been cut to a fraction of what was needed to maintain even a one-front war. Among the Nazi leadership Ribbentrop, Goebbels and even Himmler had come to terms with the inevitable and begun extending secret peace feelers to the Western Allies. But Dönitz, practically alone among the top leadership, refused to relinquish his belief in Hitler's strategic 'genius', insisting that it was still possible that the new Type XXI and Type XXIII Electro-boats might yet snatch victory from the Allies. Indeed, the overriding concern of BdU was to bring forward the day when the Electro-boats could join in the U-boat campaign; while the overriding fear of the Allies was that this day might arrive at any time.

The Allies were worried that the ocean-going Type XXIs might give the Germans the means of escalating the U-boat campaign into a large-scale endeavour reminiscent of 1942. They feared that the arrival of even 50 Type XXIs on the high seas would seriously impede the transportation of essential supplies across the North Atlantic from the USA. The prospect of the smaller, Type XXIII, coastal Electro-boats gave less cause for anxiety because their limited radius of action would restrict them to quick stabs at British coastal shipping. But while the Allies were confident that these could be contained together with the snorkel-fitted conventional boats fighting the inshore campaign, this containment could only be bought by denuding the North Atlantic of nearly all the surface and air A/S forces. In other words, the Allies simply did not have enough A/S forces to cope with two simultaneous campaigns

The Admiralty kept the closest watch on the rate at which the Electro-boats were being assembled, their chief source of intelligence coming from PR flights over the yards; while the numbers of boats commissioning was gleaned through Enigma decrypts. By 18 December 1944 NID had correctly calculated from these sources that 95 Type XXIs were being assembled or were fitting-out, and 35 had been commissioned and were working-up. Analysis of Enigma decrypts by OIC indicated that the commanders being appointed to the Type XXI boats were all experienced and well above average ability.

These portents that the Electro-boats were in an advanced stage of preparedness to enter the U-boat campaign, taken in conjunction with the alarming situation wherein Enigma was failing to provide reliable intelligence as to the intentions of BdU in regard to the U-boats' inshore campaign (brought about by the introduction of the *Sonderschlüssel* settings), prompted the Admiralty to urge heavy bombing of the Electro-boat assembly slips and berths.

But the heavy bomber forces were controlled by the Chiefs of Staff, and their order of priorities was: synthetic oil plants, transportation, tank and mechanical transport production. They argued that, to be of any value, operations against U-boat production would have to be on such a large scale that they would seriously detract from the bombing of the oil and petroleum industry; and that any relaxation in this quarter would permit vastly increased enemy activity on all fronts and would lead to a resurrection of the Luftwaffe fighter force. This was an important consideration, because by mid-December 1944 the armoured units of the German Army and the Luftwaffe's fighter force were hamstrung by the lack of fuel consequent on the systematic bombing of the synthetic oil plants. Any pause in the bombing of these plants, the Air Staff argued, would allow repairs to be effected and production re-started. No diversion from existing priorities should be countenanced unless a point were reached where the Royal Navy and Coastal Command were unable to cope with the supposed greatly increased U-boat threat.

Although the Air Staff was sceptical about NID's claims that a new and dangerous U-boat offensive was imminent, the Admiralty finally convinced the Chiefs of Staff to acquiesce in its demands to the extent that on 19 December 1944 they gave permission for the heavy bombers of the RAF and US Eighth Air Force to attack the Electro-boats' yards, but with the proviso that such operations should not be to the detriment of the

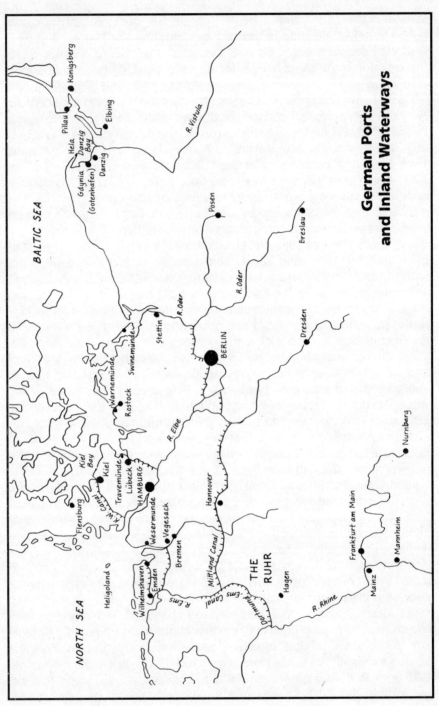

German Ports and Inland Waterways

existing priorities. The U-boat production facilities were to be attacked as secondary targets, or incidentally to major strategic objectives.

The raids did not start in earnest until 31 December, but Bomber Command jumped the gun by attacking the east Baltic port of Gdynia on the night of 18/19 December, while the Chiefs of Staff were still deliberating the issue. It was entirely a target of opportunity, because just before take-off on another mission the weather over Germany precluded all objectives except possibly in the area of Breslau and in East Prussia. The officer commanding No. 5 Group, Bomber Command selected Gdynia because HQ Bomber Command had previously given permission for attacks on naval ports if bad weather precluded the strategic objective. The raid, by 227 Lancasters which dropped 817 tons of bombs, was highly successful in that the vessels sunk included two U-boat depot ships, a torpedo-boat and five merchant ships; while a 22,000-ton oil refinery ship, the old battleship *Schleswig-Holstein* and the Type XXI *U2512* were badly damaged. The latter was about to carry out her final tactical exercises in the Bay of Danzig before becoming operational.

The first of the dedicated attacks on U-boat final assembly yards took place on 31 December, when the US Eighth Air Force dispatched 324 aircraft to attack synthetic oil plants and the U-boat assembly slips at Hamburg. For the loss of 24 aircraft, 740 tons of bombs were dropped: four Type XXI U-boats (*U2530, U2532, U2537, U2547*) were destroyed and two others (*U2515, U2556*) were badly damaged. Three of these boats had been completed and were lying alongside, the others were ready for launching. A 15,000-ton depot ship and three other vessels were also destroyed.

The German counter-attack in the Ardennes demanded a major diversion of the heavy bombers, and the marginal effort directed at the U-boat assembly yards was not resumed until mid-January. During the interim, however, a raid on the Dortmund/Ems and Mittelland Canals on 1 January put both of them out of action until 6 February, resulting among other benefits in further serious delays in Type XXI output because the prefabricated sections were brought along these canals to the yards.

The first effective attack of 1945 against the Electro-boat programme was carried out on 17 January by the US Eighth Air Force which attacked the Blohm & Voss assembly yard at Hamburg. Only three aircraft were lost and 360 tons of bombs were dropped. The yard area was hit by 132 high-explosive bombs which destroyed three commissioned Type XXIs (*U2550, U2515, U2523*) and damaged nine (*U2557, U2251, U2542, U2544, U2545, U2546,* U2548, *U2555, U2556*). In addition, five merchant ships were sunk and three damaged.

More concentrated attacks on Electro-boat production started soon after mid-February, with a dead set at the Deschimag Type XXI yard at Bremen. It was known that very little shop work was done at the Deschimag final assembly yard, so dense area attacks were considered unsuitable. Precision bombing, however, by even a few aircraft, could result in serious dislocation of output provided that accuracy were sufficient to damage the slipways on which the Type XXIs were assembled. Consequently the Deschimag yard was attacked nightly at relatively low altitudes in good visibility, from the night of 17/18 February until the end of the month, by groups of four to six Mosquitos each carrying a 4,000lb general-purpose bomb. German records confirm the damaging results that the adoption of this tactic achieved.

One of these attacks, on the night of 21/22 February, was particularly successful. Two Type XXIs (*U3052*, *U3048*), in the process of fitting-out, were badly damaged, and the launch of three Type XXIs was delayed because they were blocked in by debris. Two days later, 198 aircraft of the US Eighth Air Force also carried out an attack on the Deschimag yard. Although only one Type XXI (*U3007*), which had just been cleared for final fitting-out, was sunk, two floating cranes and the crane installation on the fitting-out quay were badly damaged, seriously delaying the fitting-out programme. Two more Mosquito attacks early in March achieved little, but a heavy attack by 407 bombers of the US Eighth Air Force on the 11th created such havoc that the Deschimag yard virtually shut down and only token activity was maintained thereafter.

Another serious blow to the Electro-boat programme was delivered in February by further attacks on the Dortmund/Ems and Mittelland Canals which were again put out of use. Repairs to the breaches were started, but a heavy raid on 3/4 March finally cut them beyond repair and they remained idle until the end of the war.

During March 1945, both Hamburg and Bremen were on the receiving end of a number of heavy raids. The yards at Hamburg were attacked twice by Bomber Command and three times by the US Eighth Air Force, during which a total of five conventional U-boats and fifteen other ships were sunk, and one conventional U-boat and eleven other vessels were damaged. The Blohm & Voss yard was devastated and final assembly of Type XXIs there was brought virtually to a standstill. Bremen received attention mainly because of the oil plants near the dock area. During the course of one of the raids on this port, on 21 March by 133 Lancasters, the recently completed 2,053-ton destroyer *Z51* was sunk alongside the quay in one of the basins. The final attack on the Deschimag yard at Bremen was made on 30 March by 319 US aircraft, when two cargo vessels, and six conventional U-boats under repair were sunk, and five Type XXI boats (*U3042, U3043, U3045, U3046, U3036*), in the process of fitting-out, were damaged beyond repair.

Other heavy attacks in March were made on Kiel (11th) by US aircraft, when three minesweepers were sunk and two Type XXIs (*U2502, U2503*) and a conventional U-boat were damaged; on Swinemunde (12th) in which US aircraft sank the 12,000-ton liner *Cordillera* and six other vessels; and on Wilhelmshaven (30th) by US aircraft whose bombs badly damaged three U-boats, including a recently commissioned Type XXI (*U3508*), the light cruiser *Köln*, and seven other vessels.

At the end of March two attacks were made on the colossal bomb-proof concrete U-boat shelter at Farge, fifteen miles down river from Bremen. On the 27th, 109 Lancasters dropped 694 tons of heavy bombs on this target, followed on the 30th by 32 Flying Fortresses which dropped special armour-piercing bombs. During the first raid two 10-ton 'Grand Slam' bombs struck the still unreinforced covering of the roof and the tremendous explosion caused it to collapse over two assembly areas. Although most of the blast dispersed upwards, the destruction of the roof considerable delayed construction of the shelter. This immense structure at Farge was part of the undertaking to put all U-boat construction under bomb-proof shelters. Four small shelters had already been completed (at Deutsche Werft, Hamburg and Kiel; and at Howaldts Werke, Hamburg and Kiel). The prefabricated U-boat pro-gramme called for the shelters at Howaldts Werke, Kiel and Hamburg to be used for Type XXI section assembly; the shelter at Deutsche Werft, Hamburg for Type XXIII final assembly; and the shelter at Deutsche Werke, Kiel for final assembly of *Seehunde* midget submarines.

Construction of the shelter at Farge, code-named 'Valentin', had begun in May 1943, and completion was scheduled for March 1945, but various delays had postponed the date to August. It was intended to concentrate in Valentin (which was 1,350 feet long and 320 feet wide) all the final assembly of the Type XXIs undertaken on the open slipways at Bremen and Hamburg, but Valentin was still incomplete when the war ended and it was never used for its intended purpose.

Consequent upon the German withdrawal before the Russian armies advancing into east Germany along the Baltic coast, Kiel became the principal German naval port, and at the end of March the heavy bomber commands were ordered to concentrate attacks on this target, with the Hamburg U-boat yards as a second priority.

The attacks on Kiel began on 3 and 4 April when 639 and 505 US aircraft dropped a total of 3,138 tons of bombs. Three Type XXIs (*U2542, U3505, U3003*) and three conventional U-boats were sunk in these two raids, as well as two liners and ten other vessels. The Hamburg yards received attention on the night of 8/9 April, when 427 Lancasters and Halifaxes dropped 1,503 tons of bombs. Five commissioned Type XXI U-boats (*U2509, U2514, U2549, U2552, U3512*) and five cargo vessels were sunk. Enormous damage was done to the Blohm & Voss and Howaldts yards, resulting in the complete cessation in both yards of any further U-boat construction. Hamburg received only three more light attacks before mid-April and no more U-boat or ship casualties resulted. Kiel was again attacked heavily on the night of 13/14 April by 467 Bomber Command aircraft, and thereafter nightly from the 21st to the 27th by groups of Mosquitos carrying 4,000lb bombs. During these raids two more commissioned Type XXIs (*U3525, U2516*) and seven conventional U-boats were sunk.

The construction programme was dealt another serious blow by the Russian advance into East Prussia. At the end of January 1945 all work was stopped at Danzig and Gdynia so that the skilled workers could be evacuated to western yards in good time. Consequently Type XXI output at the Schichau yard in Danzig, which had averaged six boats a month, ceased for good on 31 January.

The shortage of Electro-boat batteries as a result of the bombing of the production plants in Hanover and Hagen, was also a major factor in curtailing the number of boats produced. The plant at Hagen had been badly damaged in December 1944 (50 per cent of the buildings were destroyed), and when the repairs were almost completed it was damaged again during a raid in February, before being destroyed completely during a heavy raid on the night of 15/16 March. Continual air raids on Hanover destroyed all sources of power and light in the industrial quarter, so battery production was impossible, and the only other battery-producing factory, at Posen, fell into Russian hands during their advance into eastern Germany in January 1945.

Most of the electric motors for the Electro-boats were produced at plants in Berlin and Mannheim, and although both cities were frequently attacked by the bombers, the curtailed output from the damaged plants remained sufficient to match the greatly reduced number of launchings of completed Electro-boats. In comparison with the large Type XXIs, the coastal Type XXIII programme escaped direct interference by bombing, partly because the Deutsche Werft assembly at Hamburg was carried out beneath a bomb-proof concrete shelter, and partly because the other Type XXIII assembly yard, Germania Werft, Kiel, was not heavily attacked. But output suffered because the the yards were unable to obtain components, and it dropped from a steady nine per month in 1944 to four in February 1945. By the end of the war only five Type XXIIIs had been destroyed by bombing: *U2340* during a raid on Hamburg on 30 March 1945; *U4709, U4711, U4712* during a raid on Kiel on 4 April; and *U4708* during a raid on Kiel on 4 May.

The effects of the Allied air attacks on Electro-boat construction was summed-up by Vizeadmiral Karl Topp, the head of *Amt für Kriegsschiffbau* (Office for Warship Construction):

'No stoppage of U-boat production was brought about by Allied air attacks until almost the end of the war. Germany succeeded in keeping the production of new U-boat construction at a considerable level until the beginning of 1945. From the beginning of 1945, it would have been very possible from the production point of view to recommence the U-boat campaign with the new, possibly very effective Types XXI and XXIII ... 'Destruction at U-boat yards and in the supply industry certainly caused a noticeable diminution of production, but never an effective cessation of production. That this was so is due to U-boat production, including section production from *May 1945*, being carried out in the whole western area in bomb-proof shelters. Serious stoppages in U-boat production occurred only when the yards in Danzig were no longer available – through the Russian advance, and, in Hamburg, through the British advance. New U-boat construction in Bremen had been suspended, however, following the bombing of Deschimag as early as March 1945. A greater concentration of attacks on bottle-neck supplies for U-boat construction (batteries, periscopes, part-sections and sections that were only produced in one particular place) ... would have been more effective in shortening the U-boat campaign than the scattered attacks on the larger cities and neighbourhoods and on the overall armament industry.'[1]

Topp's report is far too optimistic, for it must be doubted whether, from the production point of view, the early part of 1945 could have seen a full-scale resumption of the U-boat campaign by the Electro-boats. Furthermore, the Kriegsmarine's supplies of diesel fuel, which had remained at about the necessary minimum level of 100,000 tons since the middle of 1941, had by January 1945 become inadequate following the loss of the Roumanian and Hungarian oil fields and the destruction of the Hydrierwerke synthetic oil plant. Topp was also certainly over-optimistic concerning the prospects of undisturbed U-boat production from May 1945, if the war had been prolonged after that month.

The various German statements and records of pre-fabricated output during the last four months of the war differ slightly, but NID calculated that, since the start of the programme, 116 Type XXI and 59 Type XXIII had been completed and delivered to the Kriegsmarine by 1 May 1945. In the case of the all-important Type XXI, this was far below the number envisaged in the revised production programmes; moreover only one was fully operational by the war's end. The failure of the construction programme was mainly the result of defects in the internal organization irrespective of bombing. When these had been put right in the latter part of 1944 it was then entirely due to the effects of bombing that the regular monthly quota of twenty Type XXIs a month was not delivered to the Kriegsmarine.

The following figures showing the position at the end of the war are from an NID post-war assessment calculated from various German records:[2]

Type XXI and XXIII U-Boats at the End of the War		
	Type XXI	*Type XXIII*
Number scheduled for delivery by 1 May 1945 in the revised programme.	381	95
Number not produced because of organizational troubles, faulty design and bad workmanship.	202	13
Estimated number denied by delays and damage caused by Allied bombing.	60	19
Actual number delivered to the Kriegsmarine.	118	59
Number still training, on acceptance trials or fitting-out at the end of the war.	91	38
Number at or on passage to operational bases in Norway but not yet fully operational.	12	15
Number fully operational at the end of the war.	1	6

The delays in production were compounded by the protracted training and working-up period required by the crews of the new types to bring them up to full operational readiness. Instead of the normal 3–3½ months needed to train the crew of a conventional U-boat, it was found that the complexity of the Electro-boats, in conjunction with the numerous defects and teething troubles necessitating frequent interruptions of training for repairs and modifications to be carried out, doubled the training and working-up period to 6–7 months. Further delays in training resulted from the mining of the training area by the RAF.

The Gulf of Danzig has an area of some 200 square miles, and was admirably suited to U-boat training because it was compact and, for the most part, more than 300 feet deep. Until the end of August 1944, all new U-boat acceptance and deep diving trials, all elementary training for new crews, basic tactical, technical and torpedo firing training, and rigorous working-up exercises took place in these waters. But when, on the nights of 26/27 and 29/30 August, Bomber Command Lancasters laid a total of 171 mines in the Gulf, upon which *U1000* and a patrol vessel came to grief, all the U-boat training areas had to be closed.

Preliminary sweeping located only a few mines, and the need of meticulous minesweeping caused an unavoidable delay in re-opening any of the training areas. On 6 September 1944, Generaladmiral Hans-Georg von Friedeburg, who was responsible for all U-boat trials and training, reported that the mine situation in the Gulf of Danzig was preventing him from carrying out trial schedules, particularly those connected with the new Types XXI and XXIII. He urgently requested clearance of at least the U-boat acceptance area, close off the port of Hela, and provision of adequate minesweeping escorts for U-boats proceeding via the normal channels to this area. The only outcome was that on 8 September a part of the deep water technical training area was re-opened, but with the proviso that U-boats keep at least 162 feet of water under their keel.

When the RAF laid another 75 mines in the Gulf of Danzig on the night of the 15/16 September all the training areas were closed again until 14 October, when the basic tactical training and parts of the elementary training areas and the acceptance area off Hela were re-opened. After another eight days' sweeping, the general torpedo firing area was pronounced safe, and on 8 November a second acceptance area in the southern sector of the Gulf was brought back into service.

The re-opened areas were in use for six weeks despite occasional scares when merchant ships were mined in the traffic route skirting the Gulf. Then on 15/16 and 18/19 December 1944, Bomber Command Lancasters laid a total of 113 mines in the western sector of the Gulf and, although the immediate result was damage to only one merchant ship off Gdynia, the *Seekriegsleitung* decided on the 21st that all U-boat activity in the area must be suspended.

On 1 January 1945, *Seekriegsleitung* directed that priority be given to the clearance of mines from the new U-boat acceptance areas, but after the RAF laid a further 129 mines in the Gulf on the night of 6/7 January Generaladmiral von Friedeburg called a halt. U-boat training areas in these waters were never fully re-opened, and in February all U-boat training was transferred to new areas in the bay of Lübeck, 250 miles to the west. This was an inferior location from every point of view, not least because the training area was now within range of Coastal Command aircraft which carried out regular night attacks on surfaced and snorkelling boats, completely upsetting the working-up organization and routines. The exact effect of the delay caused by the disruption of training cannot be exactly determined. 'But it seems probable that as many as twenty of the Type XXIs might have become fully operational early in 1945 had it not occurred.'[3]

The cumulative delays in production and working-up of the Electro-boats was such that *U2324*, the first of the Type XXIIIs to become fully operational, did not sail on her first operational cruise until 31 January 1945, six months after she had been commissioned; and the first of the Type XXIs to become fully operational, *U2511*, did not sail on her first operational cruise until 30 April, seven months after her commissioning.

THE INSHORE CAMPAIGN: THE FIFTH WAVE

In its essentials the inshore campaign was purely a defensive delaying action, incumbent on the Electro-boats becoming operational. In October 1944 Dönitz assured Hitler that large numbers of the revolutionary boats would be on the high seas early in 1945, but this proved to be an unrealistic forecast because only one of the 232-ton coastal Type XXIIIs was among the eighteen U-boats dispatched to British coastal waters during January.

This was *U2324*, which sailed from the Norwegian port of Christiansand on 29 January, to operate off the British east coast between Aberdeen and Newcastle, her main activity to centre off the Firth of Forth. Because her commander, Kapitänleutnant Konstantin von Rapprad, needed time to familiarize himself with the general features of his operational area, it was not until 18 February that the first contact was made with the enemy. In poor visibility off Newcastle, von Rapprad sighted a convoy and fired two torpedoes at the short range of about 1,300 yards. Gyro-angling failure caused both torpedoes to miss, and as the Type XXIIIs carried only two torpedoes, the disappointed von Rapprad had no choice but to return Christiansand where he arrived on the 24th.

This was hardly an auspicious omen for BdU's expectations of the Electro-boats' regaining the initiative at sea, but this initial cruise had proved that the Type XXIII was:

'An ideal boat for operations of short duration in coastal waters, fast, handy, easy to handle when submerged and offering a small target and little chance of location by radar. The enemy merely has a "hunch" that there's a boat about somewhere, rather than any clear proof of its presence or any precise indication of its position.'[4]

Of the seventeen conventional boats dispatched during January, nine were sent into the English Channel where six of them scored kills. The first went to Kapitänleutnant Rolf Nollmann, commander of *U1199*, who attacked a convoy off Land's End on the 21st, sinking the 7,176-ton US Liberty ship *George Hawley*. But *U1199* did not survive the convoy escorts' counter-attack which, after a short hunt, sank the boat with depth-charges off the Scillies.

Three weeks later *U1018* arrived in the western Channel, and on 11 February attacked a coastal convoy just west of Plymouth, sinking the 5,382-ton Belgian freighter *Persier*. Surviving the counter-attack, *U1018* attacked another convoy seven miles west of the Lizard at 0913 on 27 February, sinking the 1,317-ton Norwegian freighter *Corvus*. But this time she paid the price, being sunk within the hour by a frigate from an escort group.

Later that same day (1630) a USN Liberator sighted a suspicious wake in the calm sea, some 45 miles south-west of the Lizard, and the pilot decided to keep an eye on it. First, however, he contacted a nearby convoy and informed the senior escort officer. Shortly afterwards he spotted a periscope rise only 100 yards away. The periscope dipped almost immediately, but the pilot called up again and three escort groups arrived. ASDIC contact was made and twelve hours after the sighting, masses of oil and wreckage came to the surface, marking the end of *U327*, which had only just reached the mouth of the Channel.

Meanwhile, at midday on 22 February, *U1004* attacked a coastal convoy to the east of Falmouth and sank the 1,331-ton British freighter *Alexander Kennedy* and the escorting Canadian corvette *Trentonian*.

The Inshore Campaign: The Fifth Wave
U-Boats dispatched during January 1945.

Boat	Sailed	Operational Area	Returned	Ships sunk*
U1199	1 Jan 45	English Channel	Sunk	1 (7,176)
U480	6 Jan 45	English Channel	Sunk	1 (1,644)
U244	9 Jan 45	English Channel	13 Mar 45	
U275	13 Jan 45	English Channel	10 Feb 45	1 (4,934)
U1208	14 Jan 45	Irish Sea	Sunk	1 corvette
U1058	16 Jan 45	Irish Sea	18 Mar 45	
U963	16 Jan 45	Irish Sea	4 Mar 45	
U1203	17 Jan 45	English Channel	31 Mar 45	1 armed trawler
U1014	18 Jan 45	North Channel	Sunk	
U1018	21 Jan 45	English Channel	Sunk	2 (6,699)
U1276	27 Jan 45	Irish Sea	Sunk	
U1104	28 Jan 45	North Minch	22 Mar 45	
U1004	28 Jan 45	English Channel	21 Mar 45	1 (1,313) +1 corvette
U2324	29 Jan 45	Firth of Forth	24 Feb 45	
U327	30 Jan 45	English Channel	Sunk	
U1279	30 Jan 45	Irish Sea	Sunk	
U927	31 Jan 45	English Channel	Sunk	
U245	? Jan 45	North Foreland	19 Feb 45	1 (7,240)

* Expressed in number of merchant ships sunk and total tonnage.

Although she was heavily depth-charged in the ensuing counter-attack, *U1004* managed to escape, having suffered only minor damage. Two days later *U1203* sank the armed trawler HMS *Ellesmere* which was escorting a convoy of tank landing ships sixty miles south of the Lizard. This U-boat also escaped the consequences, but *U480* was not so lucky. During her return passage from the central Channel she attacked a coastal convoy off Land's End in the early hours of 24 February, sinking the 1,644-ton British freighter *Oriskany*. Having revealed her presence, *U480* was hunted down by an escort group and destroyed six hours later. At dusk on that same day an aircraft homed in on a radar contact south-east of Falmouth, and in the failing light sighted a snorkel close

The Inshore Campaign: The Sixth Wave
U-Boats dispatched during February 1945

Boat	Sailed	Operational Area	Returned	Ships sunk
U864	5 Feb 45	English Channel	Sunk	
U2322	6 Feb 45	Firth of Forth	3 Mar 45	1 (1,317)
U683	6 Feb 45	English Channel	Sunk	
U1302	6 Feb 45	Irish Sea	Sunk	4 (10,312)
U483	7 Feb 45	Irish Sea	Mar 45	
U775	8 Feb 45	Irish Sea	19 Mar 45	
U309	8 Feb 45	Moray Firth	Sunk	
U989	8 Feb 45	English Channel	Sunk	
U1064	8 Feb 45	Irish Sea	10 April 45	1 (1,564)
U399	8 Feb 45	English Channel	Sunk	2 (7,538)
U1019	10 Feb 45	Irish Sea	10 April 45	
U1278	11 Feb 45	English Channel	Sunk	
U1022	12 Feb 45	Off Reykjavik	2 April 45	1 (1,392) +1 A/S whaler
U2321	12 Feb 45	Firth of Forth	13 Mar 45	
U315	15 Feb 45	English Channel	25 April 45	2 (14,190)
U681	16 Feb 45	English Channel	Sunk	
U773	19 Feb 45	Off Reykjavik	15 April 45	
U1003	19 Feb 45	North Channel	Scuttled	
U1169	20 Feb 45	Irish Sea	Sunk	
U1021	20 Feb 45	Irish Sea	Sunk	
U1005	21 Feb 45	North Minch	21 Mar 45	
U1002	21 Feb 45	English Channel	10 April 45	
U260	21 Feb 45	Irish Sea	Sunk	
U722	21 Feb 45	Hebrides	Sunk	1 (2,190)
U953	21 Feb 45	English Channel	3 April 45	
U246	22 Feb 45	English Channel	Sunk	
U1195	24 Feb 45	English Channel	Sunk	1 (11,420)
U978	25 Feb 45	North Minch	18 April 45	
U275	25 Feb 45	English Channel	Sunk	1 (4,934)
U296	28 Feb 45	North Channel	Sunk	

ahead with thin vapourish smoke coming from it. An accurate depth-charge attack was delivered following which, in the moonlight, an ever-increasing patch of oil was seen, which marked the end of *U927*.

Two other U-boats, *U244* and *U275*, survived their patrol in the Channel, mainly because they made no attacks and thus did not reveal their positions to the A/S patrols.

Five U-boats were dispatched to the Irish Sea during January, but one, *U1279*, was sunk outward-bound when she was detected by an escort group patrolling north of the Shetlands. Only one of the surviving four boats achieved a kill. This was *U1208* which, during her return passage to base, attacked a convoy south of Waterford at 1145 on 20 February, sinking the corvette HMS *Vervain*. A supporting escort group made ASDIC contact within a few minutes, and after several depth-charge attacks were provided with convincing proof of the demise of *U1208*, when oil and wreckage welled-up to the surface.

One boat, *U1104*, was sent to North Minch but sighted nothing during her patrol which lasted from 3 to 15 March. The patrol of the single boat dispatched to the North Channel, *U1014*, was short-lived. On the day that she arrived in her operational area (4 February), she was detected by the ASDICs of an escort group engaged in a working-up exercise off Lough Foyle. Considerable quantities of clothing, paper and other wreckage of German origin, which came to the surface after a depth-charge attack by all four frigates, marked the end of *U1014*.

A new billet in the inshore campaign was occupied by *U245*, which operated off the North Foreland in the Thames Estuary from 21 January to 15 February, to attack military supply convoys plying between the Thames and the Scheldt. Despite the large amount of traffic in the area, *U245*'s commander, Korvettenkapitän Friedrich Schumann-Hindenberg, only achieved one kill; he attacked a convoy at 2025 on 5 February, sinking the 7,240-ton US freighter *Henry B. Plant*.

The loss of nine U-boats in the fifth wave reduced the exchange ratio to 0.66 merchant ships per U-boat sunk, which was a poor showing compared to the fourth wave exchange ratio of 2.3 ships per U-boat lost, but worse was to come.

THE INSHORE CAMPAIGN: THE SIXTH WAVE

The efforts of Kapitän Rösing to increase the repair, refit and berthing facilities in the Norwegian bases had begun to reap tangible benefits by the beginning of February 1945. The dispatch rate – eleven U-boats during October 1944 – had increased to eighteen during January 1945, climbing to thirty in February.

Included in the February sailings were another two Type XXIIIs that had reached *Frontboote* status. *U2322* and *U2321* sailed from

Christiansand on 6 and 12 February respectively, bound for an operational area extending from Aberdeen southwards to St. Abb's Head (twenty miles south of the Firth of Forth).

U2322 reached the area on 14 February, but her commander, Oberleutnant Fridtjof Heckel, sighted no targets until the 25th, when at 1855 he attacked a convoy south-east of St. Abb's Head, sinking the 1,317-ton British freighter *Egholm*, and getting away undetected to begin the homeward passage.

U2321 reached the operational area on 17 March, but, although she patrolled off the coast until the end of the month, she sighted no targets and arrived back in Christiansand on 14 April.

Of the 28 conventional boats dispatched during February, twelve were sent into the English Channel. Three of these were sunk outward bound, and of the nine that reached the Channel only three survived to tell the tale and only four scored a kill.

The first kill went to *U275* which attacked a convoy off Beachy Head on 8 March, sinking the 4,934-ton British freighter *Lornaston*. Two days later, while still patrolling this area, *U275* ran into a deep minefield ten miles south-south-west of Beachy Head and sank with all hands.

A fortnight later, at 1335 on 21 March, *U399* attacked a coastal convoy off the Eddystone Light and sank the 7,176-ton US liberty ship *James Eagan Layne*; while *U315* attacked a convoy off the Lizard at 1418, sinking another US liberty ship, the 7,194-ton *John R. Park*. Both U-boats got away unharmed, and *U315* struck again at 1340 next day, sinking the 6,996-ton British freighter *Empire Kingsley* north-west of Land's End, again getting away unscathed.

In the early hours of 26 March, *U399* attacked another convoy south-west of the Lizard, sinking the 362-ton coaster *Pacific*. This convoy was being trailed two miles astern by an escort group which immediately gained ASDIC contact on *U399* and destroyed her with a 'Hedgehog' attack. On the same day *U315* attacked a coastal convoy off Land's End, badly damaging one of the escorting frigates, HMCS *Teme*. She got away undetected and started homeward five days later (31 March).

The only other boat operating in the Channel to score a kill was *U1195*, which attacked a convoy to the east of St. Catherine's Point, Isle of Wight, sinking the 11,420-ton British freighter *Cuba*. But *U1195* paid the price, being located an hour later by an escorting destroyer, HMS *Watchman*, which sank her with a well-placed depth-charge attack.

Four of the six U-boats lost in the Channel (*U683*, *U399*, *U246*, *U1195*) were sunk by surface forces; one (*U275*) was mined and one

(*U681*) was bombed by an aircraft. The latter was sunk as a result of an accident. At 0900 on 11 March, *U681* was proceeding into the Channel past the Scilly Isles at a depth of 80 feet when she hit outlying rocks. The damage sustained forced her commander, Oberleutnant Werner Gebauer, to surface. Realizing that he could not continue submerged for any length of time, he made for the Irish coast at full speed on the surface. At 0926 *U681* was sighted by a USN Liberator which attacked immediately. Gebauer took violent evasive action and the stick of eight depth-charges fell short, but one exploded close enough to the stern to cause further leaks. Deciding that his position was hopeless, Gebauer gave the order to abandon ship. This was done while the boat was still under way at full speed: the ballast tank vents were opened and demolition charges were activated. The U-boat had already disappeared beneath the waves before the charges exploded, causing a great upheaval of oil and water to mark *U681*'s violent end. The U-boat's entire crew of forty were rescued some hours later by a British escort group.

Eight boats dispatched during February operated in the Irish Sea. Four were sunk and only two scored kills. On the 21st *U1064*, which entered the Irish Sea via the North Channel, sank the 1,564-ton Icelandic freighter *Dettifoss* in the entrance to the Firth of Clyde and managed to get away unscathed. A week later, *U1302*, which entered via St. George's Channel, sank the 1,926-ton freighter *Soreldoc* south of Bardsey Island, and the 646-ton coaster *Norfolk Coast* north-west of St. David's Head, within hours of each other on 28 February. Remaining in the area, *U1302* attacked a convoy north-west of St. David's Head on 2 March, sinking the 4,536-ton tanker *King Edgar* and the 3,204-ton freighter *Novasli*. After the attack an extensive hunt by several escort groups continued for five days. *U1302* stuck it out not far from the attack position, but after dark on the 7th she was finally detected by ASDIC and destroyed by a hail of depth-charges sent down by three frigates.

Eight other boats that sailed from the Norwegian bases during February operated off the Moray Firth, North Minch, North Channel, and off the Hebrides and Reykjavik. Three of these boats were sunk and only two scored kills. *U722* sank the 2,190-ton British freighter *Ingertoft* three miles west of the Isle of Skye at 0800 on 16 March. *U1022* sank the 1,392-ton freighter *Alcedo* off Reykjavik on 26 February, and the A/S whaler HMS *Southern Flower* four miles off Skagi on 3 March. The local force of A/S whalers and trawlers failed to pick up any trace of *U1022* after the attack, and a week later, at 1400 on the 10th, she attacked a group of them some fifteen miles north-west of Skagi. But while manoeuvring into a firing position she broke surface in the heavy sea and was sighted and attacked, first by gunfire and later with depth-charges. She managed to extricate herself and escape, having suffered only minor damage.

The demise of one of the three boats sunk from this group is worth recording. At 2217 on 20 March, *U1003* was snorkelling some twelve miles north of Lough Foyle when she collided with the Canadian frigate *New Glasgow*. The U-boat bottomed at once thereby escaping destruction by the subsequent depth-charges dropped by *New Glasgow* and other frigates of a nearby escort group which had joined the hunt. Examination of the collision damage disclosed a split conning-tower and smashed periscopes and snorkel, and many internal leaks. At daylight on the 21st, *U1003* came up and cruised at a depth of sixty feet all day in a north-westerly direction until dusk when, deprived of her snorkel, she surfaced to charge her nearly exhausted batteries. But she was forced to dive again before replenishment by constant alarms of approaching A/S forces. With the pumps running continuously to expel the water entering the boat through the leaks in the pressure hull, *U1003* remained on the bottom throughout the 22nd, but just after midnight the batteries gave out and without power the pumps stopped. As the interior of the boat began to fill with water, her commander surfaced and abandoned ship in the early hours of the 23rd. Soon after dawn 31 of *U1003*'s crew of 44 were rescued from their dinghies by the Canadian frigate *Thetford Mines*, the sea claiming the remainder.

The loss of seventeen boats (56.66 per cent) from the thirty dispatched during February was the direct result of the Admiralty's concentrating the A/S forces in the main U-boat operational areas around the British Isles. By the end of January these were so intensive that once a U-boat disclosed its position by attacking it was more often than not doomed to destruction, because the slow submerged speed of the conventional boats could not outrun the hunters. At a conference with Hitler on 1 March 1945, Dönitz conceded that the Allies were gaining the upper hand in the inshore campaign:

'The confining of U-boat operations exclusively to British home waters is undesirable, since it enables the enemy to concentrate his A/S forces in a small area. But, as the slow submerged speed of the old-type boats [VIIC] precludes their employment in any other region, the extension of operations to areas further afield, which might split the enemy defence forces, will only be possible when the Type XXI U-boats become operational. If we still held the Biscay coast, the Type VIIs could, of course, still operate in remoter areas such as the American coast. We do not think that the enemy has yet devised any fundamentally new methods of locating and attacking a submerged U-boat. Nevertheless, we must be prepared for increasing losses in British waters, where the enemy will apply his whole resources to mastering the U-boat menace. And in time he will meet with increasing success by virtue of the strength of his forces.'⁵

THE COLLAPSE OF THE INSHORE CAMPAIGN

At the beginning of March 1945 BdU broadcast several signals to U-boat commanders outward bound for the British coast, drawing attention to the undesirability of snorkelling on passage by day except in rough sea conditions, and reminding them that when operating in enclosed or inshore waters the periscope was to be used cautiously. Bilges were to be pumped into the diving tanks by day and only blown at night, and if it were believed that they had been detected from the air, they should change position as quickly as possible. BdU also instructed commanders to carry out night snorkelling in secluded bays, or areas with high coastlines or in neutral Irish territorial waters.

Despite these precautions the 25 U-boats that were dispatched during March were roundly defeated. Fourteen (58.13 per cent) were sunk for the small return of one 1,226-ton freighter and three trawlers (one of which had been fitted as a minesweeper).

The third Type XXIII Electro-boat to achieve *Frontboote* status, *U2321*,was among the boats that sailed during March. She operated between Aberdeen and St. Abb's Head from the 17th until the end of the month, but sighted no targets. The negative result by *U2321* and the scant returns from the seventh wave conventional boats were attributable to the following factor:

'Without the snorkel none of these patrols [in coastal waters] would have been possible but ... this fitment resulted in a limitation to do harm because the constant submergence put an end to any search for targets. The U-boats had to wait until, fortuitously, a target steamed into periscope view. Even then an attack might not result. U-boat records are full of entries that ships or convoys were sighted but on bearings from which an attack was impossible. Such immobile submerged conditions seem also to have served as a cloak to hide a lack of zeal on the part of many U-boat commanders and to provide a ready excuse for a blank report of success at the end of a cruise. During day time, air patrols could be nullified by a cautious use of the periscope or even prolonged descent to 100 feet depth while keeping a hydrophone listening watch.'⁶

The heavy losses sustained during February and March caused BdU to fear that many of the boats might have fallen prey to enemy mines which were being sown on the approach routes to and in the inshore operational areas. This danger being an unknown quantity was difficult to assess. The first indication that the British had begun laying minefields to catch the U-boats came in an *Abwehr* agent's report, received on 15 November 1944, which stated that *U1006* had been sunk by a mine off the south coast of Ireland in October (she had in fact been sunk off the Faeroes on 16 October by the Canadian frigate *Annan*). This agent, who had been operating in England for more than three years, reported on 24 November that new minefields were being laid across the entrance to the Irish Sea and in the North Channel, in small groups close to the sea bed, as a counter to the permanently submerged snorkel-fitted boats.

The Inshore Campaign: The Final Wave
U-boats dispatched during March 1945

Boat	Sailed	Operational Area	Returned	Ships sunk
U1024	3 Mar 45	Irish Sea	Sunk	
U242	4 Mar 45	Irish Sea	Sunk	
U1202	4 Mar 45	Irish Sea	27 April 45	
U714	4 Mar 45	Firth of Forth	14 Mar 45	(1,226) +1 armed trawler
U778	6 Mar 45	Moray Firth	7 April 45	
U965	6 Mar 45	North Minch	Sunk	
U1023	7 Mar 45	Irish Sea	Surrendered in UK	
U826	11 Mar 45	English Channel	Surrendered in UK	
U2321	12 Mar 45	Firth of Forth	13 April 45	
U1063	12 Mar 45	English Channel	Sunk	
U1001	12 Mar 45	English Channel	Sunk	
U905	13 Mar 45	Off Reykjavik	Sunk	
U396	13 Mar 45	North Minch	Sunk	
U774	15 Mar 45	English Channel	Sunk	
U321	17 Mar 45	English Channel	Sunk	
U325	22 Mar 45	Irish Sea	Sunk	
U249	22 Mar 45	English Channel	25 Mar 45	
U1106	23 Mar 45	Off Reykjavik	Sunk	
U218	23 Mar 45	North Channel	May 45	1 (200)
U1109	23 Mar 45	Returned to base, engine damage 6 April 45		
U776	24 Mar 45	English Channel	Surrendered in UK	
U285	26 Mar 45	Irish Sea	Sunk	
U326	28 Mar 45	Irish Sea	Sunk	
U979	29 Mar 45	Off Reykjavik	Sunk	1 (348)
U956	31 Mar 45	English Channel	Surrendered in UK	

He also reported that these deep minefields were being laid outside the declared mined zones and in mine-free passages as a trap for U-boats pursuing convoys, that more than 2,000 had been laid in September and that similar fields were being laid off Cape Clear. This information had been obtained, allegedly, from a crew member of a minelayer, but BdU placed little credence upon the reports, thinking it improbable that 2,000 mines had been laid in the North Channel where mines were very likely to break adrift in the prevalent heavy ground swell and so endanger British shipping. The reported fate of *U1006* was also doubted because BdU estimated correctly that she had been lost somewhere between the Faeroes and Orkneys.

The agent sending these reports was in fact a British double-agent, code-named 'Tate', and his reports had been carefully formulated by the Admiralty in the hope of discouraging the dispatch of more U-boats into the coastal areas. To this end, apart from the spurious reference to the cause of the loss of *U1006* and Tate's alleged source of information, the intelligence fed to the Germans was substantially correct.

In October 1944, British minelayers had begun sowing deep fields across the St. George's Channel from the south-eastern Irish coast to the north Cornish coast; off Cape Clear; across the entrance to the North Channel off Malin Head; to the north-west of the Hebrides; and five fields in the central sector of the English Channel. The broad policy was to lay deep fields on the main convoy routes, off focal points in the Irish Sea, and in areas of shallow water where U-boats might surface to fix their position. By the end of the war 17,000 mines had been laid in these fields.

BdU's apprehension of the mounting danger from mines was increased when *U260* was severely damaged by a mine on 13 March, while proceeding at a depth of 260 feet some fifteen miles south of Cape Clear. She managed to surface and report the incident by radio before her commander scuttled the boat (the crew took to the dinghies and landed on the Irish coast near Galley Head). This incident lent veracity to agent Tate's reports, and had the desired effect of making BdU withdraw the boats seaward from the coastal areas. In pursuance of this change of tactics, U-boats that had already sailed for the coastal areas early in April were diverted to new deep water attack areas 200-300 miles west of the entrance to the English Channel and 30–100 miles north of Donegal Bay.

In an attempt to tie down enemy forces in the Atlantic, six Type IX U-boats already bound for the US seaboard were formed into Group Seewolf, which was to comb the Northern Atlantic convoy routes and, it was hoped, spring surprise attacks on the weakly defended mid-ocean convoys, causing not only loss but forcing a dispersion of the Allied air and surface A/S forces concentrated around the British Isles. Group Seewolf was in fact a weak substitute for what Dönitz had always intended to do on a larger scale with his Type XXI ocean-going Electro-boats had they been ready in time.

The six boats of Group Seewolf (*U518*, *U858*, *U880*, *U805*, *U1235*, *U546*) were ordered to rendezvous north of the Azores. By 10 April they were roughly lined up on the meridian of 26°W between the latitudes 48° and 51°N, some 650 nautical miles due north of the Azores. On the 11 April they received a signal from BdU to take up precise positions in a north/south line and begin a sweep to the west-south-west along the Allied convoy routes. They were to proceed submerged at periscope depth by day and on the surface during the hours of darkness.

All orders addressed to Group Seewolf were passed in the 'Triton' Enigma key and were, consequently, decrypted and known to the Admiralty almost concurrently. As a result two US escort-carriers and twenty destroyers were ordered to form a patrol barrier across the area in which Group Seewolf had been ordered to make its westward

U-Boats Dispatched to British Home Waters during April And May 1945

Boat	Sailed	Operational Area	Returned	Ships Sunk
U636	1 April 45	NW Approaches	Sunk	
U1007	1 April 45	SW Approaches	Surrendered in UK	
U293	1 April 45	NW Approaches	Surrendered in UK	
U739	1 April 45	North Minch	4 May 45	
U2324	3 April 45	Firth of Forth	25 April 45	1 (1,150)
U825	3 April 45	NW Approaches	Surrendered in UK	
U249	4 April 45	SW Approaches	Surrendered in UK	
U1274	5 April 45	Firth of Forth	Sunk	1 (8,966)
U1305	5 April 45	NW Approaches	Surrendered in UK	
U1055	5 April 45	SW Approaches	Sunk	
U901	5 April 45	SW Approaches	15 May 45	
U2322	5 April 45	Firth of Forth	5 May 45	
U1206	7 April 45	Firth of Forth	Sunk	
U4806	7 April 45	Off Reykjavik	Sunk	
U245	9 April 45	North Foreland	10 May 45	2 (9,847)
U2329	12 April 45	Firth of Forth	26 April 45	
U1105	13 April 45	NW Approaches	Surrendered in UK	1 (878)

sweep, and the mid-ocean convoys were re-routed well clear of the danger area.

Hardly had Group Seewolf begun the search when disaster struck. Late in the evening of 15 April the US destroyers *Frost* and *Stanton* made Sonar contact with a U-boat, and a 'Hedgehog' attack resulted in a violent underwater explosion with subsequent debris appearing on the surface, marking the end of *U1235*. Shortly afterwards, in the early hours of the 16th, *Frost* and *Stanton* made Sonar contact again, a few miles to the south, and after a 'Hedgehog' attack *U880* surfaced in a crippled condition. Gunfire from the two destroyers failed to sink the U-boat before she managed to submerge again, but Sonar contact was quickly regained and after four hours of plastering the area with 'Hedgehog' mortar-bombs and depth-charges a heavy underwater explosion, followed by a surge of oil rising to the surface, provided convincing proof of the destruction of *U880*.

No further contacts were made until the night of 21/22 April, when the US destroyers *Carter* and *Neal A. Scott* picked up definite echoes on their Sonar. After a 'Hedgehog' attack several heavy under-

Boat	Sailed	Operational Area	Returned	Ships Sunk
U1017	14 April 45	NW Approaches	Sunk	
U1010	15 April 45	SW Approaches	Surrendered in UK	
U244	15 April 45	SW Approaches	Surrendered in UK	
U1277	15 April 45	SW Approaches	Scuttled	
U398	17 April 45	Firth of Forth	Sunk	
U1109	18 April 45	SW Approaches	Surrendered in UK	
U2326	19 April 45	Firth of Forth	28 April 45	
	3 May 45	Firth of Forth	Surrendered in UK	
U963	23 April 45	SW Approaches	Sunk	
U637	23 April 45	Off Reykjavik	28 April 45	
U1057	26 April 45	NW Approaches	9 May 45	
U287	29 April 45	Firth of Forth	Sunk	
U1165	29 April 45	NW Approaches	14 May 45	
U1058	29 April 45	SW Approaches	Surrendered in UK	
U2511	30 April 45	Recalled	6 May 45	
U764	1 May 45	NW Approaches	Surrendered in UK	
U2336	1 May 45	Firth of Forth	14 May 45	2 (4,669)

water explosions were felt in the destroyers, followed by the immediate loss of Sonar contact and the appearance of oil fuel on the surface in large quantities. That was the end of *U518*.

Two days later, on the morning of the 24th, *U546* torpedoed and sank one of the destroyers of the hunting group, USS *Frederick C. Davis*. This audacity on the part of *U546*'s commander, Korvetten-kapitän Paul Just, resulted in predictable consequences. The subsequent hunt by eight destroyers ended after several hours, when they forced *U546* to the surface with a hail of 'Hedgehog' bombs, where her exhausted and shaken crew abandoned ship while the U-boat was raked with gunfire.

Unaware that four of the six boats had been destroyed within a fortnight of beginning their westward sweep, BdU signalled further orders to the group on 23 April. On completion of the sweep, and if fuel permitted, three boats were to proceed to the Halifax/Cape Cod area and three boats were to operate off New York. Acting on these instructions the two surviving boats, *U858* and *U805*, made for Halifax and Cape Hatteras respectively. They reached their areas on 1 May, four days before the cessation of hostilities, and surrendered to the Canadian and American authorities.

Meanwhile, in home waters, BdU dispatched a total of 33 U-boats to areas around the British Isles from 1 April to 5 May; most of them to operate in the south-western approaches (200–300 miles from the entrance to the English Channel) and the north-western approaches (30–100 miles north of Donegal Bay).

The withdrawal of the boats from the heavily patrolled inshore waters to deep water areas reduced losses to ten boats (30.3 per cent), but success remained elusive, only seven freighters grossing 25,510 tons being torpedoed and sunk, three of these by two of the five Type XXIIIs which operated between Aberdeen and St. Abb's Head and off the North Foreland during April and May.

The first of the Type XXIIIs to reach her operational area was *U2324*, which sailed from Christiansand on 3 April bound for the North Foreland off the Thames Estuary. During his approach her commander, Konstantin von Rapprad, attacked a coastal convoy off Orfordness on the 16th, sinking the 1,150-ton cable ship *Monarch*.

The second Type XXIII to sail in April was *U2322*, which left Stavanger on the 5th, arriving off the North Foreland on the 13th. Her commander, Fridtjof Heckel, sighted no targets until the 23rd when he attacked a convoy thirteen miles east of Ramsgate just after midnight, damaging the 7,209-ton Norwegian freighter *Sverre Helmersen*. Having expended both his torpedoes, Heckel returned immediately to Stavanger which he reached on 1 May.

In mid-April both *U2329* and *U2326* were operating between Aberdeen and St. Abb's Head, but neither boat achieved anything. Having returned to base to reload with torpedoes, *U2326* set out again on 3 May, but although she sighted several targets in the patrol area she was unable to get within torpedo range.

The last of the Type XXIIIs to set out on a war cruise was *U2336* under command of Korvettenkapitän Emil Klusmeyer, which sailed from Christiansand on 1 May. Klusmeyer was a former BdU staff officer, and had been one of those responsible for developing the tactics to be employed by the Electro-boats. Anxious to put the tactical theories into practice, he had volunteered for command of *U2336*. While outward bound to the operational area he failed to receive BdU's signal transmitted on 4 May to all boats at sea, ordering them to cease hostilities and return to base. Unaware that hostilities had ceased, Klusmeyer attacked a convoy off May Island in the entrance to the Firth of Forth at 0040 on 8 May in truly academic style, sinking the 1,791-ton Norwegian freighter *Sneland I* and the 2,878-ton British freighter *Avondale Park* with a spread of two torpedoes. This attack earned Klusmeyer the accolade of being the German U-boat commander who sank the last Allied merchantmen during the Second World War.

U-Boat Dispositions, July 1944 to May 1945
According to the BdU War Diary

Column 1. French Biscay coast.
Column 2. Southern Norway.
Column 3. Northern Norway (Arctic operations).
Column 4. Baltic.
Column 5. Mediterranean.
Column 6. Black Sea.

	1	2	3	4	5	6
1944						
July	95	29	31	8	11	6
Aug	30	66	29	12	8	6
Sept	5	94	26	15	3	3
Oct	2	93	30	14	-	-
Nov	2	105	26	15	-	-
Dec	1	104	31	16	-	-
1945						
Jan	1	119	20	15	-	-
Feb	1	123	20	12	-	-
Mar	1	128	19	8	-	-
April	1	124	19	6	-	-
May (4th)	1	103	17	5	-	-

On 30 April the one and only Type XXI ocean-going Electro-boat sailed from Bergen on her first and last operational cruise. This was *U2511*, under the command of the experienced Korvettenkapitän Adalbert Schnee. She had left Kiel for Norway on 18 March, her first patrol being scheduled to begin on 26 March, but during a deep diving trial off the Norwegian coast she damaged her periscope which delayed her departure until 17 April. Then, shortly after leaving Bergen she was forced to return with diesel defects so did not finally get away until the last day of the month.

Schnee had reached a position to the north of the Faeroes when he received the order transmitted to all boats to cease hostilities, but shortly afterwards he sighted a British cruiser and her destroyer escort at long range. Closing at high speed and then reducing to silent-running speed, Schnee attained an attack position on the cruiser inside the destroyer screen, from which he carried out a dummy attack, albeit with six torpedo tubes at the ready. After a final look at the target, which was too close to miss, Schnee dived deep and, undetected by the British warships, returned to base.

The very fact that *U2511* had been able, by virtue of her high underwater speed, to overhaul ships sighted at long range and then pen-

---

Strength of the U-Boat Fleet, July 1944 to May 1945
according to the BdU War Diary

Column 1. Total strength of U-boat Fleet at end of month.
Column 2. Total number of *Frontboote* (operational boats).
Column 3. Number of U-boats training.
Column 4. New boats on trials and working-up.
Column 5. Average number U-boats at sea in Atlantic and Home Waters.
Column 6. Average number on patrol in operational billets in Atlantic and Home Waters.

	1	2	3	4	5	6
1944						
July	432	180	90	162	34	13
Aug	411	151	94	166	55	15
Sept	402	146	100	156	68	16
Oct	402	139	100	163	45	7
Nov	402	148	105	161	41	11
Dec	414	152	104	170	51	17
1945						
Jan	440	155	102	183	35	12
Feb	461	156	105	200	43	10
Mar	463	156	104	203	54	12
April	444	150	104	190	54	16
May (4th)	393	126	100	167	44	13

etrate the destroyer screen and extricate herself undetected, provides convincing proof of the narrowness of the margin by which the Allies escaped the threat posed by the Type XXIs. For if Germany had not been defeated by the land armies before the Type XXIs appeared on the high seas in large numbers, Allied sea-borne trade might well have been paralyzed and the ability to supply the Anglo-American armies on the continent might have been dangerously, or perhaps even fatally, compromised.

The danger so narrowly averted is summarized by Correlli Barnett: 'The 1,600-ton Type XXI could cruise as far as the Pacific [from German ports] without refuelling and reach a sprint speed when deeply submerged of 16 to 17 knots on her electric motors; as fast as most Allied convoy escort vessels ... Moreover, during a pursuit at this speed the noise caused by water rushing and bubbling along the pursuer's own hull would deafen his Sonars. When dived to maximum depth under attack the Type XXI could cruise for nearly 300 miles at 6 knots on her electric motors, as against barely 100 miles and 2 knots by the VIIC U-boats ... The anti-submarine forces' existing operational arithmetic of search and kill would thus be rendered null and void: whereas the area unit in searching for a traditional U-boat had been 31,400 square miles, it would be 282,000 square miles for the Type XXI. In sum, the Allied navies had no ready technical or operational answers to the Type XXI ...'[7]

Chapter 11

REAPING THE WHIRLWIND

K-VERBAND OPERATIONS: JANUARY 1945

On 1 January 1945 the first of the two-man *Seehunde* midget submarines became operational. Dönitz expected great things from these craft, as evinced by remarks he made to Hitler during a conference on 3 January:

'Assuming that out of the eighty *Seehunde* midget submarines scheduled to operate per month, only fifty are able to attack, then one hundred torpedoes will be fired at the enemy. If 20 per cent of the torpedoes hit their targets, then about 100,000 tons [of shipping] will be sunk.'[1]

Dönitz was soon to regret this boast because, as with all previous *K-Verband* operations, most of the *Seehunde* ventures would end in fiasco. *K-Verband* operations continued to be directed against Allied sea-borne supplies bound for Antwerp. To this end Konteradmiral Heye directed that *Seehunde* were to attack shipping in the Scheldt estuary, *Biber* one-man midget submarines and *Molch* manned-torpedoes were to operate in the River Scheldt, and *Linsen* explosive motor-boats were to attack shipping in the Inner Scheldt.

At 1700 on New Year's Day, seventeen *Seehunde* set out from Ijmuiden to attack shipping in the approaches to the Outer Scheldt. They proceeded at 7 knots on the surface parallel with and five miles out from the Dutch coast as far as the Hook of Holland, then made for the East Hinder Channel and their operational area north of Ostend. None was located on passage by the ubiquitous Allied air patrols, but two were sunk by convoy escorts in the operational area – one at 1710 on the 2nd, by the RN destroyer *Cowdray* off Zeebrugge, the other at 2002 on the same day by the RN frigate *Ekins* north of Ostend. One grounded at Domberg on Walcheren Island at 0300 on the 3rd, another was scuttled north-east of Zeebrugge at 1610 on the 5th to escape an attack by British MTBs. The sole success was the sinking of the 324-ton armed trawler HMS *Hayburn Wyke* off Ostend at 2225 on 2 January. Only two *Seehunde* got back to base. Seven failed to find the harbour entrance and ran ashore at various points on the coast south of Ijmuiden, but most of the crews were rescued and several other boats were subsequently salvaged. Of these, three had sighted nothing on their cruise, one had fired a torpedo at a destroyer but missed, one had survived a 12-hour depth-charge attack and another had reached the operational area only to have to return immediately because of diesel defects. The fate of the remaining four is unknown.

Eight more *Seehunde* were to have set out on the evening of the 3rd, but bad weather set in and it was not until the 6th that two put to sea, and they were forced to return soon after leaving harbour because of diesel troubles. On 10 January, five *Seehunde* left Ijmuiden bound for the Kentish coast off Margate. Two soon returned with defects and another returned after receiving damage in a depth-charge attack by unidentified surface craft early on the 11th. Of the two that pressed on with the operation, one was unable to reach the operational area because of heavy seas and frequent snowstorms, but she blundered into a small convoy in the mouth of the Thames Estuary south of the Kentish Knock shoal, and made a torpedo attack. The pilot erroneously claimed a hit, after which he withdrew and managed to reach Ijmuiden safely. The other *Seehund* reached the North Foreland where she sighted two small vessels, but was unable to attack because of heavy seas. An ever-increasing amount of water was shipped while trying to run on the diesels, but when her bilge pump became choked she was forced to beach on the North Foreland to avoid foundering.

Foul weather also prevented a planned sortie into the Scheldt by twelve *Molch* on the 10th, and two days later the weather became so bad that all further *K-Verband* operations had to be suspended until conditions improved. In the meantime reinforcements of all types were brought into Holland by rail from Germany, and by the 20th the strength of *K-Verband* vessels in Dutch ports had become quite substantial:

In Ports		Inland Reserves	
Den Helder	27 *Linsen*	Amersfoort	60 *Molch*
Ijmuiden	26 *Seehunde*	Zeist	60 *Molch*
Scheveningen	33 *Linsen*		
Rotterdam	30 *Molch*		
Poortershavn	20 *Biber*		
Hellevoetsluis	27 Linsen		

By 21 January the weather had moderate sufficiently for ten *Seehunde* to resume operations. They sailed in three groups: one of four boats bound for billets off Ramsgate; one of three boats to the South Falls area east of North Foreland; and one of three boats to the convoys' swept channel off Lowestoft. Seven returned without reaching their allotted areas -six with mechanical troubles and one after a colli-

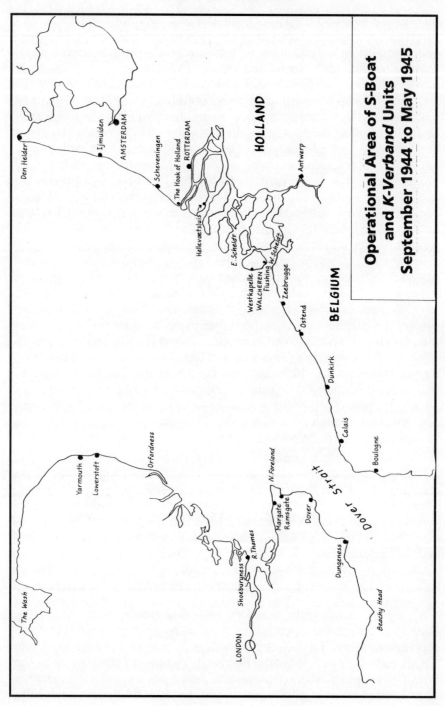

Operational Area of S-Boat and *K-Verband* Units September 1944 to May 1945

sion with a buoy. Of the three boats which continued their sorties, two operated off Ramsgate without sighting anything, and the third suffered a compass failure and blundered into the Thames Estuary. After firing at and missing a steamer at 2330 on the 22nd, the coxswain finally extricated himself from the estuary and after two days of steering blind found himself south of Lowestoft. Here the *Seehund* was sighted and depth-charged by a motor-launch. Although the boat escaped damage the coxswain decided to bottom until after dark before attempting the passage back to base. This he did, but without the benefit of a compass he set off in the wrong direction and at 0100 on the 25th he ran aground on Soroby Sands off Great Yarmouth. After spending 2½ days vainly trying to get clear, the two exhausted crew members fired Very lights to attract attention and were rescued by a boat from the Trinity House lightship *Beacon*.

After his earlier boast that the *Seehunde* were capable of sinking 100,000 tons of shipping per month, it must have been a very sheepish Dönitz who reported to Hitler on 23 January that as yet they had only accounted for one miserly 324-ton trawler. But with a mixture of bluster and irrepressible optimism Dönitz was able to make the fiasco sound like a success:

'Of the ten *Seehunde* which left Ijmuiden on 21st January, nine have so far returned. Partly because of technical defects and partly because of bad weather, their mission was unsuccessful. They underwent a severe test during their first operation, but despite negligible successes the operations were of the greatest value. All the defects which might never have been discovered in the Baltic Sea showed up under the severe conditions in the Hoofden and can thus be corrected ... They have been found to be relatively immune to depth-charges because due to their shape they offer so little resistance. They are tossed aside like a cork instead of being damaged. Thus the Seehund has proved relatively immune from enemy defences ... The crews have gained considerable confidence in their equipment, and future mass operations of the *Seehunde* under favourable weather conditions are expected to score considerable successes.'[2]

Linsen and *Biber* operations carried out in January proved to be equally unsuccessful. It was in exceptionally cold weather, with much floating ice in the Scheldt delta, that nine *Linsen* left Hellevoetsluis at 2300 on 24 January to operate in the West Scheldt. Next day the three control *Linsen* returned, having destroyed their six explosive-boats after sighting nothing. In similar weather fifteen *Biber* set out from the Hook of Holland on the night of the 29th/30th, having been towed down the coast from Poortershavn. They were undetected by Allied air patrols but were defeated by the weather. Five returned because of damage received from ice-floes, three sank after collisions with ice, one beached on return from the Scheldt near Hellevoetsluis after sixty hours at sea, and the remaining six vanished without trace.

The final *Seehunde* operation in January also started out on the evening of the 29th. Ten left Ijmuiden in two groups, one bound for the Margate area and the other for the South Falls. Only two boats reached their billets. One of these, operating well to the east of the South Falls, sighted a convoy of three ships with two escorts. Just as the sights were coming on to fire the boat had to go deep to avoid being rammed. She was ineffectively depth-charged and returned to base. The other boat reached Ramsgate, missed a ship in the roads with her torpedoes, and also returned to harbour. Of the remaining eight, two returned early with engine trouble, four returned because of damage sustained in the heavy seas, one turned back because her engineer was utterly exhausted, and one failed to find Ijmuiden harbour entrance and ran aground just south of the port.

There were no *Molch* operations during January because the intense cold was thought to lower electric battery capacity to a range of under 55 miles, which was not sufficient for West Scheldt operations. But trials completed by the end of the month proved them capable of just over 55 miles and, provided the boats could be towed as far as Goeree, this was considered adequate for future operations. Trials in launching *Linsen* explosive-boats from S-boats were also successful, and, when weather again permitted, it was intended to transport *Linsen* in this way for extended operations at the western end of the Thames-Scheldt convoy route.

Summary of K-Verband Operations: January 1945			Ships sunk	
	Sorties	Losses	Torpedo	Mines
Seehunde	44	10	1 (324)	–
Biber & Molch	15	10	–	–
Linsen	15	7	–	–
Totals	74	27	1 (324)	–
No ships were damaged by torpedoes or mines.				

SCHNELLBOOTE OPERATIONS: JANUARY 1945

According to the FdS War Diary there were 48 S-boats in Dutch ports during the first week of January, but not more than 36 were operational on any one day of the month. They were disposed as follows:

Den Helder	2nd Flotilla	8 boats
	5th Flotilla	8 boats
Ijmuiden	8th Flotilla	8 boats

Rotterdam	4th Flotilla	8 boats
	6th Flotilla	8 boats
	9th Flotilla	8 boats

The main operational task of these boats was to attack Allied supply traffic plying between the Thames and the Scheldt, a task they shared with the *K-Verband* units; or if this proved unprofitable, they were to attack shipping between the Humber and the Thames. Minelaying in these areas was considered of equal importance, but was not to be carried out in certain specified areas where it was likely to hamper the *Seehunde* operations against the Thames-Scheldt convoys. Torpedo sorties were to be made independently or in conjunction with the *Seehunde* operations, but only in close liaison between KdK and FdS directing staffs. The River Scheldt above Walcheren Island was reserved for *Biber*, *Molch* and *Linsen* operations.

Unfavourable weather prevented S-boat sorties during the first nine days of January, and a planned torpedo and minelaying sortie from all three S-boat bases on the evening of the 9th was abandoned at the last minute because of a rising gale. Consequently it was not until the night of the 14th/15th that the first operation of the year took place. Sailing from Den Helder, 2nd Flotilla's eight boats laid twenty mines off Dunkirk, while six of 5th Flotilla's boats laid nineteen mines in the Outer Dowsing Channel east of the Humber. Both sorties were detected by Wellingtons and Swordfish off the Dutch coast, but none of the boats suffered damage during the seven attacks made upon them.

Next night (15th/16th) a major effort was mounted. Nine boats of 2nd and 5th Flotillas carried out a torpedo sweep north of Cromer but sighted no convoys. They were engaged for a short time by the patrolling destroyer *Farndale* but escaped unscathed. Nine boats of 6th and 9th Flotillas attacked an east-bound convoy in the Scheldt approaches but were repulsed by the destroyer *Cotswold* and the frigates *Curzon* and *Seymour*. No damage was inflicted by either side. Eight boats of 4th and 8th Flotillas attacked a convoy off Margate and sank the 2,750-ton tank landing ship *LST 415* without loss. Both on the way out and when returning, the S-boats were sighted by Allied air patrols off the Hook, westward of Ijmuiden and off Den Helder. Nine bombing attacks were made on the boats but none was damaged and the operations proceeded unhindered.

No further operations took place until the night of 22/23 January, when 24 S-boats from the Rotterdam and Ijmuiden flotillas raided the Thames-Scheldt convoy route. One group attacked a convoy to the north of Dunkirk and sank the straggling 2,365-ton British freighter *Halo*. This led to a brief skirmish with a group of MTBs, in which one MTB was damaged but the S-boats got away without loss. Other groups of S-boats were engaged by British naval forces at different points along the route, resulting in damage to *S168* and *S175*, and farther west, in the Margate area, gunfire from the Tongue Sand Fort sank *S199*.

The Den Helder flotillas laid mines off the Humber on the following night, and although they were undisturbed by surface forces the S-boats were attacked five times by Wellingtons off Texel as they were returning to base, but all escaped damage. Another minelaying operation was carried out by eighteen S-boats on the night of 24th/25th, off Orfordness. Dense fog grounded Allied air patrols and enabled the S-boats to carry out their task undisturbed.

A spell of bad weather put a stop to further operations until the night of 29/30 January, when the two Den Helder flotillas set out to lay mines to the north of Cromer. Despite being attacked by Wellingtons shortly after leaving base, and engaged by a destroyer and a frigate while laying their mines, all the boats returned to Den Helder in one piece.

During January the S-boats had carried out 95 sorties, and for the loss of two of their number had torpedoed and sunk two merchant ships grossing 5,115 tons, and the minefields they laid subsequently accounted for five merchant ships grossing 16,361 tons, and damage to another of 1,100 tons.

K-VERBAND OPERATIONS: FEBRUARY 1945

The month of February opened on a sour note for the *K-Verband*. On the 3rd, the *Molch* reserve depot at Amersfoort was bombed during a general attack by Spitfires of 2nd Tactical Air Force on the railway system in and around the town. Although no *Molch* were damaged, the depot and its facilities was badly damaged. On the same day the *Biber* base at Poortershavn was attacked by nineteen Lancasters which dropped 12,000lb Tallboys; the base facilities were wrecked, and the heavy cranes used for lifting the *Biber* in and out of the water were destroyed. As a result, although none of the midget submarines was destroyed or damaged, no *Biber* operations could be mounted for the rest of the month.

The first *K-Verband* operation of February took place on the evening of the 5th, when eight *Seehunde* put out from Ijmuiden bound for the North Foreland area. All met with failure. One returned early with diesel problems, two beached on the Dutch coast north and south of Ijmuiden, and three returned without having reached their billets. Only two reached their patrol area, and although they sighted a great deal of shipping they were unable, because of their low speed, to get near enough to launch attacks.

Late on 10 February another eight *Seehunde* sailed for the Thames-Scheldt convoy route. Mechanical troubles caused three to return prematurely on the 11th, and another from its billet on the 12th. Three operated as ordered, but their cruises were unproductive, and one of them vanished without trace. A follow-up against the same objective was carried out by five more *Seehunde* which set out from Ijmuiden late on the 12th. Once again one boat returned early because of defects, but three reached their billets, one of which attacked a convoy off the North Foreland on the 15th, badly damaging the 2,628-ton Dutch tanker *Liseta*. One of the three failed to return, the cause of her loss being a mystery.

The next *Seehunde* operation began on the morning of the 16th when four *Seehunde* put out from Ijmuiden at 0800 to attack shipping in the Scheldt estuary. Two of these boats were never heard of again; one saw no targets and when returning to base on the 18th ran aground just north of Ijmuiden. The fourth boat attacked a convoy of landing-craft off the Scheldt on the 19th, but also ran aground off Ijmuiden while attempting to return.

That night fifteen *Linsen* left Hellevoetsluis, bound for the Scheldt. Nine returned early because of fog and the other six achieved nothing, although two of their number were lost. Late on the 21st yet another nine *Linsen* left Hellevoetsluis to seek targets in the West Scheldt. Six returned because of engine trouble and the other three failed to find any targets. The *Molch* manned-torpedoes made a belated appearance that same night; ten were towed from Scheveningen as far as Schouwen Island, and four set out under their own power from Hellevoetsluis, all bound for the Inner Scheldt. Eight returned having found no targets, two were sunk by MTBs five miles north-west of West Kapelle, one was sunk off Flushing by gunfire from a shore battery, and three vanished without trace.

The last *Seehunde* sortie of February took place on the 23rd when five boats set out for the South Falls area. All five reached their billets and they sank two ships — the 2,750-ton tank landing ship *LST 364* which went down 20 miles east of the North Foreland on the 22nd, and the 941-ton cable ship *Alert*, which sank seven miles east of

			Ships sunk		Ships damaged	
	Sorties	Losses	Torpedo	Mine	Torpedo	Mine
Seehunde	33	4	2 (3,691)	–	1 (2,628)	–
Biber & Molch	14	6	–	–	–	–
Linsen	24	3	–	–	–	–
Totals	71	13	2 (3,691)	–	1 (2,628)	–

Summary of *K-Verband* Operations: February 1945

Ramsgate on the 24th. All eight *Seehunde* returned to base, including one that had been attacked by a Beaufighter at 0948 on 28 February, about forty miles east of Orfordness, but had escaped without damage.

SCHNELLBOOTE OPERATIONS: FEBRUARY 1945

Like the *K-Verband*, the S-boats got off to a bad start, their bunkers at Ijmuiden being bombed on the 3rd and the 8th by Bomber Command, and on the 10th by the US Eighth Air Force. Tallboys were dropped in the two RAF raids, but although these bombs shattered the bunkers no S-boats were lost because they were dispersed under camouflage netting around the docks. Rocket bombs were employed for the first time in the war by the Eighth Air Force B-17 Flying Fortresses, but once again, although the port installations were badly damaged and one S-boat, *S193*, was destroyed, the rest of the boats escaped damage because they were dispersed.

Inclement weather prevented any S-boat sorties until the night of the 17th/18th, when boats of the Den Helder flotillas laid mines off the Humber and in the Wash, in foggy conditions which veiled them from both sea and air patrols. Subsequently the French destroyer *La Combattante* and the 187-ton trawler *Aquarius* came to grief on these mines and two freighters, the 8,039-ton *City of London* and the 3,517-ton *Cydonia*, were damaged.

Three nights later (20th/21st) boats from the Ijmuiden and Rotterdam flotillas attacked Thames-Scheldt traffic with torpedoes and mines, but surface and air patrols, aided by clear visibility, prevented any success. The boats were attacked by aircraft thirteen times, but all of them got back to base unscathed.

Next night 22 S-boats from all six flotillas set out to attack East Coast convoys. Sixteen air attacks shortly after they had left their bases were unsuccessful, but shadowing aircraft reports enabled naval forces to intercept and drive boats of 4th, 6th and 9th Flotillas back to base. However, the boats of 2nd and 5th Flotillas evaded the enemy forces and attacked a convoy 23 miles north-east of Great Yarmouth, sinking the 2,780-ton freighter *Goodwood* and the 1,109-ton freighter *Blacktoft*, and damaging the 1,345-ton *Skjold*. The 8th Flotilla also evaded the enemy patrols, and attacked a convoy of landing-craft in the Thames Estuary, sinking *LCP 707*. In the ensuing counter-attack by the convoy escort *S193* was sunk.

Yet again the flotillas put to sea on the third consecutive night. The Rotterdam boats were to have laid mines along the Thames-Scheldt route, but were engaged by surface forces before reaching the swept channel. The Ijmuiden flotilla was shadowed and attacked by Wellingtons from the moment they put out until they had reached a position almost halfway across the North Sea, before the commanding officer of the flotilla decided to abandon the sortie and return to base.

On the night of the 24th/25th, the fourth consecutive night of operations, the S-boats embarked on a minelaying sortie off the East Anglian coast. One group, attacked by aircraft off Ijmuiden, shot down a Wellington, and capped this by shooting down a shadowing Wellington an hour later. But before these aircraft were downed they had alerted the naval patrols that an S-boat operation was in progress. This resulted in a number of clashes as the various small groups were crossing the southern sector of the North Sea. *S167* was crippled and was scuttled to prevent capture: her crew of 23 officers and men were rescued by a British warship.

The final S-boat operation of the month took place after dark on the 28th. Boats from all six flotillas embarked on combined torpedo and minelaying sorties against shipping on the Thames-Scheldt convoy route and off the East Anglian coast. Once again the out-going boats were attacked and shadowed by patrolling aircraft, but one group managed to lay mines off Ostend although they were intercepted on their return passage by the destroyer *Cotswold* and the frigate *Seymour* which sank *S220* (26 survivors were taken prisoner). A number of other brief and indecisive skirmishes took place between groups of S-boats and British naval forces along the Thames-Scheldt route that night, but although no torpedo attacks were made on Allied shipping the S-boats were not prevented from laying their mines, which subsequently caused the loss of three merchant ships (the 4,571-ton *Auretta*, the 7,219-ton *Sampa* and the 7,176-ton *Robert L. Vann*).

During February the S-boats had embarked on 77 sorties, and for the loss of two boats had torpedoed and sunk two merchant ships grossing 3,889 tons and damaged one merchantman grossing 1,345 tons; their mines subsequently accounted for ten merchant ships grossing 19,551 tons and damaged three others grossing 11,956 tons.

K-VERBAND OPERATIONS: MARCH 1945

Between 6 and 19 March ten *Seehunde* left Ijmuiden bound for the North Foreland. They achieved nothing and lost four of their number. One was sunk by an MTB some thirty miles east of Ramsgate on the 7th; another was sunk by a Beaufighter off Goeree on the 10th; while two were sunk by the frigate HMS *Torrington* – one off Ramsgate on the 11th and the other twenty miles north of Dunkirk on the 13th.

During the same period nine other *Seehunde* were operating off the coast of East Anglia. One of these sank the 2,878-ton British freighter *Taber Park* eight miles off Southwold on 13 March. Two of these boats were sighted and attacked by Beaufighters well to the west of Ijmuiden on the 18th, but survived; another boat was sunk by an MTB 23 miles south-east of Great Yarmouth on the 22nd.

The intended scale of *Biber* operations was seriously affected on the 6th when a *Biber* pilot, while preparing for an operation, accidentally released his torpedoes in the depot basin at Rotterdam. Fourteen *Biber* were sunk in the resulting conflagration and nine others were damaged. But eleven surviving *Biber* were sailed from Rotterdam that evening to operate in the Scheldt. No Allied shipping was attacked, but none of the boats returned. One was captured by a motor-launch off Breskens on the 7th; four others were found abandoned on beaches off North Beveland, Domberg, Knocke and Zeebrugge; and another was sunk by shore gunfire off West Kapelle. The other five vanished without trace.

On the night of the 10th/11th, six *Linsen* left Hellevoetsluis to raid the anchorage off Veere on the northern coast of Walcheren Island. They were driven off by shore batteries, leaving two boats grounded on a sandbank. Next night a combined operation, by fifteen *Biber* armed with torpedoes and mines, fourteen *Molch* and 27 *Linsen*, was mounted against shipping in the West Scheldt. Again no Allied shipping was hit, but losses were heavy: thirteen *Biber*, nine *Molch* and sixteen *Linsen* failed to return.

Despite the heavy losses and total lack of commensurate results, the Germans persevered with these suicidal missions. On the night of 23/24 March sixteen *Biber* armed with torpedoes and mines set out from Poortershavn for the Scheldt approaches. It is not known if any mines were laid, but no torpedo hits were achieved and nine *Biber* failed to return.

The last *K-Verband* sorties of March were carried out by ten *Seehunde* which left Ijmuiden between 24 and 26 March. Four set out for the coastal waters off East Anglia and six to operate against the Thames-Scheldt convoy route. Most of them reached their billets but four never returned. The East Anglia group lost one *Seehund* to a Beaufighter at 1440 on the 25th, some twenty miles north-west of the

Summary of K-Verband Operations: March 1945						
			Ships sunk		Ships damaged	
	Sorties	*Losses*	*Torpedo*	*Mine*	*Torpedo*	*Mine*
Seehunde	29	9	3 (5,267)	–	–	–
Biber & Molch	56	42	–	3 (225)	–	1 (8,325)
Linsen	66	27	–	–	–	–
Totals	151	78	3 (5,267)	3 (225)	–	1 (8,325)

Hook of Holland, and another to the corvette HMS *Puffin* off Lowestoft in the early hours of the 26th. Only one *Seehund* from this group scored a kill, sinking the 833-ton coaster *Jim* on the 30th, southeast of Orfordness. One of the Thames-Scheldt group also scored a kill, sinking the 1,556-ton British freighter *Newlands* off the North Foreland at 1210 on the 26th. Shortly afterwards a *Seehund* in the vicinity was sunk by the RN motor-launch *ME 1471*, and another was accounted for by motor-launch *ML 586* to the west of Walcheren late on the 27th.

SCHNELLBOOTE OPERATIONS: MARCH 1945

The FdS War Diary gives no specific port distribution of the flotillas at the beginning of March, but it is evident that 8th Flotilla left Ijmuiden at the end of February to refit in Germany and was not replaced, thus leaving 2nd, 4th, 5th, 6th and 9th Flotillas based at Den Helder and Rotterdam with a total strength of 40 S-boats, of which no more than 25-30 were available for operations on any one day. Henceforward Ijmuiden was only used as a port of call by the S-boats, partly because the Allied bombing raids during early February had shattered a large part of the installations, and partly because the dispersal facilities were occupied by *Seehunde*. Further damage was inflicted during raids by the US Eighth Air Force on 14 and 21 March, but no S-boats nor the well-dispersed *Seehunde* were hit.

The first S-boat operation in March took place on the night of the 9th/10th, when three flotillas set out to lay mines in the Scheldt approaches. They were sighted and shadowed on their way south by air patrols and had several skirmishes with Allied naval forces, but the boats' superior speed enabled them to disengage and lay their mines. They were twice attacked by aircraft on the return passage, but no damage was sustained and they shot down a Swordfish west of the Hook of Holland.

The night of 11th/12th witnessed simultaneous operations by S-boats, *Biber Molch* and *Linsen* against the Thames-Antwerp supply line, in which, for the first and only time, S-boats were used to transport *Linsen* to a distant objective. Three control and six explosive-boats were carried and launched by the Rotterdam flotillas near the South Falls buoy to attack a passing convoy. Predictably no success was achieved by the explosive-boats and the three control boats with all nine pilots aboard made off homeward. At 0750 on the 12th, when they had reached a position off Goeree, they were sighted, attacked and sunk by Coastal Command Swordfish of No. 119 Squadron. The Den Helder flotillas laid mines off the Wash. Although both S-boat groups were reported by air patrols as soon as they left harbour, there were no subsequent encounters with enemy naval forces.

Kommodore Petersen intended to operate all five S-boat flotillas on minelaying sorties during the night of 13/14 March, but the Den Helder boats were so harried by air action that they turned back early and, as the weather suddenly deteriorated, the other flotillas were recalled and the entire operation was abandoned.

No further operations were attempted until the night of the 17th/18th, when five flotillas again put to sea on minelaying sorties. Once again air patrols gathered over them, reporting, shadowing and occasionally attacking, but this time the S-boats pressed on and were able to lay their mines off Ostend and the East Anglian coast. Only one group was intercepted by naval forces, and during a brief exchange the S-boats damaged two MTBs before making off at high speed unscathed.

Next night all the S-boat flotillas put to sea again: a total of 25 boats to operate with mines and torpedoes against the East Coast convoy route between the Humber and Orfordness. They were promptly reported by patrolling aircraft as soon as they left their bases and were shadowed all the way to Cromer, where six boats of 5th Flotilla were engaged by destroyers which damaged two boats and caused them to withdraw. The 2nd Flotilla ran into a group of British MTBs and after a fierce engagement turned back, all six of them damaged. The five boats of 9th Flotilla were fired on by destroyers off Southwold and driven away. Only 4th and 6th Flotillas reached their operational area unopposed. After laying their mines they came upon a convoy off Lowestoft which they attacked, sinking the 1,097-ton British freighter *Rogate*. One S-boat was damaged by a convoy escort during the attack.

On the night of 21/22 March all five flotillas, totalling twenty S-boats, set off once more to operate against the East Coast convoy route. The 2nd Flotilla, emerging from Den Helder, was harried by Coastal Command Beaufighters which attacked and sank *S181*, killing both the flotilla leader and the commanding officer of the boat, whereupon the remaining four boats returned to harbour with the survivors of *S181*. The S-boats shot down one aircraft. The other fifteen boats continued across the North Sea under constant air shadowing and occasional attack. On closing the British coast they were engaged by naval patrols in various positions and were driven off. Damage was claimed by each side, but in all cases it was superficial.

Next night, nine boats of 4th and 6th Flotillas sortied from the Hook to lay mines on the Thames-Scheldt route. Eight attacks were made by the watchful air patrols but without causing any damage. However, the shadowing reports enabled interceptions to be made by naval patrols and the S-boats were repulsed, two of their number being damaged.

The last operation of March took place on the night of 25th/26th, when fifteen boats from 4th, 6th and 9th Flotillas left the Hook for yet another attempt to lay mines along the Thames-Scheldt route. Reports from patrolling aircraft resulted in numerous skirmishes with naval patrols to the north of the convoy route, but five S-boats managed to penetrate the screen and lay their mines. Six air attacks were delivered as the boats were rounding the Hook but without result.

The FdS War Diary mentions the fact that by the 21st the March fuel allocation had been used up, and it was only with great difficulty that sufficient fuel was made available for the last three operations.

During March the S-boats had embarked on a total of 131 sorties, and for the loss of only one of their number had torpedoed and sunk two merchant ships grossing 3,968 tons, and eight merchantmen grossing 31,714 tons subsequently came to grief on their mines, which also damaged one merchant ship grossing 7,176 tons.

K-VERBAND OPERATIONS: APRIL 1945

By the beginning of April, the advance of the Anglo-American armies into north-western Germany had almost completely encircled Holland. Consequently it was no longer possible to send *K-Verband* reinforcements to the Dutch ports by road and rail, and only the *Seehunde* were sufficiently seaworthy to make the coastal passage from Germany. According to the KdK War Diary *K-Verband* strength in Holland on 8 April was:

29	*Seehunde*	at Ijmuiden
24	*Biber*	at Rotterdam
60	*Molch*	at Amersfoort
51	*Linsen*	at Scheveningen and Hellevoetsluis

The only potential reinforcements to this depleted force were four *Seehunde* which left Wilhelmshaven on 18 April and, despite being attacked by a Beaufighter fifteen miles north-west of Borkum, reached Ijmuiden two days later. Subsequently another seventeen left Wilhelmshaven in batches. One turned back after grounding and one foundered off Wangerooge Island, but the remaining fifteen all reached Ijmuiden on various dates up to the end of the month.

Bad weather prevented any *K-Verband* operations until 5 April, but from then until the end of the month a total of 36 *Seehunde* sorties left Ijmuiden, at fairly regular intervals, to operate off the East Coast, in the Scheldt approaches, and as far west as Dungeness in the Straits of Dover. Of the ten *Seehunde* that operated off the East Coast to the north of the Thames, six were lost for no returns. Nine operated in the

Scheldt approaches, and for the loss of three of their number, they sank the 800-ton US tanker *Y-17*. The most successful group were the seventeen *Seehunde* that operated in the Dover-Dungeness area. They sank the 7,219-ton British freighter *Samida* and damaged two other large freighters for the loss of six of their number.

The first *Biber* operation of April got under way on the 9th, when five put out from the Hook of Holland with torpedoes and mines destined for the Scheldt. Two returned with mechanical trouble on the 11th, one of these blowing up on a mine off the entrance to the harbour. The other three were sunk on the 12th to the west of the Hook — two by Beaufighters and one by a Swordfish.

Two more *Biber* left Zierikzee on the night of 11th/12th, to lay mines in the channel between North and South Beveland. One succeeded and the other vanished without trace. On the same night fifteen *Linsen* left Hellevoetsluis to operate off Ostend where they were repelled by surface patrols: the frigate *Ekins* sank two with gunfire and three explosive-boats were expended without hitting a target. A further 21 *Linsen* attempted to repeat the operation next night but were forced to to return prematurely by bad weather. A similar attempt by twelve *Linsen* on the night of the 17th/18th was again frustrated by bad weather, but six others, detailed to operate off Dunkirk, sailed despite of the conditions. They lost their way and were all eventually found hard and fast aground off Breskens.

The final *Linsen* operation of the war took place on the night of 20/21 April, when twelve put out from Hellevoetsluis to operate off Dunkirk. They were intercepted some 28 miles to the north of Ostend by British patrols, and six were sunk by the gunfire of the frigate *Ekins*. The remainder managed to return to base.

On the night of the 21st/22nd, six Biber set out from the Hook to lay mines in the Scheldt. Four returned, having laid their mines; two vanished without trace. The final *Biber* sortie, which was also the final *K-Verband* operation of the war, began at 1030 on 26 April, when four put out from Rotterdam to lay mines in the Scheldt. One grounded on

			Ships sunk		Ships damaged	
	Sorties	Losses	Torpedo	Mines	Torpedo	Mines
Seehunde	36	12	2 (8,019)	–	2 (15,756)	–
Biber	17	9	–	4 (266)	–	1 (7,191)
Linsen	66	17	–	–	–	–
Totals	119	38	2 (8,019)	4 (266)	2 (15, 756)	1 (7,191)

Summary of *K-Verband* Operations: April 1944

the way down to the sea and the others were attacked by US Thunderbolts as they were clearing the Hook. Two were sunk and one got back to base.

From start to finish the *K-Verband* operations, despite the undoubted bravery of the volunteer crews, were inept and more often than not farcical. Beyond tying down a number of Allied air and naval forces the genus did not justify the very considerable effort – both in men and *matériel* – expended by the Germans. The only possible chance of success for these unseaworthy and unsuitable craft would have been the element of total surprise. But this vital factor was very rarely achieved in areas swamped by enemy warships and aircraft.

During the entire period from 1 January 1945 until the end of the war, the *Seehunde*, *Biber*, *Molch* and *Linsen* based on the Dutch ports carried out a total of 415 sorties, and for the loss of 159 of their number sank fifteen merchant ships grossing 17,792 tons; a mere fraction of the tonnage represented by the hundreds of merchant vessels that were plying the Thames-Scheldt and East Coast convoy routes at this time. In terms of human sacrifice and *matériel* expenditure it simply wasn't worth the effort.

SCHNELLBOOTE OPERATIONS: APRIL 1945

At the end of March 5th S-Boat Flotilla was transferred to the Baltic, leaving only four flotillas in Dutch ports. Their first operation of April took place on the night of the 5th/6th, when eighteen boats left the Dutch bases for torpedo operations against shipping on the Thames-Scheldt route. One group of seven boats was sighted off the Hook by patrolling Wellingtons, but the six attacks delivered on them caused no damage. Nothing was seen of any of these S-boats near the convoy routes by Allied surface and air patrols, and the FdS War Diary makes no mention of their movements.

Next night six boats of 2nd Flotilla left Den Helder to lay mines off the East Coast. They were sighted and shadowed by air patrols from the moment they put to sea until they were engaged by a force of MTBs (at 0140 on the 7th) off Smiths Knoll. A series of violent point-blank actions followed during the next 90 minutes, during which *S176* and *S177* were rammed and sunk, and the British lost two MTBs (one from gunfire and one by ramming); another MTB was badly damaged when ramming an opponent.

Twelve boats of 4th and 6th Flotillas set out next night (7th/8th) to lay mines in the Scheldt approaches. As usual they were shadowed by air patrols until they were engaged by naval forces at 0130 to the north-west of Ostend. During the action *S202* and *S703* collided at high speed and both sank. Some 40 survivors were picked up by the pursuing frigate HMS *Rutherford* and two MTBs. Shortly afterwards *S223* struck a mine and sank about 30 miles north of Ostend. These were relatively heavy losses for the small S-boat force and no further operations took place until the night of 12/13 April, when twelve boats of 4th and 9th Flotillas put out to lay mines in the Scheldt approaches. They were shadowed and reported by Wellingtons and in due course were brought to action by a naval patrol group. A short fierce battle, at ranges as short as twenty yards, was fought with the frigate *Ekins* and two MTBs, during which *S205* was badly damaged by gunfire.

This proved to be the last S-boat operation of the war. German records state that on 16 April there were only 22 S-boats in the Dutch ports, and of these not more than fifteen were operational. A proposal to transfer 1st Flotilla from Germany was abandoned because of fuel shortage. This, and the successful combination of air and surface patrols, brought to an end what was the most successful form of attack against enemy East Coast and Scheldt-bound shipping. For during the last four months of the war the Holland-based S-boats carried out 351 sorties, and for the loss of only ten boats torpedoed and mined 31 merchant ships grossing 88,971 tons. In the final analysis, however, their effect on the Allied war effort was infinitesimal.

The whole purpose of the attacks on the Scheldt-bound shipping by the S-boats and *K-Verband* craft was to restrict supplies 'feeding' the Anglo-American armies on the Western Front, and in this the Germans failed miserably. In April 1945 alone, 1,341,610 tons of stores were discharged through Antwerp, along with 288,809 tons of petrol, oil and lubricants.

TO THE BITTER END

By the beginning of 1945, Germany was a weakened husk held firmly in the jaws of the gigantic nutcracker formed by the Anglo-American armies in the west and the Soviet juggernaut in the east. The Allied insistance on unconditional surrender, however, and the intention to

Summary of S-boat and *K-Verband* operations:
January-April 1945

	Sorties	Losses	Ships sunk Torpedo	Mine	Ships damaged Torpedo	Mine
Seehunde	142	35	8 (17,301)	–	3 (18,384)	–
Biber & Molch	102	70		7 (491)		2 (15,516)
Linsen	171	54	–	–	–	–
S–boats	351	10	6 (12,972)	25 (75,999)	1 (1,345)	7 (26,408)
Totals	766	169	14 (30,273)	32 (76,490)	4 (19,729)	9 (41,924)

split Germany into separate zones, goaded the Germans to fight to the finish. A map captured from the Allies showed that the country was to be divided at the Oder-Neisse line, which filled the Germans with the fearful certainty that unconditional surrender would entail abandoning to the Russians the entire area east of that line, together with the German troops on the Eastern Front and millions of women and children. This was the main reason why Dönitz considered it necessary for the Kriegsmarine to fight to bitter end.

The Kriegsmarine's main task in the last months of the war was to rescue from the Russians, in the short time available, as many troops and civilians as possible from the eastern Baltic provinces of Germany. Thus, from January 1945 onwards, every available merchant vessel was employed in transporting German troops and civilians from Lithuania and East Prussia, and all serviceable warships, including U-boats, were used to evacuate refugees from East Prussia and Pomerania. At the same time the pocket-battleships *Lützow* and *Admiral Scheer* and the heavy cruiser *Prinz Eugen* supported the German Army's vain attempt to hold back the Soviet advance along the north German Baltic coast by bombarding Russian positions ashore: during March alone *Prinz Eugen*, for example, expended 4,871 rounds of 8in ammunition and more than 2,500 rounds of 4.1in.

Some idea of the immensity of the evacuation carried out by the Kriegsmarine can be gained from a summary of the numbers transported, compiled by Marinegruppe Ost on 9 May 1945. According to this summary more than two million soldiers and refugees were rescued from East Prussian and Pomeranian ports and transported to ports in western Germany:

	Refugees	Troops
From Danzig, Gdynia and Hela, from 1 January to 8 May	1,047,000	300,000
From Libau, from 1 January to 8 May:	100,000	
From Königsberg and Pillau, from 25 January to 25 April:	451,000	141,000
From Kolberg, in mid-March 1945:	70,000	7,500
Total 2,116,500.		

This huge evacuation was not executed without loss: Soviet submarines and aircraft, and mines sown in the Baltic by the RAF, all took their toll of the exodus. But German records show that only 20,000 of the total transported lost their lives when the ships in which they were packed were sunk (a mere 1 per cent of the total). One of the ships sunk by a Soviet submarine was the 25,484-ton liner *Wilhelm Gustloff*, which capsized after being torpedoed on the night of 30/31 January. Most of the more than 6,000 refugees aboard her drowned in the freezing Baltic waters, making the loss of *Wilhelm Gustloff* the worst maritime disaster in history (1,500 lost their lives when the liner *Titanic* sank in 1912).

The great Russian offensive on the Oder front, which opened on the 16 April, achieved a decisive breakthrough three days later which carried the Red Army to the gates of Berlin. On the 24th, Hitler ordered Dönitz and the OKM staff to move from Berlin to Plön, 25 miles north-west of Lübeck in Schleswig-Holstein, where Dönitz was to make immediate preparations for the defence of north-western Germany.

The rapid advance of British forces to a line running between Lübeck and Hamburg caused the BdU staff to move north to Flensburg. Dönitz remained at Plön where, at 1835 on 30 April, he received a radio message from Bormann, Hitler's secretary: 'Grossadmiral Dönitz. In place of the former Reichsmarschall Göring, the Führer appoints you, Herr Grossadmiral, as his successor. Written authority on the way. You should immediately take all measures which the current situation requires.'[3]

Hitler had committed suicide a few hours before this message was transmitted from the ruined Chancellery, but Dönitz did not learn of it until the following morning. The situation demanded Dönitz seek an immediate armistice with the Allies to prevent further pointless bloodshed, but in a broadcast to the German people at 2230 on 1 May he declared: 'It is my first task [as Hitler's successor] to save Germany from destruction by the advancing Bolshevik enemy. For this aim alone the military struggle continues. As far and as long as the achievement of this aim is impeded by the British and Americans, we shall be forced to carry on our defensive fight against them as well ... '[4]

When he made this broadcast the military situation was hopeless, and catastrophic, as he well knew. The Anglo-American armies had linked up with the Red Army on the Elbe, severing north and south Germany, Berlin had fallen, and the German forces in Italy had surrendered unconditionally. German resistance was confined to a small area in the north which included Schleswig-Holstein and German-occupied Denmark, and an area in the south encompassing part of southern Bavaria and western Czechoslovakia. The only areas beyond Germany's frontiers still in German hands were western Holland, Norway and two beleaguered areas on the Baltic coast.

No doubt Dönitz believed that it was necessary to stall capitulation so as to gain time in which to save as many German troops and civilians as possible from Russian captivity, but the Grossadmiral had another motive for prolonging hostilities.

On 30 April, so as to preserve the honour of the Kriegsmarine, he had issued instructions that the fleet be scuttled: no German ships, other than those that would be required for fishing, transport and mine clearance after cessation of hostilities, were to be handed over to the victors intact. But the prevailing chaos meant that this decree would take some days to reach all naval units, hence his playing for time until this final 'honourable' task could be completed.

In the meantime all U-boats in German ports that were capable of diving were ordered to move to Norway, away from the threat of attack from low-flying aircraft, and where it was thought that their presence, in large numbers, might strengthen the hand of the German representatives in their negotiations with the Western Allies.

Since the beginning of April, Allied aircraft had been operating over the western Baltic and the Kattegat in daylight, and they had accounted for five U-boats *en route* to the Norwegian bases. The sudden exodus to Norway, swollen by the unauthorized presence of a great many U-boats that had fled the German ports even though they were in an uncompleted state and so were unable to dive, was quickly spotted and attacked by a large number of aircraft. In the total absence of German fighter opposition, these aircraft were able to pursue their hunt over the whole of the Kattegat and the Belts and even into bays and harbours, destroying in a last bloody massacre a total of 21 U-boats between 2 and 6 May. A proportion of the crews were rescued by surviving U-boats and by German and Danish patrol vessels.

Having informed all naval commanders by radio, teleprinter and courier, of his intention to scuttle the fleet, which was to be executed on the receipt of the code-word 'Regenbogen', Dönitz dispatched Generaladmiral Hans von Friedeburg,, whom he had appointed C-in-C Kriegsmarine when he was elevated to head of state, to negotiate the surrender terms with Field Marshal Montgomery at his Tactical HQ on Lüneburg Heath on Dönitz's behalf. Montgomery agreed to accept the surrender of the north German area on condition that Holland, Denmark and the German fleet were included, and that no weapons or ships were to be destroyed. The surrender, scheduled to take effect at 0800 on 5 May, was a heavy blow to Dönitz: it meant handing over every available unit of the Kriegsmarine, which in his view violated tradition and every concept of naval honour. With a heavy heart he decided that he had no choice but to accept, in order not to prejudice the chances of escape of a great part of the German eastern armies and the flood of refugees fleeing from the Russians.

In accordance with Dönitz's decision, all U-boats at sea were ordered to cease hostilities and return to base. This message was transmitted on all wavelengths continuously throughout 4 May, but not all boats received it in time to prevent them carrying out further attacks – *U853* sank *Black Point* off Long Island on 5 May, and the Type XXIII *U2336* sank two ships off the Firth of Forth on 8 May (as already recounted).

Details of the surrender terms were transmitted to all German forces at 1514 on 4 May. But the commanders of the U-boats in the western Baltic, who had already prepared their boats for scuttling in accordance with the orders for *'Regenbogen'*, and who were of the opinion that the order forbidding the sinking of their ships was contrary to Dönitz's intention and therefore must have been given under duress, scuttled their boats that night. Altogether, a total of 218 U-boats (56 per cent of the U-boat fleet) went to the bottom, including 82 Type XXIs and 29 Type XXIIIs.

After signing the surrender with Montgomery, von Friedeburg and General Jodl (chief of the OKW operations staff) went to General Eisenhower's headquarters at Reims, in the hope of negotiating separate surrender terms with the Americans, so as to gain a few more days in which to withdraw the embattled German armies on the Eastern Front to the Anglo-American front line. Their request was refused by Eisenhower who categorically demanded unconditional capitulation on both the Western and Eastern Fronts, threatening severe penalties unless the Germans signed at once. Nevertheless, von Friedeburg and Jodl managed to secure a delay of 48 hours in which to transmit the surrender orders to the far-flung army units: 48 hours in which the Kriegsmarine worked feverishly until the last minute to evacuate as many troops and refugees as they could from the remaining enclaves in the eastern Baltic.

The general surrender on all fronts came into effect at one minute past midnight on 9 May 1945. In compliance with Allied orders the U-boats at sea surfaced and, flying a black flag, proceeded to allotted ports of surrender. Of the 43 U-boats at sea on 8 May, 23 surrendered in English ports, three in Canada and four in the United States, while seven returned either to Kiel or Norway. *U1277* and *U963* were scuttled by their crews off the Portuguese coast, *U979* grounded on the Island of Amrun off the western coast of Schleswig-Holstein, *U287* struck a mine as she was entering the Elbe, and *U530* and *U977* made for the River Plate where they were interned by the Argentinian authorities. In all, 154 U-boats in Norway and Germany were surrendered intact to the Allies, including seventeen Type XXIIIs and one Type XXI.

The surface fleet was also handed over to the Allies, although there was very little left to surrender. Of the heavy ships, only the heavy cruiser *Prinz Eugen* and the light cruisers *Nürnberg* and *Leipzig* remained afloat (the latter a virtual wreck after being accidentally rammed by *Prinz Eugen* off Gdynia in October 1944). All three were in Danish ports when the war ended.

The burnt-out wreck of the pocket-battleship *Lützow*, scuttled in shallow water in Swinemunde harbour, fell into the hands of the Russians. At Kiel the British found the wreck of the pocket-battleship *Admiral Scheer*, which had capsized after being hit by five bombs during a 600-bomber raid on the night of 9/10 April, and the wreck of the heavy cruiser *Admiral Hipper*, painted in black and brick-red camouflage so that her outlines would merge with the dock-side buildings: she had settled on the bottom of the dock after being hit in the final Bomber Command raid over Germany on 3 May. Out in Kiel Bay lay the desolate, abandoned wreck of the light cruiser *Emden* which had been badly damaged during an air raid in April. British forces also took possession of the wreck of the light cruiser *Köln* lying on the bottom of the dock in Wilhelmshaven which had been bombed on 30 April.

Apart from *Prinz Eugen*, *Nürnberg* and *Leipzig*, only fifteen destroyers, eleven torpedo-boats, about two dozen minesweepers and a few dozen smaller craft were all that remained of the Kriegsmarine's surface fleet. During the course of the war the Germans had lost two battleships, two battlecruisers, three pocket-battleships, two old pre-dreadnought battleships of 1908 vintage, three heavy cruisers, four light cruisers, 44 destroyers, 56 torpedo-boats, seven armed merchant cruisers, 23 minelayers, 146 S-boats, 119 minesweepers, 163 R-boats, twelve escort-vessels, thirteen *U-bootsjagelboote*, 64 *Sperrbrecher*, 39 miscellaneous converted merchant auxiliaries, 821 patrol vessels and armed trawlers, whalers, drifters, etc., some 600 naval ferry barges and artillery barges, and 821 U-boats. The Germans also lost most of their mercantile marine: 2,035 ships grossing 3,675,655 tons.

The Allies lost 5,142 merchant ships grossing 21,543,026 tons in all theatres and from all causes including action by Japanese and Italian forces, 69.23 per cent of this huge total being accounted for by U-boats (2,927 ships grossing 14,915,921 tons, of which only 138 ships grossing 687,790 tons, or 4.71 per cent of the total, were sunk during the final year of the war). In addition, U-boats accounted for 175 Allied warships and auxiliaries (including two battleships, three aircraft-carriers, three escort-carriers and 48 destroyers) totalling some 243,000 tons.

Apart from one despicable incident, when Kapitänleutnant Eck, commander of *U852*, machine-gunned the survivors of the torpedoed Greek steamer *Peleus* on 13 March 1944, the Kriegsmarine fought bravely and fairly, preserving discipline and morale in the face of impossible odds during the final year of the war, so that when the waters finally closed over the tortured ruins of the Third Reich the black, white and red swastika ensign of the Kriegsmarine was still bravely flying.

Appendixes

GERMAN NAVAL OFFICER RANKS
AND BRITISH EQUIVALENTS

Grossadmiral	Admiral of the Fleet	*Fregattenkapitän*	no equivalent
Generaladmiral	no equivalent	*Korvettenkapitän*	Commander
Admiral	Admiral	*Kapitänleutnant*	Lieutenant Commander
Vizeadmiral	Vice Admiral	*Oberleutnant zur See*	Lieutenant
Konteradmiral	Rear Admiral	*Leutnant zur See*	Sub-Lieutenant
Kommodore	Commodore	*Oberfähnrich zur See*	no equivalent
Kapitän zur See	Captain	*Fähnrich zur See*	Midshipman

Compiled from the Naval Intelligence Division document (BR.634 G) 'Dictionary of Naval Equivalents'(1943).

TYPE XXI ELECTROBOATS
COMMISSIONED INTO SERVICE

Blohm & Voss, Hamburg

Boat	Launched	Commissioned	Fate
U2501	12 May 44	June 44	Scuttled Hamburg 2 May 45
U2502	15 June 44	July 44	Surrendered Horten May 45
U2503	29 June 44	Aug 44	Cannon/rocket fire of RAF aircraft, Little Belt 4 May 45
U2504	18 July 44	Aug 44	Scuttled Hamburg 2 May 45.
U2505	27 July 44	Nov 44	Scuttled Hamburg 2 May 45
U2506	5 Aug 44	Aug 44	Surrendered Hamburg 2 May 45
U2507	14 Aug 44	Sept 44	Scuttled Flensburg 5 May 45
U2508	19 Aug 44	Sept 44	Scuttled Kiel 3 May 45
U2509	27 Aug 44	Sept 44	Bombed RAF Hamburg 8 April 45
U2510	29 Aug 44	Sept 44	Scuttled Travemünde 2 May 45
U2511	2 Sept 44	Sept 44	Surrendered Bergen May 45
U2512	7 Sept 44	Oct 44	Scuttled Eckernforde 3 May 45
U2513	14 Sept 44	Oct 44	Surrendered Horten May 45
U2514	17 Sept 44	Oct 44	Bombed RAF Hamburg 8 April 45
U2515	22 Sept 44	Oct 44	Bombed USAF Hamburg 11 Mar 45
U2516	27 Sept 44	Oct 44	Bombed RAF Kiel 8 April 45
U2517	4 Oct 44	Oct 44	Scuttled Flensburg 4 May 45
U2518	4 Oct 44	Nov 44	Surrendered Horten May 45
U2519	18 Oct 44	Nov 44	Scuttled Kiel 3 May 45
U2520	16 Oct 44	Nov 44	Scuttled Kiel 3 May 45

Boat	Launched	Commissioned	Fate
U2521	18 Oct 44	Nov 44	Bombed RAF SE of Aarhus 5 May45
U2522	22 Oct 44	Nov 44	Scuttled Flensburg 5 May 45
U2523	25 Oct 44	Dec 44	Bombed Allied aircraft Hamburg 17 Jan 45
U2524	30 Oct 44	Jan 45	Scuttled east of Samso after cannon/rocket fire RAF aircraft SE of Aarhus 3 May 45
U2525	30 Oct 44	Dec 44	Scuttled Flensburg 5 May 45
U2526	30 Nov 44	Dec 44	Scuttled Travemünde 2 May 45
U2527	30 Nov 44	Dec 44	Scuttled Travemünde 2 May 45
U2528	18 Nov 44	Dec 44	Scuttled Travemünde 2 May 45
U2529	18 Nov 44	Feb 45	Surrendered Christiansand May 45
U2530	23 Nov 44	Dec 44	Bombed RAF Hamburg 31 Dec 44
U2531	5 Dec 44	Jan 45	Scuttled Travemünde 2 May 45
U2532	7 Dec 44	Jan 45	Bombed RAF Hamburg 31 Dec 44
U2533	7 Dec 44	Jan 45	Scuttled Travemünde 3 May 45
U2534	11 Dec 44	Jan 45	Bombed RAF Kattegat 6 May 45
U2535	16 Dec 44	Jan 45	Scuttled Travemünde 2 May 45
U2536	16 Dec 44	Feb 45	Scuttled Travemünde 2 May 45
U2537	22 Dec 44	Mar 45	Bombed RAF Hamburg 31 Dec 44
U2538	6 Jan 45	Feb 45	Mined off SW coast of Aero bei Marstal 9 May 45
U2539	6 Jan 45	Feb 45	Scuttled Kiel 3 May 45
U2540	13 Jan 45	Feb 45	Scuttled off Flensburg 4 May 45 after being attacked by RAF aircraft Great Belt 3 May 45
U2541	13 Jan 45	Mar 45	Scuttled Flensburg 5 May 45
U2542	22 Jan 45	Mar 45	Bombed USAF Kiel 3 April 45
U2543	9 Feb 45	Mar 45	Scuttled Kiel 3 May 45
U2544	9 Feb 45	Mar 45	Scuttled off Aarhus 5 May 45
U2545	12 Feb 45	Mar 45	Scuttled Kiel 3 May 45
U2546	19 Feb 45	Mar 45	Scuttled Kiel 3 May 45
U2547	Construction abandoned after being damaged in Allied bombing raid on Hamburg 8 April 45		
U2548	9 Mar 45	Mar 45	Scuttled Kiel 3 May 45
U2549	Construction abandoned after being damaged in Allied bombing raid on Hamburg 17 Jan 45		
U2550	Construction abandoned after being damaged in Allied bombing raid on Hamburg 8 April 45		
U2551	Mar 45	April 45	Scuttled Flensburg 5 May 45
U2552	Construction abandoned after being damaged in Allied bombing raid on Hamburg 8 April 45		

U2553–U2564 (twelve boats) incomplete when war ended.

AG Weser, Bremen

Boat	Launched	Commissioned	Fate
U3001	30 May 44	July 44	Scuttled Weser estuary 1 May 45
U3002	9 July 44	Aug 44	Scuttled Travemünde 2 May 45
U3003	18 July 44	Aug 44	Bombed USAF Kiel 4 April 45
U3004	26 July 44	Aug 44	Scuttled Hamburg 2 May 45
U3005	18 Aug 44	Sept 44	Scuttled Weser estuary 1 May 45
U3006	25 Mar 44	Oct 44	Scuttled Wilhelmshaven 1 May 45
U3007	4 Sept 44	Oct 44	Bombed USAF Bremen 24 Feb 44

Boat	Launched	Commissioned	Fate
U3008	15 Sept 44	Oct 44	Surrendered Kiel May 45
U3009	30 Sept 44	Nov 44	Scuttled Weser estuary 1 May 45
U3010	20 Oct 44	Nov 44	Scuttled Kiel 3 May 45
U3011	20 Oct 44	Dec 44	Scuttled Travemünde 3 May 45
U3012	13 Oct 44	Dec 44	Scuttled Travemünde 3 May 45
U3013	19 Oct 44	Nov 44	Scuttled Travemünde 3 May 45
U3014	25 Oct 44	Dec 44	Scuttled off Neustadt 3 May 45
U3015	27 Oct 44	Dec 44	Scuttled Flensburg 5 May 45
U3016	2 Nov 44	Jan 45	Scuttled Travemünde 2 May 45
U3017	5 Nov 44	Dec 44	Surrendered Horten May 45
U3018	29 Nov 44	Jan 45	Scuttled Travemünde 2 May 45
U3019	15 Nov 44	Dec 44	Scuttled Travemünde 2 May 45
U3020	16 Nov 44	Dec 44	Scuttled Travemünde 2 May 45
U3021	27 Nov 44	Jan 45	Scuttled Travemünde 2 May 45
U3022	30 Nov 44	Jan 45	Scuttled Flensburg 5 May 45
U3023	2 Dec 44	Jan 45	Scuttled Travemünde 3 May 45
U3024	6 Dec 44	Jan 45	Scuttled Neustadt 3 May 45
U3025	9 Dec 44	Jan 45	Scuttled Travemünde 3 May 45
U3026	14 Dec 44	Jan 45	Scuttled Travemünde 3 May 45
U3027	18 Dec 44	Jan 45	Scuttled Travemünde 3 May 45
U3028	22 Dec 44	Jan 45	Bombed Allied aircraft Great Belt 3 May 45
U3029	28 Dec 44	Feb 45	Scuttled Kiel 3 May 45
U3030	31 Dec 44	Feb 45	Depth-charged RAF aircraft Little Belt 3 May 45
U3031	6 Jan 45	Feb 45	Scuttled Kiel 3 May 45
U3032	10 Jan 45	Feb 45	Depth-charged RAF aircraft Little Belt 3 May 45
U3033	20 Jan 45	Feb 45	Scuttled Flensburg 3 May 45
U3034	21 Jan 45	Feb 45	Scuttled Flensburg 3 May 45
U3035	24 Jan 45	Mar 45	Surrendered Stavanger May 45
U3036	Construction abandoned after being damaged in Allied bombing raid on Bremen 30 Mar 45		
U3037	31 Jan 45	Mar 45	Scuttled Travemünde 3 May 45
U3038	7 Feb 45	Mar 45	Scuttled Kiel 3 May 45
U3039	14 Feb 45	Mar 45	Scuttled Kiel 3 May 45
U3040	10 Feb 45	Mar 45	Scuttled Kiel 3 May 45
U3041	23 Feb 45	Mar 45	Surrendered Horten May 45
U3042	Construction abandoned after being damaged in Allied bombing raid on Bremen 30 Mar 45		
U3043	Construction abandoned after being damaged in Allied bombing raid on Bremen 30 Mar 45		
U3044	1 Mar 45	Mar 45	Scuttled Flensburg 5 May 45
U3045	Damaged in bombing raid, construction abandoned		
U3046	Damaged in bombing raid, construction abandoned		
U3047	11 April 45	April 45	Scuttled Bremen May 45
U3048	April 45		Scuttled still fitting-out Bremen May 45
U3049	April 45		Scuttled still fitting-out Bremen May 45
U3050	18 April 45		Scuttled still fitting-out Bremen May 45
U3051	20 April 45		Scuttled still fitting-out Bremen May 45

U3052–U3061 (ten boats) incomplete when war ended
U3062–U3500 (439 boats) projected but never laid down

Schichau, Danzig

Boat	Launched	Commissioned	Fate
U3501	July 44		Scuttled Weser estuary 1 May 45
U3502	Aug 44		Scuttled Hamburg 2 May 45
U3503	Aug 44		Scuttled off Gothenburg 8 May 45 after attack by RAF aircraft, Kattegat 5 May 45
U3504	Sept 44		Scuttled Wilhelmshaven 1 May 45
U3505	Sept 44		Bombed USAF Kiel 3 April 45
U3506	Oct 44		Scuttled Hamburg 2 May 45
U3507	Oct 44		Scuttled Travemünde 3 May 45
U3508	Nov 44		Bombed USAF Wilhelmshaven 30 Mar 45
U3509	Construction abandoned after being damaged in Allied bombing raid Sept 44		
U3510	Nov 44		Scuttled Flensburg 5 May 45
U3511	Nov 44		Scuttled Travemünde 3 May 45
U3512	Nov 44		Bombed RAF aircraft Kiel 8 April 45
U3513	Dec 44		Scuttled Travemünde 3 May 45
U3514	Dec 44		Surrendered Bergen May 45
U3515	Dec 44		Surrendered Horten May 45
U3516	Dec 44		Scuttled Travemünde 2 May 45
U3517	Dec 44		Scuttled Travemünde 2 May 45
U3518	Dec 44		Scuttled Kiel 3 May 45
U3519	Jan 45		Mined off Warnemünde 2 Mar 45
U3520	Jan 45		Mined off Eckernforde 31 Jan 45
U3521	Jan 45		Scuttled Travemünde 2 May 45
U3522	Jan 45		Scuttled Travemünde 2 May 45
U3523	Jan 45		Bombed RAF off Aarhus 5 May 45
U3524	Jan 45		Scuttled Flensburg 5 May 45
U3525	Jan 45		Scuttled Kiel 1 May 45 after Allied aircraft attack April 45
U3526	Mar 45		Scuttled Flensburg 5 May 45
U3527	Mar 45		Scuttled Weser estuary 1 May 45
U3528	Mar 45		Scuttled Weser estuary 1 May 45
U3529	Mar 45		Scuttled Flensburg 5 May 45
U3530	Mar 45		Scuttled Kiel 3 May 45

U3531–U3695 (165 boats) incomplete when war ended
U3696–U4000 (305 boats) projected but never laid down

TYPE XXIII ELECTRO-BOATS
COMMISSIONED INTO SERVICE

Deutsche Werft, Hamburg

Boat	Launched	Commissioned	Fate
U2321	17 April 44	June 44	Surrendered Christiansand May 45
U2322	30 April 44	July 44	Surrendered Stavanger May 45
U2323	31 May 44	July 44	Mined Strander Bight 29 July 44
U2324	16 June 44	July 44	Surrendered Stavanger May 45
U2325	13 July 44	Aug 44	Surrendered Christiansand May 45
U2326	17 July 44	Aug 44	Surrendered UK May 45
U2327	29 July 44	Aug 44	Scuttled Hamburg 2 May 45

Boat	Launched	Commissioned	Fate
U2328	17 Aug 44	Aug 44	Surrendered Bergen May 45
U2329	11 Aug 44	Sept 44	Surrendered Stavanger May 45
U2330	19 Aug 44	Sept 44	Scuttled Kiel 3 May 45
U2331	28 Aug 44	Sept 44	Accidental loss off Hela Oct 44

Germania Werft, Kiel

Boat	Launched	Commissioned	Fate
U2332	18 Oct 44	Nov 44	Scuttled Hamburg 2 May 45
U2333	16 Nov 44	Dec 44	Scuttled Flensburg 5 May 45

Deutsche Werft, Hamburg

Boat	Launched	Commissioned	Fate
U2334	26 Aug 44	Sept 44	Surrendered Christiansand May 45
U2335	31 Aug 44	Sept 44	Surrendered Christiansand May 45
U2336	10 Sept 44	Sept 44	Surrendered Kiel May 45
U2337	15 Sept 44	Sept 44	Surrendered Christiansand May 45
U2338	18 Sept 44	Sept 44	Depth-charged RAF aircraft Little Belt 4 May 45
U2339	22 Sept 44	Nov 44	Scuttled Flensburg May 45
U2340	28 Sept 44	Oct 44	Bombed USAF Hamburg 30 Mar 45
U2341	3 Oct 44	Oct 44	Surrendered Wilhelmshaven May 45
U2342	13 Oct 44	Nov 44	Mined E of Swinemünde 26 Dec 44
U2343	18 Oct 44	Nov 44	Scuttled Flensburg May 45
U2344	24 Oct 44	Nov 44	Lost in collision off Heiligenhaven 18 Feb 45
U2345	28 Oct 44	Nov 44	Surrendered Stavanger May 45
U2346	31 Oct 44	Nov 44	Scuttled Flensburg 5 May 45
U2347	6 Nov 44	Dec 44	Scuttled Flensburg 5 May 45
U2348	11 Nov 44	Dec 44	Surrendered Stavanger May 45
U2349	20 Nov 44	Dec 44	Scuttled Flensburg 5 May 45
U2350	22 Nov 44	Dec 44	Surrendered Christiansand May 45
U2351	25 Nov 44	Dec 44	Surrendered Kiel May 45
U2352	5 Dec 44	Jan 45	Scuttled Flensburg 5 May 45
U2353	6 Dec 44	Jan 45	Surrendered Christiansand May 45
U2354	10 Dec 44	Jan 45	Surrendered Christiansand May 45
U2355	13 Dec 44	Jan 45	Scuttled Kiel 3 May 45
U2356	19 Dec 44	Jan 45	Surrendered Wilhelmshaven May 45
U2357	19 Dec 44	Jan 45	Scuttled Flensburg 5 May 45
U2358	20 Dec 44	Jan 45	Scuttled Flensburg 5 May 45
U2359	23 Dec 44	Jan 45	Bombed RAF Kattegat Feb 2 May 45
U2360	29 Dec 44	Jan 45	Scuttled Flensburg 5 May 45
U2361	3 Jan 45	Feb 45	Surrendered Christiansand May 45
U2362	11 Jan 45	Feb45	Scuttled Flensburg 5 May 45
U2363	18 Jan 45	Feb 45	Surrendered Christiansand May 45
U2364	23 Jan 45	Feb 45	Scuttled Flensburg 5 May 45
U2365	26 Jan 45	Mar 45	Scuttled Skagerrak 8 May 45 after being bombed by RAF aircraft
U2366	17 Feb 45	Mar 45	Scuttled Flensburg 5 May 45
U2367	23 Feb 45	Mar 45	Lost in collision with U-boat while under air attack Great Belt 5 May 45
U2368	19 Mar 45	April 45	Scuttled Flensburg 5 May 45
U2369	24 Mar 45	April 45	Scuttled Flensburg 5 May 45

Boat	Launched	Commissioned	Fate
U2370	Mar 45	April 45	Scuttled Hamburg 2 May 45
U2371	18 April 45	April 45	Scuttled Hamburg 2 May 45

Deutsche Werft, Toulon

U2372–U2377 (six boats) under construction were, all scrapped incomplete.
U2378–U2400 (243 boats) all cancelled before being laid down

Deutsche Werft, Genoa

U2401–U2430 (30 boats all cancelled before being laid down

Deutsche Werft, Monfalcone

U2431–U2445 (fifteen boats) all cancelled before being laid down

Deutsche Werft,Nikolayev

U2446–U2460 (fifteen boats) all cancelled before being laid down
U2461–U2500 (40 boats) projected but never laid down

Deutsche Werft, Hamburg

U4001–U4120 (120 boats) building, incomplete at war's end
U4121–U4500 (380 boats) projected but never laid down

Germania Werft, Kiel

Boat	Launched	Commissioned	Fate
U4701	14 Dec 44	Jan 45	Scuttled Flensburg 5 May 45
U4702	20 Dec 44	Jan 45	Scuttled Flensburg 5 May 45
U4703	3 Jan 45	Jan 45	Scuttled Flensburg 5 May 45
U4704	12 Feb 45	Mar 45	Scuttled Flensburg 5 May 45
U4705	11 Jan 45	Feb 45	Scuttled Kiel 3 May 45
U4706	19 Jan 45	Feb 45	Surrendered Christiansand May 45
U4707	25 Jan 45	Feb 45	Scuttled Flensburg 5 May 45
U4708	26 Mar 45		Bombed Allied aircraft Kiel 4 May 45 while fitting-out, construction abandoned
U4709	8 Feb 45		Bombed Allied aircraft Kiel 4 May 45 while fitting-out, construction abandoned
U4710	14 April 45	May 45	Scuttled Flensburg 5 May 45
U4711	21 Feb 45		Bombed Allied aircraft Kiel 4 May 45 while fitting-out, construction abandoned.
U4712	1 Mar 45		Bombed Allied aircraft Kiel 4 May 45 while fitting-out, construction abandoned

U4713–U4891 (179 boats) all cancelled, scrapped incomplete
U4892–U5000 (109 boats) projected, never laid down

TYPE XVIIB AND XVIIG WALTER BOATS COMMISSIONED INTO SERVICE

TYPE XVIIB Blohm & Voss, Hamburg

Boat	Launched	Commissioned	Fate
U1405	1 Dec 44		Scuttled Flensburg 5 May 45
U1406	2 Jan 45		Scuttled Cuxhaven 2 May 45

Boat	Launched	Commissioned	Fate
U1407	Feb 45		Scuttled Cuxhaven 2 May 45
U1408	Construction abandoned after being damaged in Allied air raid on Hamburg 1 Feb 45		
U1409	Construction abandoned after being damaged in Allied air raid on Hamburg 15 Feb 45		

U1410 U1416 (seven boats) cancelled 14 Aug 43

TYPE XVIIG Germaniawerft, Kiel

U1081U1092 (twelve boats) cancelled 14 Aug 43

U-boat losses May 1944 to May 1945

1944

Date	Boat	Cause and location
1 May	U277	Depth-charged by RN aircraft of escort carrier *Fencer* (842 Sqn): SW of Bear Island.
2 May	U674	Depth-charged by RN aircraft of escort carrier *Fencer* (842 Sqn): NW of Narvik.
2 May	U959	Depth-charged by RN aircraft of escort carrier *Fencer* (842 Sqn): S of Jan Mayen Island.
3 May	U852	Depth-charged by RAF aircraft (8 and 621 Sqns): SE of Socotra.
4 May	U371	Depth-charged by RN destroyer *Blankney*; French frigate *Sénégalais* and USN destroyers *Pride* and *Joseph E. Campbell*: W of Bougie.
4 May	U846	Depth-charged by RCAF aircraft (407 Sqn): N of Cape Ortegal.
5 May	U473	Depth-charged by RN sloops *Starling*, *Wild Goose* and *Wren*: NW of Palma.
5 May	U1234	Accident: collision off Gdynia: Baltic.
6 May	U66	Depth-charged by USN aircraft of escort carrier *Block Island* (VC.55) and destroyer *Buckley*: W of Cape Verde Islands.
6 May	U765	Depth-charged by RN aircraft of escort carrier *Vindex* (825 Sqn) and frigates *Aylmer*, *Bickerton* and *Bligh*: North Atlantic.
14 May	U616	Depth-charged by USN destroyers *Ellyson*, *Emmons*, *Gleaves*, *Hambleton*, *Hilary P. Jones*, *Macomb*, *Nields* and *Rodman* and RAF aircraft (36 Sqn): NE of Oran.
15 May	U731	Depth-charged by RN sloop *Kilmarnock*, trawler *Blackfly* and USN aircraft (VP.63): off Tangier.
16 May	U240	Depth-charged by RAF aircraft (330 Norwegian Sqn): 200 miles W of Trondheim.
18 May	U241	Depth-charged by RAF aircraft (210 Sqn): NE of Faroes.
19 May	U960	Depth-charged by USN destroyers *Ludlow* and *Niblack* and RAF aircraft (36 and 500 Sqns): N of Oran.
19 May	U1015	Accident: collision: W of Pillau, Baltic.
21 May	U453	Depth-charged by RN destroyers *Tenacious*, *Termagant* and *Liddesdale*: E of Cape Spartivento.
24 May	U476	Depth-charged by RAF aircraft (210 Sqn): NE of Trondheim.
24 May	U675	Depth-charged by RAF aircraft (4 OTU): W of Aalesund.
25 May	U990	Depth-charged by RAF aircraft (59 Sqn): NW of Trondheim.
27 May	U292	Depth-charged by RAF aircraft (59 Sqn): W of Aalesund.
29 May	U549	Depth-charged by USN destroyers *Ahrens* and *Eugene E. Elmore*: SW of Madeira.

Date	Boat	Cause and location
31 May	U289	Depth-charged by RN destroyer *Milne*: Arctic.
3 June	U477	Depth-charged by RAF aircraft (162 Sqn): NW of Christiansand.
4 June	U505	Captured after depth-charge attack by USN aircraft of escort carrier *Guadalcanal* (VC.8), and destroyers *Chatelain*, *Jenks* and *Pillsbury*: NW of Dakar. Naval relic at Chicago.
5 June	U987	Torpedoed by RN submarine *Satyr*: SE of Jan Mayen Island.
7 June	U955	Depth-charged by RAF aircraft (201 Sqn): N of Cape Ortegal: Salved 1971 – relic at Kiel.
7 June	U970	Depth-charged by RAF aircraft (228 Sqn): W of Bordeaux.
8 June	U373	Depth-charged by RAF aircraft (224 Sqn): off Brest.
8 June	U629	Depth-charged by RAF aircraft (224 Sqn): off Brest.
9 June	U740	Depth-charged by RAF aircraft (120 Sqn): W of Scillies.
9 June	U821	Depth-charged by RAF aircraft (206 and 248 Sqns): off Brest.
11 June	U980	Depth-charged by RCAF aircraft (162 Sqn): NW of Bergen.
12 June	U490	Depth-charged by USN aircraft of escort carrier *Croatan* (VC.25) and destroyers *Frost*, *Huse* and *Inch*: NW of Azores.
13 June	U715	Depth-charged by RCAF aircraft (162 Sqn): E of Faroes.
15 June	U860	Depth-charged by USN aircraft of escort carrier *Solomons* (VC.9): SSE of St. Helena.
17 June	U423	Depth-charged by RAF aircraft (333 Norwegian Sqn): NW of Christiansand.
18 June	U441	Depth-charged by RAF aircraft (304 Polish Sqn): 34 miles NE of Ushant.
18 June	U767	Depth-charged by RN destroyers *Fame*, *Havelock* and *Inconstant*: 10 miles NW of Pointe de Talbat.
24 June	U971	Depth-charged by RN destroyer *Eskimo* and RCN *Haida* and RAF aircraft (311 Czech Sqn): N of Ushant.
24 June	U1225	Depth-charged by RCAF aircraft (162 Sqn): NW of Bergen.
25 June	U269	Depth-charged by RN frigate *Bickerton*.
25 June	U1191	Depth-charged by RN frigates *Affleck* and *Balfour*: 25 miles SE of Start Point.
26 June	U317	Depth-charged by RAF aircraft (86 Sqn): E of Shetlands.
26 June	U719	Depth-charged by RN destroyer *Bulldog*: off NW coast of Ireland.
27 June	U998	Paid-off at Bergen after depth-charge attack by RAF aircraft (333 Norwegian Sqn): E of Shetlands 16 June 1944.
29 June	U988	Depth-charged by RN frigates *Cooke*, *Duckworth*, *Domett* and *Essington* and RAF aircraft (224 Sqn): off L'Orient.
30 June	U478	Depth-charged by RAF aircraft (86 Sqn) and RCAF (162 Sqn) air-craft: NW of Christiansand.
2 July	U543	Depth-charged by USN aircraft of escort carrier *Wake Island* (VC.58): SW of Tenerife.
3 July	U154	Depth-charged by USN destroyers *Frost* and *Inch*: W of Madeira.
5 July	U233	Depth-charged by USN destroyers *Baker* and *Thomas*: SE of Halifax.
5 July	U390	Depth-charged by RN destroyer *Wanderer* and frigate *Tavy*: Seine Bay.
5 July	U586	Bombed by USAAF aircraft: Toulon.
5 July	U642	Bombed USAAF aircraft: Toulon.
6 July	U678	Depth-charged by RCN destroyers *Kootenay* and *Ottawa* and RN corvette *Statice*: 23 miles SSW of Brighton.
8 July	U243	Depth-charged by RAAF aircraft (10 Sqn): W of St-Nazaire.
11 July	U1222	Depth-charged by RAF aircraft (201 Sqn): W of La Rochelle.

Date	Boat	Cause and location
14 July	U415	Mined: Baltic.
15 July	U319	Depth-charged by RAF aircraft (206 Sqn): WSW of The Naze.
17 July	U347	Depth-charged by RAF aircraft (210 Sqn): W of Lofoten Islands.
17 July	U361	Depth-charged by RAF aircraft (86 Sqn): W of Narvik.
18 July	U672	Depth-charged by RN frigate *Balfour*: 32 miles S of Portland Bill.
18 July	U742	Depth-charged by RAF aircraft (210 Sqn): W of Narvik.
21 July	U212	Depth-charged by RN frigates *Curzon* and *Ekins*: 47 miles SE of Brighton.
22 July	U1166	Accident, internal explosion: Kiel.
23 July	U239	Bombed by RAF aircraft: Kiel.
23 July	U1164	Bombed by RAF aircraft: Kiel.
26 July	U214	Depth-charged by RN frigate *Cooke*: 16 miles SSE of Start Point.
29 July	U872	Bombed by USAAF aircraft: Bremen.
29 July	U890	Bombed by Allied aircraft: Bremen: construction abandoned.
	U891	Bombed by Allied aircraft: Bremen: construction abandoned.
	U892	Bombed by Allied aircraft: Bremen: construction abandoned.
29 July	U2323	Mined: Baltic.
30 July	U250	Depth-charged by Russian sub-chasers *DS 910* and *MO 103* and aircraft: Koivisto Straits.
31 July	U333	Depth-charged by RN sloop *Starling* and frigate *Loch Killin*: W of Scillies.
? Aug	U996	Bombed by RAF aircraft: Hamburg: construction abandoned.
? Aug	U1196	Accident, internal explosion.
4 Aug	U671	Depth-charged by RN destroyer Wensleydale and frigate *Stayner*: 25 miles SE of Brighton.
6 Aug	U471	Bombed by USAAF aircraft: Toulon.
6 Aug	U736	Depth-charged by RN sloop *Starling* and frigate *Loch Killin*: SW of Belle Ile.
6 Aug	U952	Bombed by USAAF aircraft: Toulon.
6 Aug	U969	Bombed by USAAF aircraft: Toulon.
11 Aug	U385	Depth-charged by RN sloop *Starling* and RAAF aircraft (461 Sqn): W of La Rochelle.
11 Aug	U967	Scuttled: Toulon.
12 Aug	U198	Depth-charged by RIN sloop *Godarvari*; RCN frigate *Findhorn*; RN aircraft of *Begum* (832 Sqn) and *Shah* (851 Sqn): NW of Seychelles.
12 Aug	U981	Depth-charged by RAF aircraft (502 Sqn): Gironde estuary.
13 Aug	U270	Depth-charged by RAAF aircraft (461 Sqn): W of La Rochelle.
14 Aug	U618	Depth-charged by RN frigates *Duckworth* and *Essington* and RAF aircraft (53 Sqn): W of St-Nazaire.
15 Aug	U741	Depth-charged by RN corvette Orchis: 32 miles NW of Fécamp.
18 Aug	U107	Depth-charged by RAF aircraft (201 Sqn): W of La Rochelle.
18 Aug	U621	Depth-charged by RCN destroyers *Chaudière*, *Kootenay* and *Ottawa*: off La Rochelle.
19 Aug	U466	Scuttled: Toulon.
19 Aug	U608	Depth-charged by RN sloop *Wren* and RAF aircraft (53 Sqn): W of Ile d'Yeu.
20 Aug	U9	Bombed by Russian aircraft: Constanza.
20 Aug	U178	Scuttled: Bordeaux.
20 Aug	U188	Scuttled: Bordeaux.
20 Aug	U413	Depth-charged by RN destroyers *Forester*, *Vidette* and *Wensleydale*: S of Brighton.

Date	Boat	Cause and location
20 Aug	U984	Depth-charged by RCN destroyers *Chaudière*, *Kootenay* and *Ottawa*: SW of Ushant.
20 Aug	U1229	Depth-charged by USN aircraft of escort carrier *Bogue* (VC.42): SE of Newfoundland.
21 Aug	U230	Scuttled: Toulon.
22 Aug	U180	Mined: off Gironde estuary.
24 Aug	U344	Depth-charged by RN destroyer *Keppel*; sloops *Mermaid* and *Peacock*; frigate *Loch Dunvegan* and RN aircraft of escort carrier *Vindex* (825 Sqn): NE of North Cape.
24 Aug	U445	Depth-charged by RN frigate *Louis*: W of St-Nazaire.
25 Aug	U354	Depth-charged by RN aircraft of escort carrier *Vindex* (825 Sqn): NE of Bear Island.
25 Aug	U667	Mined: off La Pallice.
25 Aug	U1000	Mined: Baltic.
25 Aug	UIT21	Scuttled: Bordeaux.
1 Sept	U247	Depth-charged by RCN frigates *St. John* and *Swansea*: S of Land's End.
2 Sept	U394	Depth-charged by RN destroyers *Keppel* and *Whitehall*; sloops *Mermaid* and *Peacock* and aircraft of escort carrier *Vindex* (825 Sqn): S of Jan Mayen Island.
4 Sept	UIT1	Bombed by RAF aircraft: Genoa.
5 Sept	U362	Depth-charged by Russian minesweeper T116: Kara Sea.
9 Sept	U484	Depth-charged by RCN frigate *Dunver*; corvette *Hespeler* and RCAF aircraft (423 Sqn): off Inner Hebrides.
9 Sept	U743	Depth-charged by RN frigate *Helmsdale* and corvette *Portchester Castle*: NW of Ireland.
10 Sept	U18	Scuttled: Constanza.
10 Sept	U19	Scuttled: Black Sea (off Turkish coast).
	U20	Scuttled: Black Sea (off Turkish coast).
	U23	Scuttled: Black Sea (off Turkish coast).
18 Sept	U925	Unknown: Faroes/Iceland area.
19 Sept	U407	Depth-charged by RN destroyers *Garland*, *Terpsichore* and *Troubridge*: S of Mylos.
19 Sept	U865	Depth-charged by RAF aircraft (206 Sqn): NE of Shetlands.
19 Sept	U867	Depth-charged by RAF aircraft (224 Sqn): NE of Shetlands.
23 Sept	U859	Torpedoed by RN submarine *Trenchant*: off Penang.
24 Sept	U565	Bombed by USAAF aircraft: Salamis.
24 Sept	U596	Bombed by USAAF aircraft: Salamis.
24 Sept	U855	Depth-charged by RAF aircraft (244 Sqn): off Bergen.
26 Sept	U871	Depth-charged by RAF aircraft (220 Sqn): NW of Azores.
29 Sept	U863	Depth-charged by USN aircraft (VB.107): Ascension area.
30 Sept	U703	Mined: off east coast of Iceland.
30 Sept	U921	Depth-charged by RN aircraft of escort carrier *Campania* (813 Sqn): SW of Bear Island.
30 Sept	U1062	Depth-charged by USN destroyer *Fessenden*: SW of Cape Verde Islands.
? Sept	U3509	Bombed by Allied aircraft Bremen: construction abandoned.
? Oct	U2331	Accident, marine casualty: off Hela, Baltic.
4 Oct	U92	Bombed by RAF aircraft: Bergen.
	U228	Bombed by RAF aircraft: Bergen.
	U437	Bombed by RAF aircraft: Bergen.

Date	Boat	Cause and location
4 Oct	U993	Bombed by RAF aircraft: Bergen.
5 Oct	U168	Torpedoed by R.Neth.N submarine *Zwaardvisch*: off Java.
15 Oct	U777	Bombed by RAF aircraft: Wilhelmshaven.
16 Oct	U673	Accident. Collision with German minesweeper: N of Stavanger.
16 Oct	U1006	Depth-charged by RCN frigate *Annan*: W of Shetlands.
20 Oct	U116	Depth-charged by USN aircraft (VP.74): Atlantic.
21 Oct	U957	Accident. Collision with German transport: off Lofoten Islands.
23 Oct	U985	Accident. German mine: off S Norway.
27 Oct	U1060	Depth-charged by RN aircraft of fleet carrier *Implacable* (771 Sqn) and RAF aircraft (311 Czech and 502 Sqns): NW of Namsos.
28 Oct	U1226	Unknown: North Atlantic.
? Nov	U547	Mined: Baltic.
9 Nov	U537	Torpedoed by USN submarine *Flounder*: E of Surabaya (Java).
11 Nov	U771	Torpedoed by RN submarine *Venturer*: off Harstadt.
11 Nov	U1200	Depth-charged by RN corvettes *Kenilworth Castle*, *Launceston Castle*, *Pevensey Castle* and *Portchester Castle*: W of Scillies.
25 Nov	U322	Depth-charged by RN frigate *Ascension* and RAF aircraft (330 Norwegian Sqn): NW of Orkneys.
28 Nov	U80	Accident, marine casualty: Baltic.
30 Nov	U196	Unknown: Sunda Strait.
6 Dec	U297	Depth-charged by RN frigates *Goodall* and *Loch Insh*: 31 miles NE of Cape Wrath.
9 Dec	U387	Depth-charged by RN corvette *Bamborough Castle*: off Murmansk.
12 Dec	U416	Accident. Collision: W of Pillau, Baltic.
12 Dec	U479	Mined: Gulf of Finland.
13 Dec	U365	Depth-charged by RN aircraft of escort carrier *Campania* (813 Sqn): E of Jan Mayen Island.
17 Dec	U400	Depth-charged by RN frigate *Nyasaland*: 38 miles off Cork.
18 Dec	U1209	Accident, marine casualty: wrecked Wolf Rock.
19 Dec	U737	Accident. Collision German minesweeper: West Fiord, Norway.
26 Dec	U2342	Mined: E of Swinemünde.
27 Dec	U877	Depth-charged by RCN corvette *St. Thomas*: NW of Azores.
28 Dec	U735	Bombed by RAF aircraft: off Horten, Norway.
30 Dec	U772	Depth-charged by RCAF aircraft (407 Sqn): 30 miles S of Portland Bill.
31 Dec	U906	Bombed by Allied aircraft: Hamburg.
	U908	Bombed by Allied aircraft: Hamburg.
	U1011	Bombed by Allied aircraft: Hamburg.
	U1012	Bombed by Allied aircraft: Hamburg.
	U2532	Bombed by Allied aircraft: Hamburg.
	U2530	Bombed by Allied aircraft: Hamburg.
	U2537	Bombed by Allied aircraft: Hamburg.
1945		
? Jan	U382	Accident, collision: Baltic.
? Jan	U650	Unknown: off NE coast of Scotland.
? Jan	U1020	Unknown: Moray Firth.
10 Jan	U679	Mined: Baltic.
16 Jan	U248	Depth-charged by USN destroyers *Hayter*, *Hubbard*, *Otter* and *Varian*: North Atlantic.
16 Jan	U482	Depth-charged by RN sloops *Amethyst*, *Hart*, *Peacock* and *Starling* and frigate *Loch Craggie*: North Channel.

Date	Boat	Cause and location
17 Jan	U2523	Bombed by Allied aircraft: Hamburg.
	U2549	Bombed by Allied aircraft: Hamburg.
21 Jan	U1199	Depth-charged by RN destroyer *Icarus* and corvette *Mignonette*: 16 miles off Land's End.
24 Jan	U763	Bombed by Russian aircraft: Königsberg.
26 Jan	U1172	Depth-charged by RN frigates *Aylmer*, *Bentinck*, *Calder* and *Manners*: 32 miles NE of Dublin.
27 Jan	U1051	Depth-charged by RN frigates *Bligh*, *Keats* and *Tyler*: 26 miles ENE of Wexford.
31 Jan	U3520	Mined: off Eckernforde.
? Feb	U923	Mined: Baltic.
3 Feb	U1279	Depth-charged by RN frigates *Bayntun*, *Braithwaite* and *Loch Eck*: NW of Shetlands.
4 Feb	U745	Unknown: Gulf of Finland.
4 Feb	U1014	Depth-charged by RN frigates *Loch Scavaig*, *Loch Shin*, *Nyasaland* and *Papua*: North Channel.
9 Feb	U864	Torpedoed by RN submarine *Venturer*: W of Bergen.
14 Feb	U989	Depth-charged by RN frigates *Bayntun*, *Braithwaite*, *Loch Dunvegan*, *Loch Eck*: E of Shetlands.
15 Feb	U1053	Accident while exercising: off Bergen.
16 Feb	U309	Depth-charged by RN frigate *St. John*: 55 miles NE of Cromarty.
17 Feb	U425	Depth-charged by RN sloop *Lark* and corvette *Alnwick Castle*: off Murmansk.
17 Feb	U1273	Mined: off Horten.
17 Feb	U1278	Depth-charged by RN frigates *Bayntun* and *Loch Eck*: NNW of Shetlands.
18 Feb	U2344	Accident: collision off Heiligenhaven.
19 Feb	U676	Mined: Gulf of Finland.
20 Feb	U1208	Depth-charged by RN sloop *Amethyst*: 46 miles ESE of Cork.
22 Feb	U300	Depth-charged by RN minesweepers/sloops *Pincher* and *Recruit* and armed yacht *Evadne*: SW of Cadiz.
24 Feb	U480	Depth-charged by RN frigates *Duckworth* and *Rowley*: SW of Land's End.
24 Feb	U927	Depth-charged by RAF aircraft (179 Sqn): SW of Lizard.
24 Feb	U3007	Bombed by USAAF aircraft: Bremen.
27 Feb	U327	Depth-charged by RN sloop *Wild Goose*; frigates *Labuan* and *Loch Fada* and USN aircraft (VPB.112): SW of Lizard.
27 Feb	U1018	Depth-charged by RN frigate *Loch Fada*: S of Lizard.
28 Feb	U869	Depth-charged by USN destroyer *Fowler* and French sub-chaser *L'Indiscret*: off Casablanca.
2 March	U3519	Mined: off Warnemünde.
7 March	U1302	Depth-charged by RN frigates *La Hulloise*, *Strathadam* and *Thetford Mines*: 25 miles NW of St. David's Head.
10 March	U275	Mined: off Newhaven.
11 March	U681	Accident. Wrecked on Scillies: later bombed by USN aircraft (VPB.103).
11 March	U2515	Bombed by USAAF aircraft: Hamburg.
12 March	U260	Mined: 50 miles SW of Kinsale.
12 March	U683	Depth-charged by RN sloop *Wild Goose* and frigate *Loch Ruthven*: SW of Land's End.
14 March	U714	Depth-charged by RN destroyer *Wivern* and SAN frigate *Natal*: 10

Date	Boat	Cause and location
		miles NE of Berwick.
15 March	U367	Mined: off Hela.
18 March	U866	Depth-charged by USN destroyers *Lowe*, *Menges*, *Mosley* and *Pride*: SE of Sable Island.
20 March	U1003	Rammed by RCN frigate *New Glasgow*: off Lough Foyle.
20 March	U905	Depth-charged by RAF aircraft (86 Sqn): 43 miles NW of Orkneys.
22 March	U296	Depth-charged by RAF aircraft (120 Sqn): North Channel.
26 March	U399	Depth-charged by RN frigate *Duckworth*: off Lizard.
27 March	U722	Depth-charged by RN frigates *Byron*, *Fitzroy* and *Redmill*: 23 miles SW of Dunvegan.
27 March	U965	Depth-charged by RN frigate *Conn*: 23 miles W of Cape Wrath.
29 March	U246	Depth-charged by RN frigate *Duckworth*: SE of Lizard.
29 March	U1106	Depth-charged by RAF aircraft (224 Sqn): NW of Shetlands.
30 March	U72	Bombed by USAAF aircraft: Bremen.
30 March	U96	Bombed by USAAF aircraft: Wilhelmshaven.
30 March	U329	Bombed by USAAF aircraft Bremen.
30 March	U348	Bombed by USAAF aircraft: Hamburg.
30 March	U350	Bombed by USAAF aircraft: Hamburg.
30 March	U429	Bombed by USAAF aircraft: Wilhelmshaven.
30 March	U430	Bombed by USAAF aircraft: Bremen.
	U870	Bombed by USAAF aircraft: Bremen.
30 March	U884	Bombed by USAAF aircraft: Bremen.
	U886	Construction abandoned.
30 March	U1021	Depth-charged by RN frigates Conn and Rupert.
30 March	U1167	Bombed by USAAF aircraft: Hamburg.
	U2340	Bombed by USAAF aircraft: Hamburg.
30 March	U3508	Bombed by USAAF aircraft: Wilhelmshaven.
30 March	U3036	Bombed Allied aircraft: Bremen.
30 March	U3042	Bombed Allied aircraft: Bremen.
30 March	U3043	Bombed Allied aircraft: Bremen.
31 March	U682	Bombed by RAF aircraft: Hamburg.
? April	U326	Unknown: off UK coast.
2 April	U321	Depth-charged by RAF aircraft (304 Polish Sqn): SW of Ireland.
3 April	U1221	Bombed by USAAF aircraft (7 Sqn): Kiel.
3 April	U1276	Depth-charged by RAF aircraft (224 Sqn): NE of Shetlands.
3 April	U2542	Bombed by USAAF aircraft: Kiel.
	U3505	Bombed by USAAF aircraft: Kiel.
4 April	U237	Bombed by USAAF aircraft: Kiel.
	U749	Bombed by USAAF aircraft: Kiel.
	U3003	Bombed by USAAF aircraft: Kiel.
5 April	U1169	Mined: 20 miles SE of Carnsore Point.
6 April	U1195	Depth-charged by RN destroyer *Watchman*: 12 miles SE of Sandown.
7 April	U857	Depth-charged by USN destroyer *Gustafson*: W of Cape Cod.
8 April	U677	Bombed by Allied aircraft: Hamburg.
	U747	Bombed by Allied aircraft: Hamburg.
	U982	Bombed by Allied aircraft: Hamburg.
	U2509	Bombed by Allied aircraft: Hamburg.
	U2514	Bombed by Allied aircraft: Hamburg.
	U2516	Bombed by Allied aircraft: Hamburg.
	U2547	Bombed by Allied aircraft: Hamburg.

Date	Boat	Cause and location
8 April	U2550	Bombed by Allied aircraft: Hamburg.
	U2552	Bombed by Allied aircraft: Hamburg.
8 April	U774	Depth-charged by RN frigates *Bentinck* and *Calder*: SW of Ireland.
8 April	U1001	Depth-charged by RN frigates *Byron* and *Fitzroy*: 150 miles off Scillies.
8 April	U2547	Bombed by Allied aircraft: Hamburg.
	U2550	Bombed by Allied aircraft: Hamburg.
	U2552	Bombed by Allied aircraft: Hamburg.
8 April	U3512	Bombed by RAF aircraft: Kiel.
9 April	U804	Rocket fire from RAF aircraft (143, 235 and 248 Sqns): Little Belt.
9 April	U843	Rocket fire from RAF aircraft (143, 235 and 248 Sqns): Kattegat.
9 April	U1065	Cannon fire from RAF aircraft (235 Sqn): Skagerrak.
9 April	U1131	Bombed by RAF aircraft: Kiel.
9 April	U1227	Bombed by RAF aircraft: Kiel.
10 April	U878	Depth-charged by RN destroyer *Vanquisher* and corvette *Tintagel Castle*: S of Ireland.
12 April	U486	Torpedoed by RN submarine *Tapir*: W of Bergen.
12 April	U1024	Depth-charged by USN frigate *Loch Glendhu*: sank in tow 23 miles NW of Holyhead.
14 April	U235	Accident: depth-charged in error by German torpedo-boat *T 17*: Kattegat.
14 April	U1206	Accident: 30 miles NE of Aberdeen.
15 April	U103	Bombed by Allied aircraft: Gdynia.
15 April	U285	Depth-charged by RN frigates *Grindal* and *Keats*: SW of Ireland.
15 April	U1063	Depth-charged by RN frigate *Loch Killin*: W of Land's End.
15 April	U1235	Depth-charged by USN destroyers *Frost* and *Stanton*: North Atlantic.
16 April	U78	Gunfire from Russian shore batteries: off Pillau.
16 April	U880	Depth-charged by USN destroyers *Frost* and *Stanton*: North Atlantic.
16 April	U1274	Depth-charged by RN destroyer *Viceroy*: 6 miles E of Sunderland.
19 April	U251	Depth-charged by RAF aircraft: (143, 235, 248 and 333 Norwegian Sqns): S of Gothenburg.
19 April	U879	Depth-charged by USN destroyers *Buckley* and *Reuben James*: 150 miles SSE of Halifax.
21 April	U636	Depth-charged by RN frigates *Bazely*, *Bentinck* and *Drury*: 90 miles NE of Donegal.
22 April	U518	Depth-charged by USN destroyers *Carter* and *Neal A. Scott*: NW of Azores.
23 April	U183	Torpedoed by USN submarine *Besugo*: Java Sea.
23 April	U396	Depth-charged by RAF aircraft (86 Sqn): SW of Shetlands.
24 April	U546	Depth-charged by USN destroyers *Chatelain*, *Flaherty*, *Harry E. Hubbard*, *Jansen*, *Keith*, *Neunzer*, *Pillsbury* and *Varian*: NW of Azores.
24 April	UIT2	Scuttled: Genoa.
	UIT3	Scuttled: Genoa.
25 April	U1107	Depth-charged by USN aircraft (VPB.103): SW of Ushant.
28 April	U56	Bombed by RAF and USAAF aircraft: Kiel.
28 April	U1223	Bombed by Allied aircraft: off Weser estuary.
29 April	U286	Depth-charged by RN frigates *Anguilla*, *Cotton* and *Loch Shin*: off Murmansk.

Date	Boat	Cause and location
29 April	U307	Depth-charged by RN frigate *Loch Insh*: off Murmansk.
29 April	U1017	Depth-charged by RAF aircraft (120 Sqn): NW of Ireland.
30 April	U242	Depth-charged by RN destroyers *Havelock* and *Hesperus*: off UK coast.
30 April	U325	Depth-charged by RN destroyers *Havelock* and *Hesperus* and RAF aircraft (201 Sqn): N of Anglesey.
30 April	U548	Depth-charged by USN destroyers *Bostwick*, *Coffman*, *Thomas* and frigate *Natchez*: E of Cape Hatteras.
30 April	U1055	Depth-charged by USN aircraft (VPB.63): SW of Ushant.
? May	U398	Unknown: east coast of Scotland.
? May	U785	Bombed by Allied aircraft: Kiel.
2 May	U717	Scuttled at Flensburg after bombing by Allied aircraft.
2 May	U1007	Bombed by RAF aircraft and mined: off Wismar.
2 May	U2359	Bombed by RAF (143, 235, 248 and 303 Norwegian Sqns) and RCAF (404 Sqn) aircraft: Kattegat.
3 May	U958	Scuttled: Kiel.
3 May	U1210	Bombed by RAF aircraft: off Eckernforde.
3 May	U2524	Scuttled E of Samso after cannon and rocket fire from RAF aircraft (236 and 254 Sqns): SE of Aarhus.
3 May	U2540	Scuttled off Flensburg after attack by RAF aircraft (2 TAF): Great Belt.
3 May	U3028	Bombed by Allied aircraft: Great Belt.
3 May	U3030	Depth-charged by RAF aircraft (2 TAF): Little Belt.
3 May	U3032	Depth-charged by RAF aircraft (2 TAF): Little Belt.
3 May	U3505	Bombed by USAAF aircraft: Kiel.
4 May	U236	Scuttled at Schleimündung after bomb damage by RAF aircraft (236 and 254 Sqns).
4 May	U393	Scuttled after depth-charge attack by RAF aircraft (236 and 254 Sqns): N of Fyn Islands.
4 May	U711	Depth-charged by RN aircraft of escort carriers *Queen* (853 Sqn), *Searcher* (882 Sqn) and *Trumpeter* (846 Sqn): off Harstad.
4 May	U746	Scuttled in Geltinger Bight after bombing by RAF aircraft.
4 May	U2338	Depth-charged by RAF aircraft (236 and 254 Sqns): Little Belt.
4 May	U2503	Cannon and rocket fire from RAF aircraft (236 and 254 Sqns): Little Belt.
4 May	U3525	Scuttled Kiel, after attack by Allied aircraft.
4 May	U4708	Bombed by Allied aircraft: Kiel.
4 May	U4709	Bombed by Allied aircraft: Kiel.
4 May	U4711	Construction abandoned.
	U4712	Construction abandoned.
5 May	U534	Depth-charged by RAF aircraft (206 Sqn): Kattegat.
5 May	U579	Depth-charged by RAF aircraft: Little Belt.
5 May	U733	Scuttled at Flensburg after bombing by RAF aircraft.
5 May	U876	Scuttled Eckernforde after bombing by RAF aircraft.
	U904	Scuttled Eckernforde after bombing by RAF aircraft.
5 May	U2367	Accident. Collision with German U-boat while under attack: Great Belt.
5 May	U2521	Bombed by RAF aircraft (547 Sqn): SE of Aarhus.
5 May	U3523	Bombed by RAF aircraft (224 Sqn): off Aarhus.
6 May	U853	Depth-charged by USN destroyer *Atherton* and frigate *Moberly*: off Long Island.

6 May	U881	Depth-charged by USN destroyer *Farquar*: SE of Cape Race.
6 May	U1008	Depth-charged by RAF aircraft (86 Sqn): Kattegat.
6 May	U2534	Bombed by RAF aircraft (86 Sqn): Kattegat.
7 May	U320	Depth-charged by RAF aircraft (210 Sqn): W of Bergen.
8 May	U2365	Scuttled in Skagerrak after bombing by RAF aircraft (311 Czech Sqn).
8 May	U3503	Scuttled off Gothenburg after attack by RAF aircraft (86 Sqn): Kattegat.
9 May	U963	Accident. Wrecked off Lisbon.
9 May	U2538	Mined: off SW coast of Aero bi Marstal.

Source Notes

Introduction

1. For a full account of the German defeat at Stalingrad see, V.E. Tarrant, *Stalingrad: Anatomy of an Agony*.
2. All statistics in this work regarding merchant ships sunk and U-boats lost, are taken from V.E. Tarrant, *The U-boat Offensive 1914–1945*.
3. Naval Staff Historical Monograph, 'The Defeat of the Enemy Attack on Shipping', Vol. 1A, p. 90.
4. PRO Adm 234/67, Admiralty Historical Monograph, German Naval Series, 'The U-boat War in the Atlantic', Vol. II, pp. 111–12.
5. Quoted in 'The Defeat of the Enemy Attack on Shipping', Vol. 1A, p. 97.
6. Dönitz, *Memoirs: Ten Years and Twenty Days*, p. 406 (hereinafter cited as 'Dönitz').
7. Ibid.
8. Ibid.
9. Quoted in Wilmot, *The Struggle for Europe*, p. 152.

Chapter 1: A Belief in Miracles

1. Dönitz, pp. 421–2.
2. Quoted in Rössler, *The U-Boat: The Evolution and Technical History of German Submarines*, p.168.
3. Ibid., p. 179.
4. Ibid., p. 208.
5. Ibid., p. 198.
6. *Kriegstagebuch des BdU* (U-Boat High Command War Diary), entry for 10 June 1944. (Hereinafter cited as *KTB*.)
7. PRO Adm 234/68 'The U-boat War

in the Atlantic', Vol. III, p. 57.
8. Roskill, *The War at Sea* , Vol. III, Part 1, p. 16.

Chapter 2: The Sounding of The Tocsin

1. *Marinegruppe West Kriegstagebuch* (War Diary Naval Command Group West), 30 May 1944. (Hereinafter cited as *KGW*.)
2. PRO Adm 223/107, NID report 01730/43 of 15 March 1943.
3. Hinsley, *British Intelligence in the Second World War*, Vol. III, Part 1, p. 245. (Hereinafter cited as Hinsley.)
4. This section has been based on information in Hinsley, Vol. III, Part 1, pp. 238–45; and Vol. III, Part 2, pp. 41–123.

Chapter 3: The Strategy of Despair

1. This and all other quotes of Vizeadmiral Krancke in this chapter are taken from *KGW*.
2. *FdS Kriegstagebuch* in PRO Adm 223/28.
3. Ibid.
2. This section on S-boat operations is based on information contained in the *FdS Kriegstagebuch* and post-war interrogations of FdS collated by NID and bound in PRO Adm 223/28 'German E-boat Operations and Policy, 1939–1945'.

Chapter 4: Great Expectations

1. *Kriegstagebuch Seekriegsleitung* (Naval War Staff), 6 June 1944.
2. Ibid.
3. PRO Adm 234/68, p. 74.

4. 'Ultra' was the code-name given to top secret messages passed to Allied commands based on information gleaned from the decryption of German Enigma ciphers.
5. PRO Adm 234/68, p. 68.
6. PRO Adm 234/68, p. 70.
7. PRO Adm 234/68, pp. 69–70.
8. PRO Air 41/74, 'The RAF in the Maritime War', Vol. V, pp. 12–13.
9. *KTB*, 12 June 1944.
10. PRO Adm 234/68, p. 73.
11. Ibid., p. 74.
12. Ibid., pp. 74–75.
13. Roskill, *The War at Sea*, Vol. III, Part 2, p. 127.
14. PRO Adm 234/68, p. 78.
15. *KTB*, 15 September 1944.

Chapter 5: Defeat In The West
1. *FdS Kriegstagebuch* in PRO Adm 223/28.
2. Ibid.
3. Ibid.
4. Padfield, *Dönitz: the Last Führer*, p. 402.
5. *KTB*.
6. PRO Adm 234/68, p. 77.
7. Ibid., p. 80.
8. Quoted in Martienssen, *Hitler and his Admirals*, pp. 219–20.
9. PRO PG48609. Speech by Dönitz to the flag officers in *Flottenkommando B*, 24 August 1944.
10. Padfield, p. 420.

Chapter 6: Twilight In The Middle Sea
1. Roskill, *The War at Sea*, Vol. III, Part 2, p. 85.
2. Ibid., p. 108.
3. Ibid., p. 112.

Chapter 7: Death of a Giant.
1. Roskill, *The War at Sea*, Vol. III, Part 2, p. 169.
2. For a full appreciation of the influence *Tirpitz* exerted on Allied dispositions see V.E. Tarrant, *King George*

V Battleships.
3. Preserved in PRO Adm 234/250.
4. Ibid.
5. Ibid.
6. Ibid.

Chapter 8: The Setting of the Midnight Sun
1. Hinsley, Vol. III, Part 2, p. 490.
2. Campbell and & Macintyre, *The Kola Run*, p. 179.
3. Hinsley, Vol. III, Part 2, p. 491.
4. Quoted in *The Kola Run*, p. 189.

Chapter 9: Nil Desperandum
1. PRO Adm 234/68, p. 91.
2. Ibid.
3. PRO Air 41/74, pp 108–9.
4. Hinsley, Vol. III, Part 2, pp 471–2.
5. Dönitz, p. 426.
6. Quoted in Martienssen, *Hitler and his Admirals* p. 222.
7. Hinsley, Vol. III, Part 2, p. 479.
8. Ibid.
9. *FdS Kriegstagebuch*, in PRO Adm 223/28.
10. Ibid.

Chapter 10: End Game
1. Quoted in Rössler, p. 254.
2. Quoted in PRO Air 41/74, p. 176.
3. Webster and Frankland, *The Strategic Air Offensive Against Germany, 1939–1945*, Vol. III, Part 2, p. 277.
4. Report by Kapitänleutnant Klushmeier, commander of *U2336*, quoted in *Dönitz*, p. 428.
5. PRO Adm 234/68, p. 95.
6. PRO Air 41/74.
7. Correlli Barnett, *Engage The Enemy More Closely*, p. 854.

Chapter 11: Reaping The Whirlwind
1. Quoted in Martienssen, *Hitler and his Admirals*, pp. 224–5.
2. Ibid.
3. Cited in Padfield, p. 450.
4. Shirer, *The Rise and Fall of the Third Reich*, p. 1138.

Bibliography

Unpublished Sources.
PRO = Public Record Office (Kew)
Adm = Admiralty Records
Air = Air Ministry Records
Cab = Cabinet Office Papers

PRO Adm 223/88, 'Admiralty use of Special Intelligence In Naval Operations, 1939–1945'.
PRO Adm 223/6, 'Reaction to Overlord in German Naval Communication Organization'.
PRO Adm 223/28, 'German E-boat Operations and Policy, 1939–1945'.
PRO Adm 223/209, 'Receipt of Special Intelligence in the Admiralty and its Dissemination in the German Surface Units Section of the OIC'.
PRO Adm 223/34, 'Axis Merchant Shipping Losses in the Mediterranean, 1941–1945'.
PRO Adm 234/345, 'Naval Attacks on the German Battleship *Tirpitz*'.
PRO Adm 234/349, '*TIRPITZ*: An account of the various attacks carried out by the British Armed Forces and their effect upon the German battleship'.
PRO Adm 234/350, '*TIRPITZ*: Evidence for detailed accounts of damage to the German battleship'.
PRO Adm 234/288, 'German Mine Warfare, 1939–1945'.
PRO Adm 234/466, 'German Torpedo Development, 1939–1945'.
PRO Adm 234/363, 'The Campaign in North-West Europe, 1944/45'.
PRO Adm 234/366, 'Operation "Neptune": The Landings in Normandy, June 1944'.
PRO Adm 234/369, 'Arctic Convoys, 1941–1945'.
PRO Adm 234/578, 'Defeat of the Enemy Attack on Shipping, 1939–1945: A Study of Policy and Operations', Vol. IA (Text and Appendices).
PRO Adm 186/802, 'The U-Boat War in the Atlantic', Vol. I.
PRO Adm 234/67, 'The U-Boat War in the Atlantic', Vol. II.
PRO Adm 234/68, 'The U-Boat War in the Atlantic', Vol. III.
PRO Adm 239/388, 'History of German U-Boat Policy, 1939–1945'.
PRO Adm 239/467, 'German Navy: Organization and Function – Intelligence Report (1944)'.
PRO Adm 199/1566, 'Counter-measures against German E-Boats and Destroyers in Operation "Neptune"'.
PRO Adm 199/2496, 'U-Boat Warfare, 1940–1945'.
PRO Adm 199/2447, 'German Shipping Losses in North-West European Waters, 1939–1945'.
PRO Air 41/48, 'The RAF in the Maritime War', Vol. IV,
PRO Air 41/74, 'The RAF in the Maritime War', Vol V.

PRO Air 41/19, 'The RAF in the Maritime War', Vol VI: 'The Mediterranean and Red Sea'.
PRO Air 41/79, 'The RAF in the Maritime War': Statistics.
PRO Air 41/56, 'The RAF in the Bombing Offensive Against Germany', Vol VII.
PRO Cab 86/2-7, 'Anti-U-Boat Warfare Committee, 1942–1945'.
Naval Historical Branch, Ministry of Defence. FDS 65/54: 'German Small Battle Unit Operations, 1943–1945'.

Official Works – Published
Ellis, L. F. *Victory in the West*, 2 Vols., HMSO, 1962.
Hinsley, F. H. *British Intelligence in the Second World War*, Vol. 3, Parts I and II, HMSO, 1984 and 1988.
Lohmann, W., and Hildebrand, H. H. *Die deutsche Kriegsmarine 1939–1945: Gliederung-Einsatz-Stellenbesetzung*, 3 Vols., Podzun, Dorheim, 1956–64.
Molony, C. J. C., and Jackson, W. *The Mediterranean and the Middle East*, Vol. VI, Parts I, II, III, HMSO, 1984, 1987, 1988.
Webster G., and Frankland, N. *The Strategic Air Offensive Against Germany, 1939–1945*, Vol. III, Part V, Vol. IV, HMSO, 1961.
Roskill, Captain S. W. *The War at Sea*, Vol. III, Part II, HMSO, 1961.
Salewski, M. *Die deutsche Seekriegsleitung 1939–1945* Vols. I and II, Bernard & Graefe, Frankfurt, 1970, 1975.

Published Works – General
Barnett, Correlli, *Engage the Enemy More Closely*, Hodder & Stoughton, 1991.
Bekker, C. *Hitler's Naval War*, Macdonald, 1974.
Brown, D. *Tirpitz: The Floating Fortress*, Arms & Armour Press, 1977.
Campbell, Vice-Admiral Sir Ian, and Macintyre, Captain Donald, *The Kola Run*, Frederick Muller, 1958.
Churchill, W. S. *The Second World War*, Vol. VI, Cassell, 1954.
Dönitz, Grossadmiral Karl, *Memoirs: Ten Years and Twenty Days*, Weidenfeld & Nicolson, 1959.
Groner, E. *Die deutschen Kriegsschiffe, 1815–1945*, Vols. I, II, Lehmanns, Munich, 1966–8.
Jeschke, H. *U-Boottaktik: Zur deutschen U-Boottaktik, 1900–1945*, Rombach, Freiburg, 1972.
Lenton, H. T. *German Warships of the Second World War*, Macdonald & Janes, 1975.
Mallmann Showell, J. P. *U-Boats Under the Swastika*, Ian Allan, 1987.
Martienssen, A. *Hitler and his Admirals*, Secker & Warburg, 1948.
O'Neill, R. *Suicide Squads of World War Two'*, Salamander Books, 1981.
Padfield, Peter, *Dönitz: The Last Führer* Victor Gollancz, 1984.
Rohwer, Jurgen. *Axis Submarine Successes, 1939–1945*, Patrick Stephens, 1983.
Rössler, E. *The U-boat: The Evolution and Technical History of German Submarines*, Arms & Armour Press, 1981.
— *U-Boottyp XXI*, Lehmanns, Munich, 1967.
— *U-Boottyp XXIII*, Lehmanns, Munich, 1967.
Rössler, E., and Kruska, E. *Walter-U-Boote*, Lehmanns, Munich, 1969.
Shirer, W. L. *The Rise and Fall of the Third Reich*, Secker & Warburg, 1960.
Stern, R. C. *Type VII U-Boats*, Arms & Armour Press, 1991.

Tarrant, V. E. *The U-Boat Offensive, 1914–1945*, Arms & Armour Press, 1989. German edition *Kurs West: Die deutschen U-Boot-Offensiven, 1914–1945*, Motorbuch Verlag, Munich, 1993.

— *King George V Battleships*, Arms & Armour Press, 1991.

— *Stalingrad: Anatomy of an Agony*, Leo Cooper, 1992.

Terraine, John, *Business in Great Waters: The U-Boat Wars, 1916–1945*, Leo Cooper, 1989.

Porten, E. P. von der, *The German Navy in World War Two*, Arthur Barker, 1970.

Whitley, M. J. *German Destroyers of World War Two*, Arms & Armour Press, 1991.

— *German Coastal Forces of World War Two*, Arms & Armour Press, 1992.

— *German Capital Ships of World War Two*, Arms & Armour Press, 1989.

— *German Cruisers of World War Two*, Arms & Armour Press, 1987.

Wilmot, Chester, *The Struggle for Europe*, Fontana, 1979.

Index